BIC 1218

MW01222657

5

The Real New Age and the Opposition: Biblical Eschatology for Today

According to the Bible, the struggle between good and evil is not an even match because God is more powerful than evil. In fact, God has already defeated evil and this clear defeat has been marked on the calendar and in human history by a cross and an empty grave. Nevertheless, we humans continue to have to struggle against evil because the Opposition to the New Age brought by Jesus Christ is active and we are subject to the influence of that Opposition. This struggle intensified in the last age of history that was introduced by Jesus Christ. The Bible gives some important guidance for us in our struggle, which interestingly is clarified for us today by insights gained from the social sciences and from history. The task given to Christians to represent Jesus Christ in the world in this last age has been carried out very imperfectly largely because the Opposition to Christ has been able to influence large groups of Christians distorting the witness to the gospel of Jesus Christ and life in his New Age. The purpose of this book is to provide help for Christians and others who feel drawn to Jesus Christ and his New Age and want to participate more fully in his victory. This is in the knowledge that our victory will not be complete in this life, but under God and together we may be able to clarify the gospel of Jesus Christ to the world.

BOOKS BY ROBERT L. MONTGOMERY

The Diffusion of Religions: A Sociological Perspective

Introduction to the Sociology of Missions

The Lopsided Spread of Christianity: Toward An Understanding of the Diffusion of Religions

The Spread of Religions: A Social Scientific Theory Based on the Spread of Buddhism, Christianity, and Islam, First Edition

Why Religions Spread: The Expansion of Buddhism, Christianity, and Islam With Implications for Missions, Second Edition

THE REAL NEW AGE AND THE OPPOSITION

Biblical Eschatology for Today

ROBERT L. MONTGOMERY

CROSS LINES PUBLISHING
18 PARKVIEW DRIVE
ASHEVILLE, NC 28805

Author: Robert L. Montgomery
Author Email: rmontgo914@aol.com
Author Blog: www.scientificstudyofmissionsproject.org

Copyright ©2012 Robert L. Montgomery

ISBN: 978-0-615-69639-3

PRINTED BY: LIGHTNING SOURCE

Cover Design: Laura Gaines, Orchard Street Creative

Excerpts Taken From:

New Revised Standard Version of the Bible, Copyright 1989,
Division of Christian Education of the National Council of
Churches of Christ in the United States of America.

Used by Permission. All Rights Reserved.

Dedicated to

Yu-Shan Theological College and Seminary
Taiwan

TABLE OF CONTENTS

CHAPTER 7

CHAPTER 8

ACKNOWLEDGEMENTS

The Christian Mission is intimately related to eschatology or the doctrine of last things since this Mission is the task given to the followers of Jesus Christ for the last stage of human history which Christ introduced. I supplemented my study of missions (the many efforts carried out by Christians to fulfill their Mission) with the study of the social sciences. This was because I felt that important insights could be gained from these fields, which were developed only in the last two centuries. For this book I owe a special debt to scholars both in theology-missiology and in the social sciences. I always believed that as important as the secular social sciences are, it was essential that in theological thought we wrestle with and incorporate findings and insights from the social sciences. This brings me to acknowledge the influence on my thinking for this book of Walter Wink's (1984, 1986, 1992) trilogy on "The Powers": (1) *Naming the Powers: The Language of Power in the New Testament;* (2) *Unmasking the Powers: The Invisible Forces That Determine Human Existence;* and (3) *Engaging the Powers: Discernment and Resistance in a World of Domination.* His thought led me to see the link between the terminology of the social sciences and the terminology in the Bible related to "the powers." Although I did not fully agree with Wink's assessment of the social sciences, I felt that he did a very useful work in enabling theology to incorporate valuable concepts and theories from the social sciences.

There are many other scholars who have influenced my thought, but I must mention especially James Davison Hunter (2010) as providing one of the best examples I know of placing social scientific theories into a broader theological perspective. My use of the term "socio-cultural forces" presupposes his thorough description of what is behind such a term, which is much more than is often meant by such terms as "culture" and "worldview." Arend Th. van Leeuwen (1964) and Rodney Stark (1997 [1996], 2001, 2003, 2007) have influenced greatly my view of human religious history along with Christian Smith (2003a, 2003b, 2010), who has also broadened my view of the human capacities for faith and moral formation. Most recently, I became acquainted with the work of John R. Hall especially in his 2009 book, *Apocalypse: From Antiquity to the Empire of Modernity.* I was delighted that he shows convincingly that apocalyptic thought, closely related to the concerns of this book, has had a powerful influence in human history from at least the millennium before Christ to the present. Of course, although obtaining ideas from many sources I take responsibility for the views expressed in this book. There are other theologians and social scientists whose writings have influenced my thinking and the References will show some of them, but there are others, too many to mention.

In addition, I owe personal thanks to several people. My wife, Mary Taylor Todd, was a great help in correcting the text, but especially by being patient during long hours of writing. Margo and Kent Smith helped me substantially. Margo is a teacher of English who helped me greatly in editing the manuscript. Kent is an extremely accomplished Biblical scholar who made numerous suggestions for making the best use of my Scriptural references and in interpreting the Bible. Of course, I take responsibility both for my writing mistakes and for all the views expressed.

I also appreciate the invaluable help of Laura Gaines and Orchard Street Creative in creating the design of the cover and in formatting the text in preparation for printing.

PREFACE

About 40 years ago I began an intellectual exploration trip to try to discover major reasons why people respond so differently to the Christian message about Jesus Christ. The exploration was prompted by my experience as a missionary among the aboriginal people on Taiwan from 1956 to 1972. The simple fact is that they were very receptive to the Christian message that was brought to them, while the surrounding majority society was not. I wanted to know why they were so much more receptive than most people in Asia, including the people where I lived as a child of missionary parents in China. (The response has increased greatly in China in the last few decades.) Since everything in our lives is interrelated, this intellectual exploration affected and even intertwined with my spiritual and emotional life. My exploration was into the social sciences, in particular sociology and anthropology; to see what light they could shed on why there were such great variations in response to the Christian gospel. The social sciences are not a normal part of training for most ministers. They were certainly not for my training as a minister of the Presbyterian Church. I had to go back to graduate school and did not complete my PhD program in social scientific studies of religion at Emory University until I was 47 years of age. I set my goal to develop a subfield in the sociology of religion that I called, "sociology of missions." Toward that end I have written four books with a Second Edition for the last one (1996, 1999, 2002, 2007, 2012) and also maintain a blog website (www.scientificstudyofmissionsproject.org).

The social sciences apply the secular methods of science to the study of human behavior. Since I believed that God is at work in all conditions of life, I felt that the social sciences could throw light on the conditions that affected the response of people to the gospel even though in science no reference can be made to God as a causative force in human life or historical events. Thus, while my sociology of missions had to stand on its own and be evaluated by others in the social sciences, in my theology I was prepared to incorporate valid effects of social conditions on the religious responses that I had seen in Taiwan.

Thirty-six years after leaving Taiwan, I was invited to return to give three lectures and a Commencement address at Yu-Shan Theological College and Seminary, where I had taught part-time. This is a school that specialized in training leaders for the aboriginal churches. I gave the lectures in June of 2008 and also had the opportunity to visit a number of churches. The ideas for the present short book grew out of my experiences among the aboriginal Christians, the latest being the lectures that I gave at Yu-Shan in 2008, which I greatly expanded for this book. Preparing the lectures and writing this book required me to study the Bible anew and to seek to integrate what I could learn from the Bible with what I had learned from the social sciences. This meant going beyond a strictly social scientific approach to a more encompassing theological approach in which I was originally trained. In studying the spread of religions for my previous writings I had to review a great deal of history. The time had come to relate that history and social scientific findings to a theological perspective. The Bible states, "And this good news of the kingdom will be proclaimed throughout the world, as a testimony to all the nations; and then the end will come" (Matthew 24:14). Thus, missions, history, and the doctrine of last things (eschatology) are all bound up together. My study of missions had brought me to where I needed to deal with the Biblical view of human history that necessarily includes eschatology and then relate that view to what I had learned through both historical studies and the social sciences. It is not surprising, then, that the study of missions and history should drive me to wrestle with the difficult subject of eschatology.

I gave the lectures in Taiwan, which I entitled, "The Last Days," because I wanted the young people preparing for ministry in the aboriginal churches to know the basic eschatological message (*eschatos* referring to "last") of the New Testament. I believed this would help them continue with the excitement and enthusiasm of the previous generation of church leaders I had known. I also wanted them to know that it was not only independent churches with "prophecy preachers" that could speak about "the last days." There was a legitimate use of the term in their preaching. At the same time, I wanted the students to avoid the misinterpretations of preachers of "the last days," who tend to see the world as ending very soon and who see little value in seeking to improve the environment and unjust conditions in the world. Also, there is an unfortunate tendency of the preachers of "the last days" to emphasize violence and to give undue attention to the State of Israel as a sign of the imminent return of Christ. I hasten to add that I also think it is important for members of churches in the United States and elsewhere in the world to be aware of the eschatological message of the New Testament and to develop a Christian view of history that takes in the "big picture" of the world and of human history. In the biblical view of history there is a beginning and an end. Facing the latter reality is the major reason for writing this book.

My four previous books referred to above that examined the spread of religions had been inspired by the remarkable movement to Christianity among the aboriginals on Taiwan. Although comprising less than two percent of the population on Taiwan, they make up approximately forty percent of the membership in the Presbyterian Church in Taiwan within which I worked. Initially, I wanted to see what the social sciences could say about this movement, but ended up surveying the last two thousand years in which Christianity had spread, as well as the spread of Buddhism and Islam during this same period. Based on their demonstrated capacity to spread widely crossing numerous socio-cultural and geographical boundaries, Buddhism, Christianity, and Islam are called the "missionary religions" (Arnold 2006 [1896]; Ellwood 2003:49). This review of history from a social scientific perspective made me also seek to connect what I found with what the Bible teaches about history. The result was what I presented in a preliminary way in my lectures in Taiwan.

The eschatology of the New Testament actually presents a philosophy of history or at least a special viewpoint about history. I have had a lifelong interest in history and majored in it in college. I took my interest in history with me in my exploration of the social sciences, which has a subfield known as the sociology of history. I had to make use of the sociology of history because I was basically interested in understanding why and how Christianity and the other missionary religions had spread over the last two thousand years, as well as more recently. Some of the same kinds of variations took place in response to the other missionary religions as to Christianity. I should add that the spread of religions I studied refers to their spread by propagation and the acceptance by new peoples of a religious identity not previously held. In other words it did not include spread by immigration, although immigration could be a catalyst to people accepting a new religion.

In reviewing the long yet relatively short history (in relation to the long history of humankind) of the spread of Christianity and the other religions I was particularly struck by all that Christians had done to hinder that spread. It seems a miracle that the Christian faith has spread at all and that almost one third of the earth's population now confesses to being Christian. This made me think more about what the Bible says concerning the period of history introduced by Jesus Christ, which the Bible calls "the last days" and makes clear that it marks the climax of history characterized by both the spread of the gospel and opposition to Jesus Christ, an opposition arising first from *within* Christianity (or within a Christian context) that has done much to hinder the spread of Christianity. The present book, then, is an outgrowth of my lectures to the aboriginal students in Taiwan, but it goes considerably beyond these lectures and presents thoughts, as controversial as some may be, that I believe people in all lands need to ponder.

INTRODUCTION

The title for Chapter 1 and a basic concept for this book came from New Testament passages mentioning the "last days" (Acts 2:17; II Timothy 3:1; Hebrews 1:2; I Peter 1:5, 20; I John 2:18). These passages all use terms based on "eschatos" meaning "last." A particularly beautiful passage is Hebrews 1:1, 2: "Long ago God spoke to our ancestors in many and various ways by the prophets, but *in these last days* he has spoken to us by a Son." This places eschatology at the center of the message of the New Testament and the Christian message to the world.

The "New Age" in the title of the book, of course, is what has been introduced by Jesus Christ in "these last days." I am using the term because of the current interest in "New Age" religion. I believe Christ introduced the "Real New Age" in his Kingdom, the arrival of which he announced at the beginning of his ministry and often spoke of during his ministry. This Kingdom came with Jesus and is still coming, but it exists within the world where his authority is recognized and his sovereign rule is followed. This means his Kingdom is continually coming and so we continue to pray, "thy Kingdom come, thy will be done." Even though no one fully follows Jesus Christ, by faith we are "transferred" (Colossians 1:13) into his Kingdom that is continually coming in power in these last days.

By calling the Kingdom brought by Jesus Christ "The Real New Age," I am contrasting the Kingdom or Rule of Christ with the modern popular phenomena called "New Age" religion. I believe that the concept of a "New Age" draws ultimately on the concept of "the Messianic Age" that followers of Christ believe was introduced by Jesus the Messiah with his Kingdom. I am using the term "New Age" to catch the attention of people who have been attracted to some of the features of "New Age" religion. There is, of course, much confusion about what is meant by "New Age" religion in contemporary use. It is sufficient here to say that "New Age" religion may draw on one or more of the following concepts: (1) a new age has arrived or is arriving, for example, "the Age of Aquarius," which replaces the old age of people seeking domination and brings in harmony and peace; (2) the truth should be approached through total immersion in reality rather than through the analytical methods of science; (3) an energy force to which individuals are connected, permeates reality or the cosmos; (4) people have an inner spirituality that may be considered divine or making them part of the divine. Some will recognize ideas imported from Eastern religions and pre-Christian European tribal religion, but some ideas may be found also in Christianity. It is not necessary to reach agreement on what is included in "New Age" religion. "New Age" religion will remain a vague concept and there will always be different understandings of it. To some extent people who are "into" "New Age" religion are reacting against what they perceive to be "organized religion" and particularly what they perceive to be "narrow" and "authoritarian religion," namely, principally what they perceive in Christianity. "New Age" religion is generally loosely organized. Of course, "New Age" religion is not really "new," but is as old as the mystery religions, Gnostic religions, and nature religions of the ancient world.

Since "New Age" is so much in the vocabulary of many religiously and spiritually oriented people, my purpose is to set forth the Biblical view of the "New Age," which I believe actually contains some elements of the notions in "New Age" religion and even inspired some of them. Some religious people in traditional denominations simultaneously hold to some ideas of New Age religion. Nevertheless, many popular notions of "New Age" are not equivalent to the Biblical view of the Kingdom of God and in some respects, perhaps many respects, are opposed to it. Certainly, from my perspective, inner peace and harmony together with energy supplied by the Spirit of God may be found in Christ's Kingdom, even if only imperfectly experienced. Nevertheless, I believe strongly in the need for the visible Church with its inevitable human organizational characteristics. My purpose in referring to the "Real New Age" is not only to draw some attention to this book, but to emphasize the Christian view that the world has been different over the last 2000 years because of the coming of Jesus Christ, who introduced a time for a worldwide turning to God. We do live in a New Age and need to experience it ever more fully. Although the world has benefited greatly from the worldwide turning to God represented by the spread of the gospel of Christ, there is still much more turning to God needed.

"The Opposition" part of the title of the book comes from the teachings that are encountered in the Bible regarding the appearance of Opposition to Christ and his Kingdom in "the last days." I capitalize Opposition to indicate its special nature. The term "antichrist" is used in some passages (only in the letters of John) regarding this Opposition, but not in all of the passages. I sought to incorporate an examination of these passages about Opposition to Christ because I felt they have been largely neglected by many Christians due to their misuse by other Christians and their difficulty of interpretation.

When I was in seminary in the early 1950's, we would occasionally discuss beliefs about the second coming of Christ, the supposed millennium, and especially the distinctive set of beliefs known as "dispensationalism" (the theory behind "the rapture" and other doctrines regarding the church, history, and its ending). Our theology professor, Felix B. Gear (1944:126), had chaired the Committee of the General Assembly of the Presbyterian Church U.S. (my church) that stated: "Dispensationalism …is out of accord with the system of the doctrine set forth in the Confession of Faith, not primarily or simply in the field of eschatology, but because it attacks the very heart of the

Theology of our Church, which is unquestionably a Theology of one Covenant of Grace."

Many, if not most people in churches today, especially in the older denominational churches, have never heard of dispensationalism. However, almost everyone has heard of "the rapture" and "Armageddon." Many have read or heard of the exciting "Left Behind Series" books. Some may remember seeing or using Schofield Reference Bibles in homes and churches. These terms and these books come directly out of the dispensational movement. In the 1950's I expected dispensationalism to fade away or at least be of negligible influence among Christians. I was completely wrong. Not only has dispensational thought not faded away, but it has also grown in influence even to the extent of influencing thinking in the highest levels of government. However, it is not simply dispensationalism that has influenced the views of many about the Middle East, particularly regarding the meaning of the establishment of the State of Israel in relation to the Second Coming of Christ. Irvine H. Anderson (2005) has written in considerable detail how knowledge gained in Sunday schools and churches of ancient Israel's occupation of Palestine predisposed the British and American public to welcome the establishment of the State of Israel. At the same time, the public is relatively ignorant of the history of Palestine from Biblical times to the present. Nevertheless, "dispensational premillennialism" or "Armageddon theology," appears to have impacted a smaller but more activist group – especially in the United States" (Anderson 2005:41). Anderson (2005:47, 48) summarizes:

> In retrospect, there appears to have been several
> levels of understanding of the relationship between
> the Jewish people and land of Palestine. There has
> been a generalized knowledge that Palestine was the

historic home of the Jews in biblical times. This may not have caused many to take action in support of a restoration, but neither has it caused them to oppose actions taken by others. Then there has been the idea that God really promised the land to the Jewish people. Some fundamentalist individuals and groups have taken this to be a divine decree that should not be questioned. In a few cases, this belief by itself has led to active support of the restoration. And then there has been the belief that we are living in the End Times and the ingathering of the Jews to Palestine is a prelude to the Second Coming. Some people of this persuasion have been extremely active in support of that return.

The second and third levels of understanding mentioned in this summary are both part of the dispensational perspective and probably have had some influence on American foreign policy toward the Middle East.

My purpose in this book is not specifically to try to refute dispensationalism, although I have a very different interpretation of the Bible and of history, as I show in the whole book. Given the assumed necessity by dispensationalists of using a literal interpretation of the Bible, especially of Old Testament promises about the land occupied by ancient Israel (an interpretation that is not made by the New Testament), it is known to be a rather difficult task to change the minds of dispensationalists (Poythress 1987). To turn from dispensationalist views, people need to accept a whole new perspective toward the Bible, one that interprets the Old Testament in the light of the New Testament itself and especially in light of the belief that all the promises of God have their fulfillment in Jesus Christ and his Kingdom. Thus, in the New Testament there is not one set of promises for believers in Christ and one set for Israel as seen in dispensationalism. To turn from dispensationalism also requires accepting a view of history that replaces the complex, but mechanical scheme presented in dispensationlism. In a time of worldwide changes and tensions, when wild speculations on the future of the world are rife, the biblical perspective on history is much needed.

Perhaps because of the growing influence of Christians with strong views about the "the end times," "millennial studies" are beginning to be taken seriously by scholars. The term "millennial" comes from the one place in the Bible that speaks of a one thousand year reign of Jesus Christ (Revelation 20:4), but "millennialism" has come to refer to a wide variety of ideal, utopian, or transformed ages envisioned by different groups of people. Kenneth G. C. Newport and Crawford Gribben (2006) have edited a book that calls attention to the increase in influence of "millennial studies." Gribben (2006:239) states:

> Millennial scholars are no longer the intellectual quacks who keep their heads down and elaborate their analyses only among the remnant of the faithful. Our moment has come. The "semiotic arousal" [dealing with signs] of "apocalyptic time" is extending the field of our millennial inquiry, while geopolitical crises are priming our peers to see the significance of eschatological thinking in contexts that might formerly have been considered mundane. Specialists in millennial studies have never had as much to contribute to the scholarly discussion of the academy – and, perhaps to the safe continuance of the many and varied societies in which they live and work.

"Eschatology" is a more comprehensive term than millennial, but the general field of "millennial studies" has become defined by scholars as the field that examines thought, primarily religious thought, about the future, especially the end of the world. Whatever terms are used, my interest is in developing a perspective on history that incorporates its beginning and end, as well as the time between. This immediately introduces the need for the study of belief or theology because no one knows the future, certainly not any remote future, but not even the immediate future. The rapid changes in the world are reason enough to consider how history should be viewed in the light of the Bible, but it is also time for people of faith who are not dispensationalists or simply have not thought much about the "end times" to clarify their views that are in contrast to those who confidently proclaim what is going to happen. Historically people who are in comfortable circumstances are not likely to think much about the end of the world or even welcome any change in their circumstances. This includes many people in mainline Christianity. However, we have come to a time when the pervasive sense of insecurity and uncertainty gives even the formerly comfortable a strong incentive to think of the world's destiny and their place in it. As a sign of modern insecurities, movies and television are constantly confronting people with end of the world scenarios and also often including the comments of those who thrive on wild speculations about the future, particularly giving their "explanations" that unravel the secrets of Scripture.

More ominously, John R. Hall (2009) has shown the tremendous impact of apocalyptic thought in Western history up to the present. Drawing on the violence found in apocalyptic writings, opposing and warring sides have justified their use of violence against each other. This includes not only extremist Muslims and Christians, but also broad publics that have been influenced, often by political leaders, to picture "their side" as the "righteous ones" in conflict with the dark forces of evil. The many speculations about the end time, but especially the appropriation of apocalyptic images to justify acts of violence by opposing forces, provides a major rationale for this book. Basically of course, I wish to initiate conversation and study to move toward an understanding of the eschatological view of the Bible.

In the first chapter I review my view of the eschatological viewpoint of the Bible in the context of world history. The New Testament is considered an eschatological book that tells us we are living in the "last days" introduced by Jesus Christ. I want to retake the "last days" talk for the majority of Christians who have tended to leave it to those who think of the "last days" in terms of the next few years and "the end" as being in the near future.

Since I have mentioned dispensationalism, I seek in the second chapter to give some sense of what it is and to account for its influence. Many earnest Christians are dispensationalists and I bear them no personal animosity. In fact, they have had a zeal for prayer, evangelism, and missions often lacking in other Christians. However, I believe the system of thought in dispensationalism is at odds with the Biblical view of history and the end times. Because of the sensitivity of disagreeing with fellow Christians, I seek as much as possible to use a social scientific perspective to analyze the dispensational movement. In fact, it bears all the marks of a religious movement that has put to shame the complacency and unexciting approaches of many traditional Christians in established churches. In the book as a whole I seek to set forth an interpretation of the Bible that I believe is a better interpretation than the one offered in dispensationalism and furthermore gives a better understanding of history.

In the third chapter I discuss what actually has been happening in the last two thousand years since Jesus Christ came. History is both discouraging and exciting, but it needs to be faced honestly. I believe part of that honesty is to submit ourselves to the open and honest scrutiny of secular historians and social scientists. This requires a secular and scientific methodology that makes no theological affirmations, but the affirmations of secular scholars seek to be objective. In this book I will include my own theological perspective and make a number of theological affirmations. Nevertheless, I seek to avoid mixing the social scientific and theological perspectives so that readers will know when I move from one to the other.

In the fourth chapter I consider the issue of evil on a macro scale and how evil fits into the biblical view of reality. In this chapter I make the connection between the biblical view of realities that are greater than individuals and impinge on the lives of everyone and the social scientific discoveries related to society and culture. This is basic to understanding the power of evil (the Opposition) to influence large numbers of people, who are not necessarily "bad" people, but are quite "normal."

In the fifth chapter I take up the question discussed in a number of passages in the New Testament of the Opposition to God. In I and II John this Opposition is identified by the term, "antichrist." This term has clearly been much misused by being applied to various figures in history and because of that misuse tends to be avoided by many. However, since "the Opposition issue" is discussed in several passages of the Bible, I believe it is an important teaching that needs to be considered.

The sixth chapter is apt to be the most controversial chapter because in it I provide historical examples of when the Opposition to Christ and the New Age (his Kingdom) became particularly strong. The expected appearance and reappearance of the Opposition to Christ is an important part of the larger eschatological message of the New Testament.

The seventh chapter discusses how to recognize and defend against the Opposition to Christ and the New Age in a rapidly changing world. The Opposition has actually already been defeated or has been given a death blow. At the same time, like a snake that has been killed, it still retains the ability to move and it continues to influence human life. A defensive stance is the appropriate stance. I present a number of current challenges of the Opposition, again a controversial subject.

The eighth and ninth chapters set forth the basic tasks that lie before Christians, which are (1) to follow, to listen, to receive, and to love and (2) to live and work in and with the Community of Faith. When these are done faithfully, the Opposition will have the least effect because Christians will be living the life to which they are called. The best defense against the Opposition is a living relationship with Jesus Christ in fellowship with his followers that issues in service to Christ's Kingdom in the world. It is especially important that this not be understood as only the task of individual Christians, but especially of Christians working together.

In the tenth chapter I offer some principles to guide Christians in living with and relating to other religions in a world in which inter-religious contacts are increasing and especially in a world in which the content of religions will come under increasing scrutiny. This content includes both beliefs and experience. The fact that Christians are being called to be especially thoughtful about their faith and life is a major reason for writing this book.

CHAPTER ONE

IN THESE LAST DAYS

AN ESCHATOLOGICAL BOOK

It could be said that the New Testament is an eschatological book, namely a book about the beginning of the last days of the history of the world. The New Testament must be seen in relation to the whole Bible and even all of human history since the New Testament represents the climax to all that preceded it and the opening chapter of what is to come. The eschatological perspective of the New Testament requires viewing the whole of history from beginning to end.

THE LONG RANGE VIEWPOINT OF THE BIBLE

There is a distinctive view of time and history offered in the Bible. For one thing, the biblical view of time requires taking a long-range view of history and of our lives. This is a good thing since we now know that the history of the cosmos and of the human race is much longer than seen in a literal reading of the Bible. The Bible says, "With the Lord one day is like a thousand years, and a thousand years are like one day" (II Peter 3:8). In other words, 1000 years is not much time in God's calendar. At the same time 1000 years may be compressed into a day. We are actually seeing how time is being compressed in the sense that change is speeding up. Change that used to take hundreds and even thousands of years is taking place in a few years, sometimes days. Probably in the last 100 years as many changes have taken place in the world as in the previous 1000 years or more. Although this applies obviously to technology, such as with transportation and communication, the main concern of the Bible is the spread of the knowledge of God first, as it was revealed to God's people in the Old Testament and then, to all "nations" (peoples) through the gospel of Jesus Christ in "the last days."

In fact the spread of the gospel of Jesus Christ in the world, although taking place for approximately the last 2000 years, has greatly accelerated just in the last 50 years. With only one third of the population of the world identifying as Christian, there is obviously much more needing to be done in the witness to Jesus Christ. Previously Christianity had the reputation of being a "Western religion" in popular thought and even among scholars with the exception of missiologists and most missionaries themselves. This claim can no longer be justified, as the historian, Philip Jenkins (2002), made clear in his book, *The New Christendom: The Coming of Global Christianity*, a welcome change to Christians who have winced under some of the associations of Christianity with the West. Even the term "Christendom" is enough to make many wince.

I remember a reporter who was interviewing me when I was traveling in the United States speaking on overseas mission work. She asked me, "Why should we take our religion to others when they already have their religion." The peculiar, but common notion she expressed was that Christianity was "our religion." Most people in the United States have forgotten that Christianity was brought to their forebears by missionaries. Christianity originated in the Middle East, certainly not in the West, as any reader of the Bible can see. The Bible is clearly not "in the Western world" or is it a Western or American book!

The greatest factor breaking the identification of Christianity with the West has been the rapid spread of the Christian gospel following the collapse of Western colonialism after World War II. Although under the radar of many observers of globalization, this rapid spread of the gospel is the most momentous change to have taken place recently in world history. While Christianity has appeared to lose strength, especially in Europe, it has increased dramatically in numbers in China and Africa. How do the accelerating changes of the last two thousand years fit with the Biblical view of history?

THE LAST PERIOD OF HISTORY

The most important view in the Bible regarding time is that we have entered the last period of history. It was initiated by the coming of Jesus Christ, prepared for and anticipated throughout the history of Israel. The "last days" or the last stage of history that was introduced by Christ is also the time for the New Age in the world that is preparatory for the "new heavens and a new earth" (II Peter 3:13) to be established at the end of history. This New Age contains the foretaste and prefiguring of what is to come at the end of history. The New Age was announced by Jesus in the beginning of his ministry as the coming of the Kingdom of God. The "Kingdom of God" is the term Jesus used for what I am calling "the New Age. It is clear that we are to begin to experience the Kingdom of God on earth now, meaning that we can live now in the New Age introduced by Jesus Christ. And we can know some of the major characteristics of this New Age and also demonstrate them to the world. Ephesians (3:5-10) and Colossians (1:26) both make reference to what was hidden for many ages as now being made known to believers and through believers to "rulers and authorities in the heavenly places" (Ephesians 3:10).

The clearest evidence of the arrival of the New Age is the

resurrection of Jesus Christ and the experience of resurrection in the lives of believers. He is "the first fruits" (I Corinthians 15:20) of the age to come, but we also become "a kind of first fruits" (James 1:18). This is because we begin to experience the effect of Christ's resurrection now as stated in the Letter to the Ephesians, where it refers in the past tense to a resurrection experience for all believers: "But God…made us alive together with Christ…and raised us up with him and seated us with him in the heavenly places in Christ Jesus" (Ephesians 2:4-6). This is one of the clearest passages teaching "realized eschatology" or the current experience of the promised age. So the Kingdom of God should also be called the New Age because it has a real connection to the new heavens and the new earth, meaning "new everything," that will come at the consummation of history. It is clear that we can begin to experience that future now through faith.

The New Testament message is an eschatological message and Jesus was an eschatological preacher. This was because he envisioned the last days as having arrived with his coming. Many think of Jesus as simply an ethical teacher, who taught people to be kind and good. He was such a teacher, but first, he was an eschatological preacher who came announcing the arrival of the New Age that was to be the Last Age. Albert Schweitzer (1968 [1906]) in his book, *The Quest for the Historical Jesus*, made this plain for the scholarly world in the early part of the last century, but it has taken a long time to sink into Christian consciousness and is still not there for many Christians, especially "comfortable" Christians, who would rather not think of the end of the world as we know it.

The apostles understood this eschatological message and continued to proclaim it. However, neither Jesus nor the apostles knew when the Last Age, which he inaugurated, would reach its end and the new heavens and new earth be initiated. They only knew that because of what Jesus had done, dying for our sins and rising again, the whole creation had now entered its last period of history to be followed by a new creation of everything–"the heavens and earth." Although the full new creation is yet to come, the Kingdom that Christ brought deserves to be called "the New Age" because in it we can begin to know something of what "the new heaven and new earth" will be like.

THE LONG HISTORY OF HUMANS

Science gives us tools for understanding certain aspects of the work of God in the world and at the same time correcting misunderstandings that people have from reading the Bible in the wrong way. Recently scientists have thrown light on the long history of humans on earth, as well as the long history of earth itself. This long history enables us to understand better why the Bible should be understood as presenting an eschatological message. Even the history of Israel presented in the Hebrew Scriptures should be considered as very recent human history. Science provides strong support for the view that the last 2000 years since the incarnation of Jesus Christ is a very short time in human history. We now know that human beings like us have been on the earth for at least 50,000 to 70,000 years, maybe longer. The People of Israel and especially Christ himself came at the end of a very long period of human life on earth. The 2000 years since Christ walked the earth seems like a very short time compared to 50,000 or more years. Even the old civilizations that existed in China, India, Mesopotamia, and Egypt are seen to be relatively recent developments. For tens of thousands of years, all human beings lived in caves or simple huts and lived and hunted with stone, bone, and wooden tools.

We know now clearly that the development of civilizations with cities and writing has nothing to do with some people being more intelligent than others. Humans simply did what they needed to do as they began to produce food, instead of primarily gathering food, with the result that populations increased. It is foolish for people to wonder if their ancestors were less intelligent than other people because they did not develop extensive agriculture, build cities, or use writing People did not need these human developments. Agriculture was developed because the conditions were present for planting and harvesting and there was a simultaneous need for more food. These conditions were greatly enhanced with the development of some form of irrigation in river valleys. People developed civilizations with cities because so many people were living together supported by agriculture and at the same time developed trade with one another. They had to develop some system of writing in order to make records, and to communicate more effectively. Trade encouraged the development of specialized skills. People did not develop such civilizations with cities in most places simply because they did not need to. They could live more easily by hunting and fishing and perhaps some supplementary farming In fact, the people living primarily by hunting and fishing generally had a better life than most "civilized" people in the cities, who built monumental buildings and carried out other projects for their rulers. While we greatly admire these monumental structures, the people in the ancient civilizations toiled in their fields or lived in crowded cities, probably in greater misery and with poorer diets than the "uncivilized" people, who lived in the forests and mountains. Religion appears also to have declined in the civilizations from the more spiritual expressions of pre-literate peoples to religions that centered around temples with priests. Worst of all, rulers claimed divinity or semi-divinity and established oppressive empires.

In light of this long history of human beings on earth, another 100, 1000, or several thousand years beyond the present would still be a short time.In just the last 2000 years the gospel of Jesus Christ has spread around the world and it has been accompanied by very many changes, many of which it influenced. However, we see that there are many changes still needed in the world if people are to live under "liberty and justice" and to have the freedom to witness to and to accept Jesus Christ as the Savior of the world. Furthermore, the gospel of Christ needs to be disassociated from some of the terrible behavior of Christians. The bringing of freedom to all people so that they may respond to Jesus Christ also should be accompanied by a number of other changes, such as a halting of the degradation of the earth that is also accompanied by a lifting of people from poverty, hunger, war, and various forms of oppression.

Even though most nations have declared themselves as favoring democracy and often claimed that they have freedom of religion, many do not practice what they preach. Francis Fukuyama (2006 [1992]:70) wrote his book, *The End of History and the Last Man*, largely on the basis that there was no "*coherent* [italics his] alternatives to liberal democracy." Certainly, as he recognized, important history is yet to occur because it is clear how far short of this goal many nations are. Also, many changes are needed in how well humans care for their environment, natural and created, before people can live in safety and health and flourish as God wants for humans. Then there are the numerous injustices that people suffer in all societies around the world, including in the technologically advanced nations, injustices that God abhors. There is much to do in the next 100 or 1000 or more years before Christ comes; the most important task being to spread the gospel of Jesus Christ through word and deed, which certainly includes demonstrating the concern of God for the well being of all people.

This view of history as extending into what seems to many to be a distant future contradicts the warning of those who like to proclaim, "the end is near" or "Christ is coming soon." My saying that "the last days" may extend hundreds or even thousands of years into the future will be criticized by some as destroying the sense of urgency Christians need in order to carry out evangelism or even to remain faithful. I recognize this problem, but I counter that this need not be. Actually, the "end is near" for each individual as Christ pointed out in his parable about the rich fool (Luke 12:13-21), who built new barns, filled them with grain and goods and then died. The eschatology of the New Testament is that the coming of Christ includes both many comings and a final coming. In fact, at Pentecost the promise of Jesus was first fulfilled when he said, "Truly I tell you, there are some standing here who will not taste death until they see that the kingdom of God has come with power" (Mark 9:1). Except for those who are expecting Christ to set up a kingdom on earth, we can see that in the last two thousand years there have been many times when the kingdom of Christ has come in a special and powerful way. These are the times when the gospel of Christ gained special recognition among new groups of people. Actually, we are in such a time currently following the collapse of colonialism and the special spread of Christianity in Africa and China.

The most basic word in the Bible about the timing of the end of the present age is the statement, "And this good news of the kingdom will be proclaimed throughout the world, as a testimony to all the nations; and then the end will come" (Matthew 24:14). But what can be said to be a true and an effective proclamation of the gospel of Jesus Christ? Large portions of the world, for example the Muslim world, may have heard the name of Jesus Christ, but has the witness to Christ really been given to them? The Christianity encountered by people in the Middle East, among whom Islam originated, was primarily that of the Byzantine Empire, a "Christian Empire" that existed for over 1000 years, but where faith and often cruel political power were closely allied. Many in the Middle East and around the Mediterranean saw a sword of domination or attempted domination in the Christianity they encountered rather than Christ's cross of love and forgiveness. The Crusades of the eleventh and twelfth centuries reinforced this perception, as did the colonial era of the last few centuries. The recent wars in the Middle East have certainly not helped to clarify the gospel of love and forgiveness. Even in the so-called "Christian West" many people know the name of Jesus Christ, but their image of Christians is very far from being a witness to what Jesus Christ is like. It could be said that the Church may have passed through a childish stage and an adolescent stage, but has not yet reached the mature personhood in Jesus Christ that is needed for a clear witness to be given to the world.

Reviewing the history of Christianity, it may be seen that the temptation that Christ rejected in the wilderness was yielded to by the church in the fourth century. The subsequent association of faith and political power has done much to distort the gospel as Christianity has spread throughout the world. The state church was perpetuated in Europe after the Reformation and would have been in the United States except for the providential conditions (from a secular perspective, an accident of history) of a mixture of religious groups that prevented any one group from dominating through state power. As the gospel spread around the world, unfortunately this spread was often in close association with outside coercion in the perceptions of the receivers of the gospel. Only about one third of the people of the world now say that they believe in Jesus Christ. Before we consider why this is so in more detail in the chapter on the spread of Christianity (Chapter 3), let us look at the last 2000 years as a whole.

THE COMING OF A MEDIATOR

The Bible tells us why the last 2000 years are different from all previous time. The arrival and the action of Jesus Christ in dying for the sins of the world and rising from the dead made the difference between all previous time and the time since Jesus Christ. This made him the Mediator that humans need and long for between themselves and God. Now most of the world counts time from when Christ came, even if the calculation is probably mistaken by 3 or 4 years. This is why it was so foolish to get excited about the year 2000, which was really not exactly 2000 years since the birth of Christ. This is aside from the fact that there is clearly so much more that needs to be accomplished in the world to witness to Christ and to teach "everything I [Christ] have commanded you" (Matthew 28:20).

The coming and the work of Christ have required a response from human beings over the centuries, even though this response has been very halting and imperfect. In the case of Christians themselves the response has been less than complete, but many others have had a negative response to the Christianity that represents Christ and his Kingdom so poorly to the world. In the first place, if the response to Christ from Christians had been complete the gospel probably would have spread out evenly from where Christ first sent out his disciples, just as the ripples from a stone that is dropped in water. In other words, the gospel would have spread out in a great circle. Instead it spread in a lopsided fashion. This fascinated me and I (2002) wrote a book about Christian history called *The Lopsided Spread of Christianity*. We will consider more carefully in the third chapter the total spread of Christianity over the centuries.

The basic view of the New Testament is that now that Jesus Christ has come, "the mystery hidden throughout the ages and generations has now been revealed to his saints" (Colossians 1:26; cf. Ephesians 1:9).

It is now up to human beings to respond to God's action. The Apostle Paul preaching to the Athenians (Acts: 17:30, 31) said it this way:

> While God has overlooked the times of ignorance, now he commands all people everywhere to repent, because he has fixed a day on which he will have the world judged in righteousness by a man [a human being] whom he has appointed, and of this he has given assurance to all by raising him from the dead.

By the word "now" we see the centrality in time of the entrance of Jesus Christ into history and the consequential demand placed on all humans to turn to God. Most importantly, we see the centrality of "a man" or "a human being" to the purpose of God in human history. God has reached out to humanity through a *single human being* and showed us what God is like and what God expects us to be like. We are serving God in the present age when we show (witness) to the world this single human being, who is the Great Mediator (II Corinthians 5:19-21) between God and humans. Let us think about how important this is.

When I became interested in the variations in how people had responded to Christianity in the last 2000 years, I came to realize that there were two other religions that had spread widely. Scholars sometimes call the three religions the "missionary religions", even as long ago as the nineteenth century (Arnold 2006 [1896]). In historical order they are Buddhism, Christianity, and Islam. I examined and compared their spread and first wrote about it in an article (1991) and then in a book called, *The Diffusion of Religions: A Social Scientific Perspective* (1996). I wanted to write something that would stand up under social scientific scrutiny. In it I paid special attention to how domination by one society of another hindered the spread of a religion from the dominant to the dominated society. This is because I was particularly aware of the sense of domination created in many lands by colonialism, including where I lived in the Far East.

Recently I was able to write more comprehensively in two books. One in 2007 and then a Second Edition with some additional material in 2012 which I called, *Why Religions Spread: The Expansion of Buddhism, Christianity, and Islam With Missionary Implications.* I isolated seven causes or factors affecting the spread of religions over primarily the last two thousand years. (Buddha lived some 500 years before Christ, but Buddhism did not begin spreading widely until probably the time of Emperor Asoka in India, who was ruling some 250 years after Buddha.) In my research into the various causes for the spread of religions I made a discovery, which enables us to understand the power of the gospel of the coming of a Mediator.

Before describing this discovery, I will give some important background that led to the discovery. It is good to begin with the fact that almost all peoples of the world have realized that there is a God above and beyond the created world, namely a transcendent God. Besides this "high God" they were conscious of "powers" above and beyond ordinary human life. These were often worshipped as divinities. Social scientists have long recognized the pervasiveness of religion among all peoples. There is even recognition by some scholars that earlier religions were more pure than they became later as civilizations developed. Rodney Stark (2007:63) has placed new emphasis on the fact that "there seems sufficient reason to accept that at some point many cultures abandoned belief in High Gods and embraced a flock of smaller Gods." Of course, it can be accepted that some individuals doubted the existence of God (Psalm 53:1), but in reviewing the history of religions, irreligion or doubt in the existence of God, became a strong movement only in the modern era in which it appeared, significantly, in a Christian context before spreading around the world (Montgomery 2012: 293-341). In other words, Christians were instrumental in driving people away from God or at least giving them an excuse for rejecting the gospel of Jesus Christ.

For many ancient peoples, God seemed to be fairly close, even as part of the world around them, but as civilizations developed and certainly by the first millennium before Christ, God and the associated transcendent realm seemed further away from what had become a world under the domination of authoritarian rulers and full of human misery. As already noted, many lived in crowded, dirty, and disease-ridden cities. Throughout history and especially as misery spread with civilizations, people tried to get in touch with or get access to the distant God and to gain spiritual power and deliverance from their miserable lives. Since a "high God" seemed distant, people did their searching through creating numerous divinities that they could see and touch. "Seeing and touching" became very important.

A sociologist provided me with a clue about human yearnings to contact God. Sharon Sharot (2001), a sociologist of religion, analyzed the religions of the world in terms of elite and popular religions. All the religions of the world developed these two versions or expressions of religions, including Christianity. Elite religion is the religion of the powerful, who rule over others. The rulers are interested in order, unity, continuity, and maintaining orthodoxy or correct belief, all of which support their rule. The religious leaders, in cooperation with the rulers, produce literature and monumental buildings, the latter partly to impress the people. What do the elite want from God? As rulers, they want approval and legitimacy for their reign over others. One important way of obtaining legitimacy is by claiming to have a direct connection between themselves and the Divine. This was usually done with the help of religious specialists or priests. Arend Th. van Leeuven

(1964:165-173) describes this kind of rule as an autocratic state that sees the life of society as a kind of pyramid or mountain that touches the cosmos and the Divine through the ruler. Often the accompanying ideology emphasizes the value of harmony, under the elite of course.

In contrast to elite religion, popular religion or the religion of the population at large is based primarily on the desire to survive in the difficult and miserable conditions existing for most people in the ancient civilizations. The people sought healing from the diseases that constantly attacked them in the crowded cities and poor villages. They also sought food, good crops, good hunting, and children to grow up and help them, and safety from the many dangers of life. Since the transcendent God seemed far away, they looked for immanent, tangible, and concrete manifestations of God or gods that would enable them to obtain the help and power "from above" to overcome or simply survive the difficulties experienced in their miserable lives. Initially, as preliterate peoples, they looked for God in objects, such as mountains, rocks, sacred trees, something they could tie around their necks or arms, and even in birds and animals, but especially in ancestors or heroic humans having special powers. They began to make objects to represent God that would allow them to get some of God's power for their lives. As people developed art, these objects were turned into what we call "idols." The point I am making is that human beings wanted to be able to see and touch God or some representation of transcendent power. They wanted access to God, even if primarily on their own terms and for their own purposes.

You can see the desire for a tangible representation of God in the Bible where the people, in spite of the command not to create objects to worship as all the peoples around them had done, nevertheless constantly did create idols to worship. When we read the Bible carefully, we can see that the people of Israel did worship idols representing various gods, especially up to the time of the destruction of the Temple. The destruction of the Temple and of Jerusalem, followed by the Exile, provided the blow that more than anything else destroyed idolatry among the people of Israel. However, even the faithful people of Israel used words that show how they longed to have direct contact with a tangible God or representation of God. For example, we read in Psalm 42:1,2:

> As a deer longs for flowing streams, so my soul longs
> for you O God.
> My soul thirsts for God, for the living God.
> When shall I come and behold the *face of God*?
> -Psalm 42:1,2

The writers of the Hebrew Scriptures often spoke of seeing the "face of God." In Psalm 27:8, 9 we read: " 'Come' my heart says, 'seek his face! Your face, Lord, do I seek. Do not hide your face from me.'"

These words give us an important clue about a pervasive desire among human beings. Human beings long for direct contact with God found in some tangible representation. I found important empirical evidence for this in the three religions that spread widely. What I have said above is background for what I call "my discovery." Although Buddhism, Christianity, and Islam are very different, they have something in common. They each lift up a *single human being* who in some way gives people access to God.

Buddha did not claim to be Divine, but people came to regard him as such and millions of people worshipped him. John Noss (1949:172) wrote movingly that even though the people did not understand the sophisticated philosophy found in Buddhism, they became interested, "not in the teaching, but in the man...a personality that could be adored...Fortunately for the future of Buddhism, its founder balanced the arahat [saint] ideal of self-salvation with the ideal of compassionate goodwill toward all living beings, and practiced the compassion himself." More than any other human figure Buddha became adored across Asia and more recently has found followers in the West.

The believers also added many helpers (bodhisattvas), just as Christians added other intermediaries (Mary and the saints). But most importantly people believed Buddha had compassion for their suffering and provided each individual a way of escape from suffering. I remember a picture of Buddha on a brochure of a Buddhist organization (a picture in a Buddhist hospital) in which Buddha is depicted ministering to a sick disciple in a fashion often shown in pictures of Christ. This is a Buddha people can feel near to and have access to.

Muhammed is not believed to be Divine, but he is considered to be a very special and sacred person. Historically, Muhammed was a great religious leader, who was also a military leader and statesmen. He provided inspiration to tribal peoples that enabled them to defeat the armies of two great empires, the Byzantine and Persian Empires. Muslims actually liberated many Christian people in Syria and Egypt from the persecution of other Christian people, namely the "Christian Empire" based in Constantinople. The triumphs of these tribal people inspired the Arabs and other peoples (Central Asians, Africans, and Southeast Asians) to create new orders with a new religion. The rise of Islam could be characterized as a "revitalization movement." But beyond all of these accomplishments carried out by Muhammed and his network of followers, Muhammed was given a special status as a "friend of God." In addition and adding to the sense of God's immanence through Muhammed, the Koran was considered to be the dictation of God through the mouth of Muhammed. The Koran became like an extension of God into human life. It is through Muhammed and the tangible divinely dictated Koran that Muslims feel close to God. It is important that salvation is offered *to every individual* who submits to the all powerful and compassionate God of Muhammed.

What about the fact that other religions besides the three missionary religions have had outstanding leaders, many of whom were worshipped? None of them claimed to provide people a *means of direct access to God* and to do so on a universal basis, namely to every individual human. The other founders were sages, teachers, or prophets, but not personal representatives of the Divine with a universal message of compassion and salvation for each individual. Although all religions, including the missionary religions, tend to become identified with certain ethnic groups, the three missionary religions crossed numerous ethnic boundaries while religions other than the missionary religions became *primarily* identified with one group or a limited number of groups of people. In fact, the identification with a single ethnic group for Christianity has been a major hindrance in its spread, as we shall see.

Now, with this background to understand why the three missionary religions have spread more widely than any other religions, we can also see why Christianity, while often failing to be accepted by new groups, has spread still more widely than even the other missionary religions. Christianity has also been a major influence in bringing about more changes in the last 2000 years than any other religion, which is not to say that its influence was always for good.

Of all religious figures, Jesus Christ is set forth more clearly than any other person as the Great Mediator between God and humanity. More detail is given about his compassionate life than about any other religious leaders. Christians believe that Jesus Christ is God come to earth and that he not only came to earth, but that he specifically opened up a new and living way to God above. The letter to the Hebrews makes this very clear (Hebrews 4:14-16). He is the Mediator and the Intercessor based on his death on the cross and his resurrection in power. No other leader or founder of a major world religion died for human sins and rose from the dead for our salvation. Furthermore, the one who died and rose again is at the right hand of God making intercession for us. The Bible even tells us that Jesus Christ existed from the foundation of the world (John 1:1-4; Colossians 1:15-20). All things were made through him. He is the image of God showing us what God is like and what God wants us to be like and will make us like, namely like Jesus Christ. Jesus Christ reveals both the original and final plan of God for humans. I came to the conclusion that other religions, particularly Buddhism and Islam, also demonstrate the longing of humans for a tangible compassionate Mediator between them and God, enabling them to spread quite widely.

The coming and work of Jesus Christ is what makes the last days or the final period of history different from all previous time. The mystery of God's purpose for humans is a mystery no longer. Because of the coming of Christ it is now an open secret. God's purpose for us fulfills the longing of the human heart to have direct access to God and somehow to become what we should be, creatures remade in God's image. God has turned idol making on its head. Instead of humans making images of gods who are like us, God is making humans into God's own image. This is the exciting work of God in the "last days," the days for the coming of the New Age that follows the previous Old Age in which humans did not know God's plan and what God was doing. The purpose of the preparatory work under the people of Israel in the Old Covenant is now clear. Christians can learn from the Hebrew Scriptures about God's mercy toward and judgment of the People of God and also the typical mistakes of God's People that Christians are repeating. But now the Mission to the world has been made clear through Jesus Christ and the Spirit of God has been given to carry out that Mission through God's people.

CONCLUSION

The rule or kingdom of Jesus Christ deserves to be called "The New Age" because it brings a new clarity and a new experience of God's presence and work in human life. Speaking simply empirically, the years since Jesus Christ mark a distinct turn in human history in which change has been accelerating, the most distinct change for believers in Jesus Christ being the spread of his gospel and Kingdom. What was not clear before, whether God cared about his creation, especially human beings, has been made very clear in Jesus Christ. Since humans could not come to God, God has come to humans. The real question for humans is not whether to believe in God since the devils believe and tremble. Thus the argument over the existence of God is really a distraction. The real question is whether humans can respond to the God who comes looking for them (Genesis 3:8, 9). Since God could not force people to both believe in and love "Ta" (I prefer the Chinese which can be either "him" or "her"), it makes sense that God would come as Jesus Christ, the "suffering Servant," to win our hearts. This cannot be proved and it is not based on reason, but it is reasonable or "makes sense" that a Creator God would seek to win human hearts this way. And it is exactly what God did as Jesus Christ came among us showing great mercy for all and then dying for our sins and rising again to glory and to receive "all authority in heaven and on earth" (Matthew 28:18). The yearning for contact with God that we see throughout history and all over the world is fulfilled explicitly through Jesus Christ, the Great Mediator.

The eclectic and vague religions that are called "New Age" represent the yearning, but not the fulfillment of the human desire for a direct relationship with God. It is also true that New Age religions are not "new" at all, but are like many religions that have existed through the centuries. In New Testament times most of these were called Gnostic religions because they claimed to have a secret knowledge (gnosis) of the path to eternal life.

If it is so clear that Christ is the fulfillment of human yearning through the centuries, why has this not been accepted more widely in the last two thousand years? In fact, the gospel of Jesus Christ has been accepted widely, but there are specific conditions, especially Christian failings, that have blocked the acceptance of the Good News of Christ and entrance into the New Age he introduced. In the third chapter I will review the last two thousand years to clarify what has happened to both spread and block the spread of the Good News of Christ. However, before that I discuss a view of the Bible and history that has misled many Christians.

CHAPTER 2

THE CONTINUING INFLUENCE OF DISPENSATIONALISM

MORE THAN A SET OF IDEAS

Most Christians are not familiar with the term "dispensationalism," but many have heard the terms, "rapture" and "Armageddon." Many are also aware of the *Schofield Reference Bible*, perhaps in their home or church. They may have heard the preaching of "Christian Zionists" and be among those who see the founding of the State of Israel as being a special sign of the soon-to-be return of Christ. Other influences that may be considered more positive have been the establishment of numerous independent churches and organizations promoting evangelism and missions. All of these ideas and activities are evidence of the influence of dispensationalism or of its milder component, pre-millennialism, even if the terms are not used or understood. Dispensational ideas have remained influential among Christians, especially among those who think and preach about "the end times." However, dispensationalism is really more than a set of ideas, but may be regarded as a religious movement with a strong eschatological emphasis in its message. Of course, as we have seen in Chapter 1, Christianity itself had a strong eschatological message from the beginning, which many Christians up to the present have neglected. Dispensationalism filled a gap in the Christian thought of many, but with an unfortunate elaboration of the Christian message.

THE DISPENSATIONAL MOVEMENT

Millennialism, sometimes referred to as chiliasm (from the Greek word for 1000), has a long history in the Church going back to the Montanists, the followers of Montanus of Phrygia. In 156 C.E. he proclaimed himself as the one through whom the dispensation of the Holy Spirit had begun. His message appealed to those who opposed the increasing worldliness of the church, which included the early church theologian, Tertullian (c. 160–c 220 C.E.). The desire to increase the intensity of Christian life has been a major goal of the various millenarian movements in history. It is not surprising that eschatology should figure largely in the thought of those who would like to raise the temperature of Christian faith since eschatology is about raised expectations. Probably the Dispensational Movement is the most influential such movement in the modern era.

Dispensationalism as a system of thought was given its first full statement by John Nelson Darby (1800-1882), a founding member of the Plymouth Brethren Church in Great Britain, in the 1830s. True to the pattern of leaders of religious movements, he felt that the established church was greatly lacking in spirituality and could even be considered apostate. Barbara Rossing (2004) has written an excellent theological analysis of dispensationalism, showing its numerous misinterpretations of the Bible. She also notes the important fact that dispensationalism has had an influence even on American government policy toward the Middle East, although the extent of its influence is a matter of debate. That is, politicians and religious leaders may be primarily using each other to gain influence. I would like to emphasize that apart from being a special theological and historical perspective, dispensationalism should also be regarded as a religious movement, especially in North America. This helps us to understand the continuing influence of dispensational thought.

A social or religious movement is aimed at bringing about change of some kind. As already noted, millennial movements are usually aimed at changing the Church in the direction of being purer and more earnest, in short, being "more spiritual." Dispensationalism has exactly this aim and for this reason it has often attracted people who are looking for a more intense religious experience than they had previously known in some established denomination. The emphasis on prayer, personal discipline, evangelism, and world missions has been especially attractive to people.

Every movement requires articulate leaders, actually a network of leaders, who exhibit "charisma." Beginning in the 1870s, Darby attracted a number of American religious leaders, among who were D.L. Moody (1837—1899), J.R. Graves (1820—1893), James Brookes (1830—1897), A.B. Simpson (1843—1821), A.J. Gordon (1836—1895), R.A. Torrey (1856—1928), C.I. Schofield (1843—1921), and James M. Gray (1851—1935). These men were very effective speakers and most were active in organizing and speaking at numerous conferences. Among these were the Niagara Conferences (1870 to the early 1900s) and the American Bible and Prophetic Conferences (1878 to 1914). These kinds of gatherings and organizing are also characteristics of movements.

Further development in organization is seen in the institutionalization that took place with the establishment of numerous Bible Institutes and Schools beginning in the nineteenth century. Early examples of these were the Nyack Bible Institute–now Nyack College and Alliance Theological Seminary (1882), Moody Bible Institute (1886), Boston Missionary Training School (1889), Columbia Bible School—now Columbia International University (1923), and Dallas Theological Seminary (1924). As the years passed, the development of Bible Institutes, now mostly Bible colleges or universities, mushroomed, so that many of the larger cities in North America contained at least one such institution. The Association of Biblical Higher Education reported in 2011, "More than 120 years after the first Bible School was started, there are more than 1200 Bible schools and colleges in the United States and Canada" (www. abhe.org). Bible colleges finally began to raise their educational standards by the 1970s. However, since then many people in the larger Evangelical community have turned away from looking primarily to Bible colleges to obtain their ministerial leadership. Nevertheless, the institutional expression and base of the movement in schools and training centers was already well established.

In addition to articulate leadership and the development of the means of influencing large numbers of people through conferences and institutions, the dispensational movement has been very effective in publishing its viewpoints and in using electronic media as it developed. The single most effective publication of the movement has been the *Schofield Reference Bible*, first published under the leadership of C. I. Schofield in 1909 by Oxford University Press. Additional popular expressions flowed from the movement. The message of the movement changed over time. In spite of the emphasis by Darby on the "ruin of the Church," namely the apostate condition of the older established churches, most of the American leaders of the movement did not initially promote separation from established churches. However, with the development of the fundamentalist-modernist struggle beginning after 1917, dispensationalists became the major flag carriers among fundamentalists. George Marsden (1987:37) states, "John Nelson Darby, who in the nineteenth century had brought dispensationalism to American, had urged separation from existing denominations; but until the controversies of the 1920s, relatively few of his American followers paid much attention to his separatist doctrine." It was then that dispensational publications began to gain great circulation. Milton and Lyman Steward, two devout and wealthy dispensationalists, were the major contributors to the distribution of three million copies of The Fundamentals. "As Lyman wrote to Milton after learning that the American Tobacco Company was spending millions of dollars distributing free cigarettes in order to give people a taste for them: 'Christians should learn from the wisdom of the world'" (Ruthven 2004:12).

As the electronic media began to develop in the 1920s and 30s, dispensationalists, ever mindful of the Biblical mandate to evangelize, gave a major effort to using the various forms of electronic media. The use of auditoriums that could hold very large gatherings and benefit from electronic media became a hallmark of evangelism by dispensationalists. Dispensationalists became leaders in radio and then television broadcasting, becoming much more adept in their use than the established churches. Jerry Falwell, now deceased, and Pat Robertson, both dispensationalists, became famous modern broadcasters and television preachers, as well as political activists.

It almost goes without saying that people in the Dispensational Movement or those simply influenced by it have shown an entrepreneurial spirit in setting up numerous evangelistic and overseas mission oriented organizations. An example of one of the most imaginative and successful organizations has been Operation Mobilization (OM) initiated by George Verwer (2008) with the support of close friends. Over a number of years several ships were purchased and refurbished to carry large numbers of short-term missionaries and missionary interns to visit ports throughout the world and to carry on a variety of mission activities. Verwer, a convert of Billy Graham in 1955 and a 1960 graduate of Moody Bible Institute, is an example of an independent Christian leader who appears quite moderate, making no mention of his eschatological views in his 2008 book about his missionary experiences.

I have not given in detail the actual beliefs advanced by dispensationalists, but it is true that an effective movement must have an ideology that appeals to many people at least over some period of time. Even so, the *presentation* of the ideology may have as much or more to do with its effectiveness as the actual details of the ideology. Very briefly, there are traditionally seven dispensations, although some dispensationalists mention fewer, a dispensation being God's way of dealing with humans (God's "economy") in a particular age. Without entering into the complex discussion of the characteristics of the various dispensations (See Ryrie 1995 [1966]), what is most important to know is that we are presently living in the next to last dispensation, the dispensation of grace, sometimes called "the age of the Spirit," and we are awaiting the final dispensation of the millennial Kingdom. In this Kingdom, the Lord Jesus Christ "will personally take charge of the running of the affairs of the world"(Ryrie 1995 [1966]:6). At the end of this period, a rebellious army will attack the seat of government, but be defeated and the rebels cast into everlasting punishment. Although all do not agree, a common belief is that there will be a rapture of believers before the first return of Christ to be followed by a period of tribulation of those remaining during which a certain number will repent. The exact content of dispensational beliefs are not as important as the fact that they have appealed to many people because of their systematic and detailed explanation of history, as well as their claims to give descriptions of future events. This is combined with a very specific, disciplined, and open piety or religiosity emphasizing Bible study, prayer, personal discipline, and preaching, especially preaching of an authoritative kind. Both the nature of the content and the strong and efficient presentation of dispensational beliefs have proven effective in influencing large numbers of people.

ADAPTABILITY OF DISPENSATIONALISM

Dispensationalism has been responsive to the rapid and often revolutionary social and political changes that have been taking place since the late eighteenth century and increasingly in recent years. Premillennialism, the belief that the return of Christ will be followed by his 1000-year reign on earth, can also be included as being responsive to these great changes. All dispensationalists are premillennialists, but not all premillennialists are dispensationalists. That is, premillennialists do not necessarily believe in the seven dispensations. Richard Kyle (2006:92) speaks of the "suitability" of dispensationalism in noting its growing influence after World War I:

> These years after 1914 gave dispensationalism a tremendous boost. This era witnessed tragedy after tragedy. But "things were never better for American premillennialism" [Weber 1979]. The basic prophecies of the early dispensationalists in the nineteenth century began to take concrete form in the early twentieth century. In the eyes of dispensationalists, world war, the return of the Jews to Palestine, the Russian Revolution, the redrawing of the European map, and the rise of totalitarianism were all predicted in Scripture. Indeed, most of the major themes so conspicuous in modern popular dispensationalism had taken shape before World War II, the only exceptions being the threat of nuclear annihilation and control of the masses by the Antichrist through television and computers.
>
> The apparent fulfillment of ancient biblical

prophecies enabled dispensationalism to take solid root in the evangelical subculture. Within premillennialism the tenet of an any moment rapture had prevailed over posttribulationalists [the rapture after a time of tribulation]. In Pentecostalism and early fundamentalism, premillennialism had taken hold. Further, the modernist-fundamentalist conflict of the 1920s fragmented many denominations. What emerged was a separatist fundamentalism with its own churches, schools, mission agencies, and publishing houses. Dispensationalism thus had a subculture and a substantial institutional structure to perpetuate itself.

Kyle lists the same movement characteristics noted above, but especially draws attention to the ideology that presents a view of history, which seems to fit the turbulent modern times. The seven dispensations of dispensationalism cover all of history from the beginning of the Bible to the present and to eternity. What gives particular strength to this perspective on total human history is that it is based on an interpretation of the Bible, which at least purports to give the highest possible honor to the Bible. Dispensationalists like to emphasize that their views are based on "taking the Bible as it is."

Accordingly, dispensationalism and the fundamentalism with which it became associated focus very much on literally interpreting a Bible that is "without error." Here is how Charles Ryrie (1995 [1966]:20), a convinced dispensationalist, describes the basis of dispensationalism: "For now it suffices to say that dispensationalism claims to employ principles of literal, plain, normal, or historical-grammatical interpretation consistently." Later in Chapter 5 of his book, Ryrie (1995 [1966]:79-95) discusses "The Hermeneutics of Dispensationalism" stating quite clearly, "Dispensationalists claim that their principle of hermeneutics is that of literal interpretation." Furthermore, he claims that while other Christians may be literalists, dispensationalists are distinguished in their consistency in literal interpretation, concluding, "Classic dispensationalism is a result of consistent application of the basic hermeneutical principal of literal, normal, or plain interpretation. No other system of theology can claim this" (1995 [1966]:85).

The self-proclaimed "taking the Bible as it is" approach of dispensationalists enabled them to take over the leadership of the Fundamentalist movement in the 1920s, but also eventually to become a major influence among Evangelicals and to gain a major voice among Christian conservatives in the United States. The more scholarly, but also more complex, approach of the historic mainline churches employed historical and literary criticism to interpret the Bible as was being done in Europe, much to the dismay of "Bible believers."

It was after World War II that the liberal-conservative divides in society and the churches became particularly apparent with the struggles of the 1960s and 1970s. The mainline churches became tagged as "liberal" because they, particularly in their leadership, took the "liberal" side in their support of civil rights, opposition to the Vietnam War, and in other social issues, such as women's rights and abortion. James Davison Hunter (1991) wrote of a deep struggle in America, which he called "the culture wars," that was (is) a struggle on how America should be defined. Without going into the complexities of this struggle and the ambiguities in the terms "liberal" and "conservative," it is obvious that there has been a rise in influence of Evangelicals (of whom the dispensationalists have been a major part) beginning especially with the presidency of Ronald Reagan. D. Michael Lindsay (2007) provides important data to demonstrate how Evangelicals have become a major influence in the United States along with the rise of conservatives in politics. Although Lindsay does not distinguish the dispensational branch within Evangelicalism, it is clear in the names he lists that dispensationalists have been a major influence within Evangelicalism and have thus ridden the wave of conservatism in society. To what extent this wave has been slowed and even reversed in some areas with the presidential election of November 2008 remains to be seen. However, in the mid-term elections of 2010 there was a resurgence of conservatism. Whatever the case and the outcome of elections, the struggle over different views of American identity and values is clearly an ongoing contemporary struggle. In his recent book, Hunter (2010) describes how the struggles between the "right" and the "left" Christian perspectives hardened by becoming politicized.

One can see how dispensationalism or the Dispensationalist Movement has remained influential by recalling the heavy emphasis it places on the literal or "plain" authority of the Bible. Some kind of authority is necessary for the religious, spiritual, and moral life. While older and more liturgical churches provide religious authority to a relatively great extent through the church community and its official leaders (the Pope providing a very personalized authority), the Protestant movement and especially the Evangelical wing of Protestantism elevated the written Scriptures to highest authority. However, strong and authoritative preachers, who constantly base their authoritative approach on "what the Bible says", have also characterized the Dispensationalist Movement. It is therefore understandable that dispensationalism should be especially appealing to people who feel the need for a direct written authority from God for their religious-spiritual life, even though in fact it is usually mediated through an authoritarian spokesperson.

There are other conservative Evangelicals, who equally

emphasize the authority of the Bible with the dispensationalists, but who are generally more highly educated and sophisticated in their interpretation of the Bible and usually consider themselves traditional Reformed or Calvinistic theologians. These traditional Evangelicals, also called "Covenant theologians," have been less well known and influential on the popular level than the dispensationalist Evangelicals.

In addition to being highly adapted to the conservative affinity for authoritarian direction to life, the ideology of dispensationalism turned out, at least in North America, to be especially well adapted to the spirit of independency and localism and the entrepreneurial spirit that exists in society. It has already been noted that the Dispensational Movement took over leadership of the fundamentalist branch of Evangelicalism in the time of the Fundamentalist-Modernist controversies of the 1920s. With the doctrine of the "ruin of the church" that had existed from the beginning of the ideology under Darby, dispensationalists found that it was not difficult to separate themselves from organized churches in order to set up "more spiritual churches" that placed greater emphasis on the spiritual disciplines such as prayer and witnessing, as well as on "taking the Bible as it is." Independency in religious organization is very compatible to American culture's localism and individualism. Consequentially, dispensationalists and those strongly influenced by them feel free in setting up their own independent churches free of "control" of denominational organizations (the hated bureaucracies), which in any case are likely to be considered liberal and even apostate.

If one looks at dispensationalism in the light of the 2000-year history of Christianity, the Dispensationalist Movement may be seen as one of many movements, going back as far as the second century Montanists, that has attempted to revitalize the faith. Thus, from the beginning dispensationalists took a critical stance toward the historic churches as being too "worldly" or too much in league with the secular world. The leaders and followers in the Dispensationalist Movement in the nineteenth century were seekers of an intense spiritual experience. The same is true of many, if not most, of the followers of the Movement to this day.

One of the great appeals to the Christian public of the Dispensational Movement along with those who follow the milder eschatological belief of Pre-millennialism has been the emphasis given to prayer, righteous individual behavior, and evangelism, traditional Christian disciplines. Again, these disciplines may often be lacking among Christians at large. Many dispensationalists and people influenced by them have been successful in establishing Christian agencies carrying out extensive work. The sending out of missionaries overseas has been a hallmark of such agencies. It is also true, based on my personal observation and reading that some leaders of these agencies or para-church organizations become more moderate in their views and less judgmental of others over time. This may come from long experience in dealing with human nature, including their own and their followers, and with recognizing devout Christians in established churches. Also, contact with needy and suffering people has helped many conservative Christians shift away from an overemphasis on doctrinal issues alone.

Of course, given the pluralistic religious condition of American society, there are expressions of intense spiritual experience other than that found in the Dispensationalist Movement. Richard Flory and Donald Miller (2008) describe four types of "post-boomer" generation (ranging in age from their twenties to their forties) Christians, all of whom are serious about their faith: *Innovators, Appropriators, Resisters, and Reclaimers.* In brief, the *Innovators* foster spiritual growth in which individuals are embedded in communities that make much use of the body, story telling, and art. The *Appropriators* make the most use of modern technology and adapt many features of modern culture found in entertainment, the mall, and popular music to attract people to hear their messages. The *Resisters* tend to be very rationalistic and to place a great emphasis on correct verbal expression of the faith. Finally, the *Reclaimers* place themselves in the context of the older historical churches, such as the Orthodox and Anglican Churches, and are inspired by their rich liturgies. Of the four groups, the *Appropriators* have been the most likely to be part of the Dispensationalist Movement or at least be highly influenced by it. This is because the great emphasis on evangelism in dispensationalism has made it very open to adopting modern methods of communication, as well as features of popular culture that will attract people. The other most conservative group, the *Resisters*, is more likely to be represented by the traditional Calvinists among the Evangelicals.

FLAWS IN DISPENSATIONALISM

In Chapter One, I set forth what I believe to be the Biblical perspective on "the end times," which is quite different from the view of dispensationalism. However, I will state a few of the major flaws that I see in the dispensational perspective. Dispensationalism is undercut primarily by the Bible's own interpretation of itself, particularly the New Testament view of the Old Testament.

Christian interpretation of the Bible should begin with Jesus Christ, the living Word. Jesus Christ showed no interest in controlling territory or setting up an earthly Kingdom. He specifically rejected such a kingdom at the time of his temptation in the wilderness (Matthew 3:8-10) and before Pilate (John 18:36-37), as well as by the nature of his ministry. The apostles followed their Lord in their activities and writings in showing no interest in the establishment of a kingdom in Jerusalem or in any other specific place on earth.

Rule over territory was never a concern of Christ and stopped being a concern of his followers after the coming of the Holy Spirit.

When Gentiles started receiving the gospel in Antioch, an important meeting was called in Jerusalem to discuss what should be done about requiring the Gentiles to follow Jewish religious practices (Acts 15:1-21). After hearing the reports of Peter, Barnabas, and Paul, James the leader of the Jerusalem church stated that the coming to faith in Christ by the Gentiles was a fulfillment of the words of the prophets where it is said:

> After this I will return, and rebuild the dwelling of David, which has fallen, and from its ruins I will rebuild it and I will set it up, so that all other peoples may seek the Lord—even all the Gentiles over whom my name has been called. Thus says the Lord, who has been making these things known from long ago (Acts 15:16,17).

Interestingly, the original Hebrew from Amos 9:11, 12, speaks of possessing "the remnant of Edom," but James leaves this out. The leader of the church in Jerusalem wants to make clear that the real purpose of God is to restore his Kingdom by drawing the Gentiles of all nations to Christ. The "dwelling of David" is seen as the growing Church, not the people of Israel as such and specifically not the physical city of Jerusalem with its temple.

Dispensationalists like to say that other Christians weaken the promises of the Bible by "spiritualizing" them or considering them merely metaphorical. Here, the Bible itself "spiritualizes" the promise about the restoration of the kingdom of David. It is certainly not to be an earthly kingdom centered in Jerusalem. Furthermore, the fulfillment of the promise to restore Zion was seen as beginning in those very early days of the preaching of the gospel of Jesus Christ.

The "rebuilding of the dwelling of David" was seen to be taking place in the conversions in Antioch.

The whole book of Hebrews is useful for its perspective on the fulfillment of the Old Testament practices through Jesus Christ. The wilderness experience in which rest in the Promised Land was refused to the people because of their lack of faith is used as a metaphor to encourage seeking rest through the present life of faith in Christ (Hebrews 3:7-19). Furthermore, the Book of Hebrews is well known for its description of how the Old Testament sacrifices foreshadowed the sacrificial work of Jesus Christ. To look forward to the reestablishment of the former sacrifices in Jerusalem, as some dispensationalists have done, is really unthinkable, even a denial of the efficacy of the one sacrifice of Christ.

One of the clearest passages in the Bible that reduces the importance of the earthly Jerusalem in the kingdom established by Jesus Christ is found in Hebrews 12. After speaking of Mt. Sinai, that was such a terrifying place for the ancient Hebrews, the writer adds these words, contrasting the New Jerusalem with the ancient source of the Law:

> But you have come to Mount Zion and to the city
> of the living God, the heavenly Jerusalem, and to
> innumerable angels in festal gathering, and to the
> assembly of the first born who are enrolled in heaven,
> and to God the judge of all, and to the spirits of the
> righteous made perfect, and to Jesus, the mediator
> of a new covenant, and to the sprinkled blood that
> speaks a better word than the blood of Abel.

This is the Bible interpreting the Bible. It clearly shows that the Jerusalem of human history points beyond itself. Where is Jerusalem now? It is where we meet Jesus and receive the forgiveness of God.

Jerusalem is throughout the world, the world that "the meek inherit" (Psalm 37:11; Matthew 5:5). What do believers "possess" now? All things! "For all things are yours, whether Paul or Apollos or Cephas or the world or life or death or the present or the future—all belong to you, and you belong to Christ, and Christ belongs to God" (I Corinthians 3:22-23).

A basic error of dispensationalism is misunderstanding the meaning of true possession of "the land" or any part of creation that is taught throughout the Bible. The world belongs to God. We only truly possess anything in the world when we live by faith and offer all that we are and have up to God. This is the lesson God has been teaching his people since the call to Abraham. From the beginning, the promise to possess the land was based on living faithfully as God's people. In the New Testament, the promise to Abraham that his descendents will possess the land was not revoked; it was expanded by Jesus Christ to include the whole world. God is not interested in our (Christians or Jews) "possession" of anything in the sense of control or ownership, of some earthly title to land; however, God is interested in the sense of our recognizing the world as God's and using the world for the glory of God and the benefit of all. That is the true meaning of being in Zion and "possessing the land." As for "spiritualizing" meanings in the Bible, the Bible itself in both the Old and New Testaments speaks of "circumcising of the heart" (Deuteronomy 10:16; 30:6; Romans 2:29; Colossians 2:11). Of course, physical circumcision as a religious act was given up in the New Testament. The same is true of the meaning of "possessing the land."

CONCLUSION

It may seem strange to place a discussion of dispensationalism at this point in a book on "The Real New Age." The reason for doing this is that dispensationalists have gained more attention than any other Christian group in their emphasis on eschatology or "last days." In this doing this, they filled a vacuum in Christianity left by the older established churches, which largely neglected talk of the "last days." It has helped them create excitement, intensity of commitment, and evangelistic zeal. The price has been high in terms of a misinterpretation of what the Bible teaches about "the last days" and in terms of overemphasizing a verbal witness and underemphasizing a holistic witness to Christ and the gospel. A clear distinction and separation was made between the promises to Israel and the promises to the Church, the former promises being interpreted in a very materialistic manner and the latter in a very spiritual manner. The result of this distinction in perspectives is the setting forth of two Covenants when the Bible really presents one covenant of grace for God's people. This was the major reason for the declaration of the Presbyterian Church, U.S. (now part of the Presbyterian Church U.S.A.) that dispensationalism was out of accord with the Reformed Faith. One effect of this separation of promises has been to give support to groups who separate from established churches in this "Age of the Spirit" in order to form "more spiritual" bodies. A rationale is provided for schism.

In the end, what the Bible teaches about the last period of history or the New Age of Jesus Christ is an important part of Biblical teaching that is neglected at the peril of weakening Christian faith and action and fostering divisions in the Church, particularly as some Christians fill the gap of neglect of eschatology by developing non-Biblical eschatological perspectives.

CHAPTER 3

THE SPREAD OF CHRISTIANITY BECAUSE OF AND IN SPITE OF CHRISTIANS

THE BEGINNING OF THE SPREAD OF THE GOSPEL OF CHRIST

This chapter takes up the story begun in the first chapter. My purpose there was to make clear that based on the Biblical view of history we have been in the last days, the last period of history, for the last two thousand years. In other words, Jesus Christ introduced a New Age, namely his Kingdom that now exists in the present period. No one knows how long the New Age will continue before it is brought to a final consummation in a new creation of all things. Even if the last days continued for another one hundred or a few thousand or even ten thousand years, that would still be a short time in human history. What is important is that the presence of the New Age makes the period of history since Jesus Christ different from all previous periods of human history.

The major phenomenon affecting more people than any other phenomenon in this last period of history is the beginning of the spread of the gospel of Jesus Christ throughout the world. I say "beginning" because there are many areas of the world, and especially aspects of human life, to which the gospel has not spread and the Kingdom has not come. There is still much teaching to do if the commandment is to be fulfilled: "teaching them to obey all that I have commanded you" (Matthew 28:20). As we look at these last two thousand years we have to say that there would be many more Christians if Christians had represented Jesus Christ more clearly by following his will more fully or at least been more conscious of the perceptions of people that were created by how Christians behaved or presented themselves. Many people have heard the words of the gospel in their minds, but have not really heard the gospel in their hearts. They have heard the name of "Jesus Christ," but they don't really see Jesus for who he is or understand what he has done, much less follow the teachings he commanded. The believers themselves, who are children of the New Age, have often failed to live according to their Lord's will, especially in not showing the compassion of Christ toward others, including other Christians. In other words, people have not seen Jesus Christ in us clearly—we who are designated to be witnesses to him.

THE SPREAD OF CHRISTIANITY

Although we are quick to say that Christianity is not identical to the Kingdom of God or even the Universal Church of Jesus Christ, we Christians are identified as belonging to a religion known as "Christianity." That label is likely to stick even though it carries a great amount of cultural baggage. It is more accurate to speak of "Christianities" since there are so many versions associated with so many cultural groups, sub-groups, and various movements. Nevertheless, like it or not, people will continue to speak of "Christianity" because of a common identification with Jesus Christ.

Christianity in its various forms has spread in three great waves and is now in its fourth wave. The first wave was its spread throughout the Mediterranean Basin, occupied primarily by the Roman Empire. This was in the first 300 years of the first millennium C.E. The second great wave was the spread of Christianity northward to the European tribes in Western and Eastern Europe over the next approximately 700 years. Smaller waves went south and east, even as far as China and perhaps further, but the effect was much smaller than the wave to the north, where Christianity became foundational to Western Civilization. After 1000, Christianity lost much of its momentum for almost 500 years. Its institutional aspect clearly dominated its movement aspect so that its missionary drive was lost. The third great wave took place beginning about 1500, increasing in strength in the nineteenth and twentieth centuries, and lasting up to the collapse of colonialism after World War II. After the collapse of colonialism, Christianity is now in the fourth great wave of spreading and has become a truly worldwide religion in representation by numbers of believers around the globe for the first time.

I mentioned earlier, that a few years ago I began to wonder why Christianity had spread in such a lopsided fashion; spreading at first primarily to the west instead of to the east. Should it not have spread out evenly? In working on my (2002) book, *The Lopsided Spread of Christianity*, I learned that the failure of Christians was one of the main reasons that Christianity did not spread out evenly. It was not simply the convenience of spreading in the Roman Empire, as often thought. It is understandable that the travel possibilities in the Empire facilitated the spread of Christianity, but a great failure of Christianity in the fourth century greatly hindered the spread of Christianity eastward. Christianity became identified with the Empire in the fourth century, which not only could be coercive and cruel, but which became the sworn enemy of many peoples in the Middle East and North Africa. This was the beginning of a major failure to represent a God and a Savior who are non-coercive. On the other hand I learned that the spread of Christianity was not as lopsided as I had thought because Christian missionaries, primarily the Nestorians, went eastward and people were converted in many areas of Asia.

Small kingdoms were converted to the north and east of Jerusalem, including much of Syria and the kingdoms of Armenia and Georgia. Various Arab tribes were converted. Soon many people were converted in Persia (Iran). Later, people were converted in India and also China. In particular, in Central Asia, Mongols were converted, including at least a whole tribe. There was a strong Christian presence among the Mongols who conquered most of Asia and much of the Middle East and Eastern Europe. Kublai Khan's mother was a Christian. The wife of Hulegu (Hulagu), the Mongol ruler of Persia, was a Christian. A leading Mongol general in the Middle East was a Christian. Nestorian Uigar Christians served as scribes for the Mongol Khans. Christianity had already been introduced to China under the Tang Dynasty by Nestorian Christians in the sixth century and it was introduced again by the Mongol rulers. However, the fall of the Tang dynasty in the beginning of the tenth century and of the Mongol (Yuan) dynasty in 1368 was followed in each case with the virtual disappearance of Christianity in China, where it never lost its identity as a foreign religion.

While there was a mix of success and failure to the east, Christianity spread mainly westward throughout the Mediterranean Basin and then northward to the European tribes. Making Christianity the official religion of the Roman Empire in the fourth century aided its spread, but at the same time established a tremendous barrier to its spread. The spread of Christianity after the decline of Roman power among the tribes took some seven hundred years to the year 1000 and even later to the Baltic nations. Individual and small groups of missionaries were crucial. However, an apparent short-term advantage, but a major drawback to the on-going witness to Jesus Christ was that the spread of Christianity took place in Europe along with the commonly accepted concept, especially by rulers, that everyone in a particular territory should be of the same religion. Christianity became obligatory as a territorial religion as in every land it joined forces with governmental coercive powers. The first three hundred years of non-coercive and voluntary Christianity came to an end as church leaders fell for the temptation that Jesus rejected at the beginning of his ministry, namely to become allied to governments, which by definition exercise coercion.

A MAJOR CHRISTIAN FAILURE

Territorial Christianity was based on the major Christian failure of the fourth century. This Christian failure has had negative effects up to the present day. Not only is this mistake not usually recognized; it is even celebrated as a major triumph of Christianity—"the winning of the Roman Empire." In falling for the temptation that Jesus rejected in the wilderness, the witness to Jesus Christ became severely clouded. Christians accepted the help of governmental power to gain control of a whole region, which was the Roman Empire of the day. It was a sin based on a common human desire for power and it was a failure common to all the religions of the world. This great human failing is the attempt to augment religious authority with governmental power.

Throughout the history of the world, religions and governments have been drawn to each other. One scholar, N. J. Demerath (2001), compares this mutual attraction to the attraction of the moth to the flame. Both religion and government can be the moth or the flame because when they combine they damage each other, even though the damage may not be obvious at first. It works like this. Governments have a monopoly of force, but it is very expensive and troublesome to rule by raw force alone. Therefore, governments seek to have widely recognized authority or legitimacy for their rule. Legitimacy is the recognition by those who are ruled of the *right* of a government to rule them. When governments have authority as well as power, it is much easier and cheaper to govern since they do not have to use raw force or power to rule. What is the highest authority? It is God and religions are supposed to have access to God. Therefore, governments typically throughout human history have approached religions with the offer, "You give us the approval of the Divinity and we will give you protection. In fact, we will eliminate or keep out of our territory all of your religious competition; we will do this by making you the official religion." Religions, for their part, have typically welcomed and even sought this arrangement because they then became religious monopolies over a given territory ruled by the government. As is well known, many, if not most, of the ancient rulers and some modern rulers were designated as being divine or at least semi-divine. Where this has been impossible because of religious beliefs, as in later European history, kings claimed to rule by "divine right."

In the fourth century, Constantine recognized that Christianity had spread throughout the Empire. It is thought that Christians made up about 16 percent (Stark 1997 [1996]: 13) of the population of the Roman Empire at this time, but they were spread throughout the Empire with churches in most cities and were the most effective Empire-wide network of non-governmental organizations. The Roman government had lost much of its former power and had undergone a re-organization under the previous emperor, Diocletian, to centralize its power. Although Constantine tolerated non-Christian religions, he saw Christianity as an ideology to unite the Empire under him. He used the Christians to give him legitimacy, but then Christians used him and his successors to establish Christianity as a monopolistic religion. Before the end of the fourth century, under Theodosius, it was made illegal not to be a Christian. At the same time, the Roman

Empire began to be invaded by the tribes to the north, some of which were Arian Christians. Rome fell to the mostly Arian Christian Goths in 410, but the government of the Empire had already been transferred to Constantinople. The Roman Empire in the West ceased to exist in 476 allowing the Church to exercise considerable political power in the resulting power vacuum. In effect the Western Empire fell into the arms of the Roman Catholic Church, while the government of the Eastern Empire continued to dominate the churches, which later became associated with particular nations as "autocephalous churches." Byzantium became the face of Christianity to the peoples further to the east and it was certainly not the face of Christ.

Many people think that Christianity spread to the European tribes through the power of the Roman Empire. This is not true. The gospel spread typically through the efforts of traveling monks, who themselves were usually from the tribes. A good example is that of Patrick, who as a Celt from Britain carried the gospel to the Celts of Ireland. Later, Celtic and British Saxon missionaries carried the gospel to the tribes of England and to the Continent. In spite of this spread of the gospel mostly without the accompaniment of governmental power, the sin of the fourth century was immediately repeated among the tribes. As the local European tribal rulers were converted they became "little Constantines" and forced the Christian faith on their fellow tribes' people, as well as on those they sought to dominate. Again, they made the assumption that a people in a given territory should have one religion—the religion of the rulers. This assumption lasted for many centuries, in fact up to recent times. In the Protestant Reformation, the Protestants accepted the same principle. This was the basis for the Peace of Westphalia of 1648 at the end of the Thirty Years' War between nations associated with Roman Catholicism and Protestantism. They agreed on which countries should be Roman

Catholic and which Protestant, although the struggle was based very much on developing nationalism. Christianity continued to be considered a territorial religion and the non-biblical concepts of "Christendom" and coercive Christianity were perpetuated. In spite of this distortion of what Christianity should be, the peoples of Europe learned through the gospel of their worth as distinctive peoples. A major result of the spread of the gospel to the European tribes is that at the western end of the Euro-Asian land mass many nations came into being whereas in the eastern and southern parts of this land mass, enduring empires ruled over diverse peoples.

Let us go back, however, to the great negative effect of the sin of the fourth century on the spread of the gospel to the east. In the fourth century, the government of the Roman Empire was shifted from Rome to Constantinople. There followed approximately one thousand years of a "Christian Empire"—the Byzantine Empire. One of the saddest stories of Christian history is the fighting and oppression ("Jesus Wars") that took place as a result of the doctrinal disputes in the fourth through the sixth centuries (Jenkins 2010). What a terrible representation of Jesus Christ to the world!

The historian of Eastern Christianity, Samuel Moffett (1992:137), notes that as soon as the Byzantine Empire became a "Christian Empire," the Persian Empire began a very severe persecution of Christianity. Why? Obviously, because Christianity was considered the religion of their enemy. We may also say that the success of Islam in the seventh century was at least in part due to the oppression by the Byzantine Empire of the people, especially the Christians in the Eastern Mediterranean, who differed from the Orthodox Faith and many of whom welcomed the Muslim "tribal liberators." The Arab tribes, with Christians among them, united to defeat both the Persian and the Byzantine Empires. The victory of the desert tribes over these great empires convinced many tribal people that Islam offered a religion of strength and moral order that would enable them to defeat their enemies. It did much to raise the self-esteem of many peoples as in what has been recognized as "revitalization movements" (Wallace 1956, 1967). Following the typical pattern, Islam also fused religion with governmental power and this has remained its policy to this day. Thus, a "Christian Empire," along with the "Zoroastrian Empire" of Persia, helped to spawn an "Islamic Empire." Creating a so called "Christian Empire" may have helped to spread Christianity, at least of a nominal kind, in the territories of the Empire, but at the same time it created great opposition to Christianity outside the Empire. This opposition to Christian domination continued and later spread during the "colonial era" of the West. Of course, opposition to the so-called "Christian West" in the Middle East has continued to the present. Christianity actually adopted the policy of "holy war" during the Crusades with resulting persecutions against internal heretics and Jews and external invasion of "infidel territory."

After the combination of Christianity and governmental power in the fourth century, much of the voluntary spirit that had permeated Christianity in the first three hundred years was lost. The voluntary spirit was maintained primarily by the monks and nuns in the religious orders, who carried the gospel to the various tribes in the north. However, at the same time the religious orders helped to establish a "two-class Christianity" made up of those who voluntarily entered the priesthood or monastic orders or convents for special service in contrast to the rest of the Christians who lived "ordinary" or "secular" lives. Parish priests actually became known as "secular priests" while monks and nuns became "the religious." Religious specialists were naturally considered more holy than ordinary Christians. People thought that the priests, monks, and nuns gained special merit and holy status by their vows of celibacy and poverty. They were also considered to have special intermediary power with the transcendent God along with Mary and the saints. Intermediaries became almost necessary as Christ became identified with dominating and coercive power. He was given the name, "Pantocrator" or "Ruler of All."

As we know, Europe became officially Christian, but there was recurring resistance to the official version. Although this resistance was largely crushed with governmental help, opposition to "official Christianity" grew until in the Protestant Reformation governments themselves in the spirit of nationalism decided they wanted to be free from the domination of the official monopolistic Roman Catholic Church. Thus German princes protected Luther. The Dutch Protestants fought to gain independence from Roman Catholic Spain. Key English and Scottish rulers wanted to be free of domination from Rome. The Scandinavian countries also broke away from the authority of Rome. Even nations that continued to grant monopolistic powers to the Roman Catholic Church, such as Spain and France, exacted major concessions from Rome in granting a greater measure of national authority to the church in their lands. The Eastern Orthodox churches had long since gained independence for their national churches ("autocephalous churches"), but Orthodox Christianity was under constant pressure, domination, and invasion from pagan tribal powers in the north east and Islamic powers to the east. Note that the most successful breakaway churches and their countries, namely those to the north, were generally the most distant from Rome, as well as from the threat of Islam in the south and Mongols in the east. Outside threat creates internal unity and over dependence on authoritative and protective power. Nevertheless, even the Protestant churches accepted the principle of the state church as "normal" for their versions of Christianity and did not hesitate to fight "outside enemies" and internal "heretics."

Even before Europe was splitting religiously, the Islamic Turks overran the remnant of the Byzantine Empire, conquered much of Southeastern Europe, and threatened what the Southern Europeans called "The Holy Roman Empire." The claim to be "The Holy Roman Empire" was the attempt in Europe to maintain the heritage of the Roman Empire, but it only succeeded in being maintained in southern Europe. The Russians also claimed the same heritage in calling their ruler, "Czar" or "Caesar."

As noted, the Protestants were aided greatly by the spirit of nationalism in which the various nations of northern Europe sought to be independent of the authority and power of the Roman Catholic Church and its allied nations. France, even though it succeeded in remaining largely Roman Catholic after the cruel religious wars of the sixteenth century, was a leader in advancing the cause of nationalism. Protestant nations felt threatened by the nations to the south as plans or attempts were made to reclaim the breakaway Protestant nations. The initial explorations from Europe began from the wealthy nations in the south, Venice, Portugal and Spain. However, the northern European nations began to overtake and pass them in economic and political power in the seventeenth and especially in the eighteenth and nineteenth centuries.

In the sixteenth and seventeenth centuries, Christianity was carried to India, Indonesia, Latin America and the Philippines by the Portuguese and Spanish conquerors together with their monks. After considerable initial success in Japan in the latter part of the sixteenth century and early seventeenth century, Christianity was crushed in Japan. The Japanese had seen what had taken place in the Philippines under Spanish rule and did not want to be similarly colonized. The Dutch came to Indonesia and Taiwan. However, they were thrown off of Taiwan in the seventeenth century, but not from Indonesia until the twentieth century. In the eighteenth and especially the nineteenth and twentieth centuries, the English established themselves by force in many places including India, Burma, Malaysia, Indonesia (for a short time), and China making them the most successful colonial power. The French established their power in what is now Vietnam, Cambodia, and Laos.

In the nineteenth century the European countries divided up Africa. At the end of the nineteenth century, the United States joined the European powers as a colonial power in the Philippines. This association of Christianity with imperialism and colonialism distorted the gospel for numerous peoples around the world and created great resistance to the Christian message, especially in the ancient civilizations of the Middle East, India, Southeast Asia, China, Japan, and Korea. (Korea, along with the Pacific Islands and numerous minority groups in Asia became a different story more recently.) Africa, although lacking in a continuous civilization since ancient times (somewhat like the European tribes in the first millennium C.E.), was also generally resistant to the "white man's religion."

THE MODERN MISSION MOVEMENT

In the eighteenth century great changes came across Europe and also spread to America where many Europeans had settled. Two movements took place and they continue to have their influence to the present. One was a movement that included many anti-religious elements, but when looked at closely, also showed influences from Christianity and was supported by many Christian people. This movement is called "The Enlightenment," but it also was a stimulus to the "secularization movement" that has resulted in the weakening of the power of state-sponsored Christianity, as well as creating numerous secularists, who left the churches. Nevertheless, many Christian people, especially in the United States, supported the movement to separate the power of government from religion. Of course, the "accident of history" or from the Christian viewpoint, the providential work of God, made it advantageous to both governmental and religious leaders to secularize the government.

The Enlightenment was a movement, which introduced freedom of thought, especially religious, thought, to much of the modern world and should more properly be called (somewhat awkwardly) "the human rights movement." However, among intellectuals the eighteenth century Enlightenment is given entirely too much credit for the modern developments of democracy and science. Both of these important institutions had their origins in the previous sixteenth and seventeenth centuries in important movements in which Christians were active. In France and later elsewhere, the Enlightenment contained a strong anti-religious spirit in opposition to the authoritarian church so that it aimed not simply at freedom of religion, but freedom from religion, meaning primarily Christianity. Much of this anti-religious spirit, typically maintained by intellectuals and academics, was (is) based on the longstanding association of religion with state power and numerous injustices. Liberated intellectuals in the West wanted to maintain their intellectual freedom over against the perceived threat of religious authority. In spite of the contribution of intellectuals to freedom of religious thought, there is a danger of attributing too much influence on subsequent religious freedom to philosophic ideas of freedom. Many scholars attribute the rise of religious liberty to philosophic views of what they call "the Enlightenment," but Anthony Gill (2008:7) raises serious questions about this conventional "history of ideas" view:

> Although the path toward religious liberty has
> often been considered a natural outgrowth of more
> 'modern' thinking (i.e. the triumph of Enlightenment
> philosophy) over traditional thought, the overarching
> thesis presented here argues that interests play an
> equally important if not more critical role in securing
> legislation aimed at unburdening religious groups
> from onerous state regulations.

In his careful study, Gill demonstrates that political actors changed
governmental regulations of religions based on their own perceived
interests. His analysis does at least two things relevant to our review
of the spread of Christianity: (1) It raises in importance the choices
of networks of actors in governments based on their perceptions of
what will be most beneficial to their own interests; and (2) it makes
changing social conditions of major importance in setting the stage for
individual actors to make decisions having far reaching consequences
for or against religious freedom. Thus, on the one hand, the religious
freedom movement of the modern era released anti-religious
sentiments and actions in societies, at the same time it produced
conditions in which new, intense, and diverse religious sentiments and
actions could take place. This dual effect has made the understanding
of the Enlightenment, together with secularization and modernization,
all fields for furious debate among scholars. This is because of the
different and even contradictory effects each one of these historical
phenomena has had. Gill (2008) has performed a great service by
placing an emphasis on networks of actors in governments and the
social conditions that affect their choices and criticizing an overly
intellectualistic ("history of ideas") interpretation of history. Also,
the "great man theory" of history is undercut because government
leadership typically belongs to a network of the elite.

A second important movement beginning in the eighteenth century, alongside the movement for religious freedom, was a movement among Christians and their churches. Those enamored by the Enlightenment often overlook this movement. Like the human rights movement, this other movement has been given various names and has had various manifestations. "The Pietistic Movement" in Germany and the "Wesleyan Movement" in Great Britain, both in the eighteenth century were part of this movement. A broad name given to it is the "Evangelical Movement." It emphasized that Christianity was not just a matter of having correct beliefs (orthodoxy), but of experiencing and maintaining a relationship of faith in God through Jesus Christ. Before that, the characteristics of elite and scholastic religion had become dominant in Protestantism after the Reformation. Religious scholasticism was encouraged during the religious wars of the sixteenth and seventeenth centuries when nations struggled over what doctrines would become official beliefs of various national territories. The Evangelical Movement of the eighteenth century with its emphasis on Christianity being based on a personal and ongoing faith in Jesus Christ in vital Christian communities reacted against scholasticism and rigid orthodoxy.

Because of the Evangelical Movement, numerous mission societies sprang up and missionaries were sent out to the whole world in the nineteenth century. Concurrent with the Evangelical Movement and continuing up to the twentieth century, European nations were establishing colonies throughout the world and dominating many societies. This nineteenth century imperialism and colonialism was made possible because of the industrial revolution, but also the new prosperity also financed missionary efforts. In spite of much tension and even conflict between colonial governments and missionary organizations and individual missionaries, the inevitable viewpoint of most receiving peoples was that Christianity was associated with domination and the destruction of local culture. Thus colonialism became a large albatross around the neck of the missionary movement, not broken until World War II.

At the same time as the missionary movement and other social movements, for example, the abolition movement against slavery and the women's movement were taking place as a result of the Evangelical Movement; religious freedom was given a major boost by the new social situation in the United States. For the first time the old principle of the state religion that had distorted and hindered the spread of the gospel was formally broken in the United States where church and state were separated in the Constitution. (The term "separation" is not used, but is an effect of the "no establishment" and "free exercise" of religion phrases.) It was not due to human intelligence or even faith that people abandoned the state church concept. As already noted, it was due to the "accidental" circumstances or conditions in which people of various beliefs were mixed together in North America so that political and religious actors saw the benefits of separating religious and governmental authority. For Christians, this is an example of God working through historical social conditions. Although two of the churches, the Congregationalists and the Anglicans, tried to establish themselves as state churches, they were prevented from doing this by members of other churches through the new laws. In North America no one could claim a territory for their religion, as they did in Europe. As a result in North America religious diversity and religious competition became the dominant pattern. In this respect, a return to the first three hundred years of Christianity was brought about.

As already noted, colonialism practiced by Western countries in which Christianity was associated with the colonial powers created tremendous opposition to Christianity around the world. However, we must note the marked exceptions to this dominant pattern of resistance. In the old civilizations in the Far East there existed minority peoples who were dominated by the majority people in those lands. These minority peoples usually did not perceive the Western powers as bringing them harm. Instead, they felt pressure from the majority peoples. The outside Western powers may have even lightened the domination the minorities felt from the majority societies. At least the Western powers were not perceived as the primary threat. Throughout Asia, therefore, in the nineteenth and twentieth centuries, many minority peoples were very receptive to Christianity coming to them from the West. In Christianity they actually affirmed their distinctive identities.

In the special case of the "minority nation" of Korea, which had often been dominated by China and was a colony of Japan in the first half of the twentieth century, Christianity was especially welcomed as a support against outside domination and as favoring Korean nationalism (Montgomery 1996, 2012; Kane and Park 2009). There are also many examples of minority peoples being receptive to Christianity within majority societies that were highly resistant to Christianity and foreigners generally. These examples are found in India, Burma, China, Malaysia, Indonesia, Vietnam, and Taiwan. There is also the example of large numbers of the "untouchables" of India who were receptive to the outside religion. Even in the Pacific Islands people receiving the gospel were usually able to distinguish the missionaries from those exploiting them with the result that most islands became majority Christian. This pattern seen most clearly in Asia and the Pacific shows very clearly that people will perceive the gospel of Jesus Christ most clearly when it is not associated with domination and force. A clearer witness is given to a non-coercive Savior, who knocks at the door of hearts (Revelation 3:20). It may be remembered that the spread of Christianity to the European tribes to the north came after the collapse of Roman power and when the Byzantine Empire exercised little power toward the north.

THE FOURTH PERIOD
OF THE SPREAD OF CHRISTIANITY

Now we see why Christianity has spread both because of and in spite of the behavior of Christians and of the various Christianities. Of course, even in the times of the worst forms of Christian domination there were faithful missionaries who witnessed to the love and compassion of Jesus Christ. This was true of the many monks in Europe, even though they may have been accompanied by the forces of the neighboring Christianized tribe. This was not as true of monks who traveled eastward to Asia; witnesses to the natives of the Americas were clearly associated with invading Europeans. This was true for many of the missionaries of the nineteenth and twentieth centuries who witnessed to Christ during the colonial period, even though they were often in opposition to or in tension with the colonial powers. However, events and conditions are now breaking the old association of Christianity with domination so that as a result the fourth great wave in the spread of Christianity has begun. It began soon after the collapse of colonialism during and after World War II. Although missionaries had been in Africa for several hundred years, in 1900 only about 10 percent of the population below the Sahara was Christian. With the collapse of colonialism after World War II, Christianity grew explosively in Africa. Now, the majority of populations of most African nations south of the Sahara are Christians and Christians make up 46 percent of the total population of the African continent, surpassing the continent's Muslims, who are primarily in the northern part of the continent (Bonk 2009: 58).

Another great area of explosive growth has taken place just in the last few decades in China. The picture is very complicated and total figures are not available because of the large number of unofficial churches, but the basic fact is that there may be between 5 to 10 times as many Christians now in China than there were in 1950 and this is a more conservative estimate than made by many.

We are in just the beginning of the fourth period of the spread of Christianity. For the first time since the conversion of the European tribal peoples there are more Christians outside of the West than in the West. Christianity can no more be considered a "Western religion," but must be considered as belonging to the whole world, as much or more African or Asian as Western.

CONCLUSION

What can we learn from the last two thousand years of the spread of Christianity? The gospel of Jesus Christ has spread throughout the world primarily because of who Jesus Christ is and what he has done. It is a unique and compelling story that has demonstrated its inherent power to win believers from among all peoples. Surprisingly, people accept the story of Jesus Christ from complete strangers, even from those sometimes associated with their enemies. However, Christians have done much to hinder the spread of the gospel by misrepresenting Jesus Christ, often by their behavior or more often, by the behavior of those with whom they were associated. People at the receiving end of missions often could not distinguish missionaries from the colonial rulers since they looked alike and were often closely associated.

Falling for the temptation that Christ rejected, Christians confused the power of the cross with the power of government beginning in the fourth century with the result that the same confusion was created in the minds of the hearers of the message of the gospel of Christ.

This confusion has created an anti-religious and anti-Christian movement beginning in the West and then spreading around the world in association with Western domination. Significantly, this movement began in the context of European Christianity. What can we do?

We can begin by supporting the separation of religion from governmental coercion. There is a great misunderstanding and ongoing debate as to what this means. This does not mean the separation of God and government because religion is not identical with God. Religion is the human response to God, which almost inevitably is organized in some way. Unfortunately, many Muslims in particular think that the separation of religion from civil government is taking God out of government, but this is a view shared by many Christians in the West as well as by people in traditional societies, for example, India. It was and is assumed that the government should promote "true religion". Some fundamentalist Christians in the United States and traditional Christians in Europe share this viewpoint and seem to have a hard time giving up the need to have a "religious aura" around the government and the public sphere in general. They are most comfortable when religious language is used by government officials and in public civil occasions. They feel that God's favor will be obtained when public officials openly recognize God. Instead, separating religion, including religious language, from government and civil occasions is recognizing that religion in its human form includes sin and we are in constant danger of taking God's name in vain by referring to God in relation to particular political policies. Political and civil gatherings should not "ape" the Church by calling on God's name and seeking to give a "religious aura" to their actions. Instead, government officials should let their just actions speak for themselves. The same is true of the public policies advocated by Christians. They should let truth and justice be self-evident and stand the test of time.

The doctrine of sin is really the basis for democracy because this doctrine recognizes that not only should religions not be given the power of state governments nor governments act as religious bodies, but governments themselves should have internal checks on the exercise of power. This is why we should both keep organized religion out of government and support a secular democracy with divided powers. Let the right and wrong of government actions be self-evident and not covered with religious language or given special organized religious approval. It is basically the recognition of human sin that is the basis for dividing the power of governments and letting the various units of government check one another, as well as preventing governments from using religion for its purposes. At the same time, a vigorous civil society is supported where there can be open criticism of government and of those with power in society. The separation of government power from religion is to protect both governments from bad religion and religion from being associated with or using coercive power.

The witness to Christ is a witness to the power now released in the world in its last days that power being found in the New Age introduced by Jesus Christ. The power of the cross and the resurrection of Christ make all things new and we can begin to experience it now. This has become clear now more than ever before. And it will become even clearer in the years to come.

CHAPTER 4

OPPOSITION
ON A MACRO SCALE

EVIL—MORE THAN AN INDIVIDUAL PROBLEM

Beginning in this chapter I turn specifically to the subject of the Opposition to God and the New Age of Jesus Christ, especially as it appears on a large scale. One of the main purposes of this book is to help people think of sin and evil in some new ways, even though I recognize that taking up this task may appear to be a rather negative goal. Since the Bible deals with the subject, I think there is a place for seeking to understand something about what is against God and us as humans and especially as Christians. I do not attempt to deal with all aspects of sin and evil, but rather those aspects usually affecting large numbers of people that we often do not notice.

I spell the Opposition with a capital "O" to distinguish it from individual sin infecting all people that is also in opposition to God, but on a micro level, primarily affecting individuals and also often those people who are connected to the individual. This is not to deny that individuals, such as people with more power than most people, may bring harm to many people, but I am more interested in the conditions that enabled such individuals to gain their power and influence over many people. In short, I am looking at the Opposition that is on the macro level, both expressed by and affecting large numbers of people. Individuals—many times good persons—are affected by the

Opposition and often give support to it and help to perpetuate it. This is why it is important to understand as much as possible about the Opposition to Jesus Christ that is deceptive by its nature.

TREPIDATION

I enter the subject of this and the following chapters with trepidation because of the warning in Genesis 2:17 not to eat of "the tree of the knowledge of good and evil." I take this as a warning not to assume too much knowledge about what is good and evil, right and wrong. We are not wise to claim to be ethical or moral experts. In addition, the Opposition represents realities that are beyond our abilities to know and fully understand. Only God can really know and deal with the Opposition. The Opposition is too subtle and deceptive (Genesis 3:1-7) for us to out smart and defeat. Thankfully, it has already been defeated so that we can talk about it, as long as we do not assume too much confidence in our own views, but depend on the "Word and Spirit," meaning Christ, the Bible, and the leading of the Holy Spirit in interpreting both the Bible and human history and most importantly, in guiding our attitudes and behavior.

There is a great dependence of many interpreters of the Bible on apocalyptic literature in talking about the Opposition to God and Jesus Christ. I will not neglect the perspectives revealed there, but I believe our major reliance should be upon the non-apocalyptic writings of the Bible. With that in mind, I will begin by looking at how the Bible views total reality and compare that reality to that part of reality explored, described, and explained by science, particularly the social sciences. It is important to do this because I will make use of concepts from the social sciences, but place them within the larger context of theological knowledge gained from the Bible.

REALITY IN THE BIBLE AND THE SOCIAL SCIENCES

The Bible posits two basic realities: God and creation. For the reality of God, this book assumes the Trinitarian God, Father, Son, and Holy Spirit, as will be seen. Those who do not accept the reality of the Trinity, as I accept it, may still agree with what I have to say about the other reality–the created order. The created order consists of "heaven and earth," which means that God's creation includes both the supernatural and the natural, the latter being what we call "nature" or the total universe from the tiny atoms (possibly the strings) to the most distant part of the universe. The created supernatural consists of all that is "beyond this life or world," but not God. The human being, which has the capacity to communicate with God and is eternal, is actually part of the supernatural order. This may be difficult for some people to accept, but humans are both supernatural and natural. After death the human being awaits the resurrection of a new body and the creation of a new heaven and earth, although this reality is completely mysterious and may involve entirely new dimensions of time, space, and form of individual identities. The natural existence of humans is subject to influences from the supernatural part of creation. It is these influences, particularly influences for evil that are of special interest in this book.

The Triune God influences the natural order, which God created and is working to redeem. This influence can be both direct and indirect, but the human knowledge and experience of this influence is always incomplete and faulty. It is a knowledge that can only be known through the supernatural part of humans, namely through the faith that connects them to God. Although a great deal can be learned about the work of God in the world from the Bible in the story of salvation told there, human knowledge of it will always be "through a glass darkly" (I Corinthians 13:12). What is also revealed in the Bible is that there are mysterious influences from the created supernatural that are both good and bad. The good influences from the created supernatural are identified in the Bible as angels, literally "messengers from God," as when it is said that an angel announced the birth of Christ (Luke 1:26-28), ministered to Jesus in the wilderness (Mark 1:13), could be called upon by Jesus to defend him (although he did not call upon them) (Matthew 26:53), or announced Jesus resurrection (Matthew 28:5-7). I will label the good influences "Support" as distinct from "the Opposition." I must add that my interpretation of the Bible is that we can and should assume the reality of Support, whether direct from God or through God's messengers, but not seek to communicate with the representatives of this supernatural created reality, as well as humans who have gone on before us after physical death. In other words, the supernatural part of creation, whether it is angels or those who have gone before us and are in a realm (often called "heaven") awaiting the resurrection and the new creation of all things, should not come between us and God or function as intermediaries between us and God. Our communication should be directly to God through the Mediator God has provided, Jesus Christ. We do not need and should not seek any other intermediary or intermediaries.

The Opposition is even more mysterious than the Support since it is also part of the supernatural part of God's creation. I cannot answer the question of how something God created and was originally good became an evil force. In some sense evil is less real or is a negative reality because God's creation is good. It may be compared to "cold," which is really the "absence of heat." Nevertheless, the Bible recognizes and humans certainly experience evil as a real and influential force in the world, just as cold is experienced. Although the evil forces of the Opposition are more powerful than humans, they are not equal to God or a "second Divinity" and they have been defeated. I will deal with this fact later. This book is particularly interested in identifying and defending against the influences of evil or the Opposition, but again, I am not encouraging anyone to seek to identify, much less interact with, a specific or personal manifestation of evil. Jesus and the apostles referred to a personal evil as Satan (Matthew 4:10; Mark 8:33; Acts 5:3; II Corinthians 2:11), but it is not wise and spiritually dangerous for believers to seek to directly identify Satan or the Devil. This raises the question of what I am trying to do in this book. How can I speak of "the Opposition" and identify some of its influences, as I do in this and the next two chapters. As I have already said, I do so with trepidation. Nevertheless, I believe we can understand and speak in some generalities about evil and even with caution and humility identify some of its typical characteristics and activities.

In summary, the Bible conveys the fact that the created order includes much more than what is ordinarily meant by the term "nature" or the empirical universe. Much of the empirical world that humans inhabit can be observed directly and its patterns identified, which is what science seeks to do. There are patterns and regularities in the natural world that when learned may be used to benefit humans, but unfortunately also harm them. The empirical world includes natural human life, much of which is internal and not directly observable, for example, emotions, motivations, viewpoints, and attitudes. Although faith is a gift from God and is based in the supernatural part of humans, it also belongs to the internal life of humans and is expressed in observable ways. The social sciences especially seek to identify and explain patterns in human life, including the internal life, as difficult as this may be because the internal life is not directly observable. The internal life of humans cannot be separated from human social and cultural life because this internal life is highly affected by socio-cultural forces that are associated with social structures and cultural traditions. These forces are important both for the work of God and the Opposition against God's work.

Thus both God and the Supporting forces of the supernatural operate in and through the natural world inhabited by humans, but so does the Opposition to God. It is highly important, therefore, to understand the natural order that is subject to ordinary observation, but also to the more systematic study of the academic disciplines. The New Testament scholar, Walter Wink (1989 [1984], 1986, 1992), has probably done more than anyone else to draw attention to the realm of creation that is beyond the observable world of nature. His interpretation of Biblical teaching about evil on a macro scale is particularly interesting to me because it is closely related to what the social sciences have identified and seek to analyze in human life.

SUPRA INDIVIDUAL FORCES IN THE BIBLE AND THE SOCIAL SCIENCES

Before introducing Wink's thought, which focuses primarily upon New Testament teaching regarding "the powers," I would like to point to the Old Testament or Hebrew Scriptures teaching that God's creation includes powers that are above individual human life, but that are subject to God. These powers are linked to the supernatural realm of God's creation and it is not surprising that they were given the status of being divinities, even though it turns out that they are in some senses false, at least in being considered divine. In other words, the Hebrew Scriptures recognize that there are powers above and beyond individual humans that nevertheless have direct influence on human life, a fact made clear in recent centuries by the social sciences. To some extent, the social sciences confirmed the earlier insight of the Bible, as well as of most religions regarding "higher powers."

An example of the very early expression of the powers that

influence individual human life "from above" is found in the short Psalm number eighty-two. Their God takes his place in "the divine council." The "council" is made up of "gods," whom God proceeds to judge as being unjust and then calls on them "to give justice to the weak and the orphan; maintain the right of the lowly and the destitute; rescue the weak and the needy; deliver them from the hand of the wicked." It is declared that these "gods" "shall die like mortals, and fall like any prince." In spite of the strong assertion that there is only one true God, this passage recognizes that there are powers in the world above ordinary individual human powers, at least the powers of ordinary people. These "powers" included ancient kings who claimed to be divine and actually exercised great powers, but like the "gods" of the Psalm, they were mortal and would die. The language may be primitive, but the viewpoint is highly realistic, a precursor to what the modern world has learned. The New Testament has a more sophisticated, but nevertheless equally realistic expression of how individuals are influenced from above and beyond themselves. This realistic view of human life is found in the doctrine of the "heavenly powers" or "principalities and powers."

One of the best-known passages referring to the supra-individual powers with which humans have to deal is in the Letter to the Ephesians. In Ephesians 6:12 we read, "For our struggle is not against enemies of blood and flesh, but against the rulers, against the authorities, against the cosmic powers of this present darkness, against the spiritual forces of evil in the heavenly places." These are clearly not earthly rulers and authorities. Earlier in Ephesians reference is made to the "ruler of the power of the air, the spirit that is now at work among those who are disobedient" (Ephesians 2:2). Then, in Ephesians the purpose of God is said to be "to make everyone see what is the plan of the mystery hidden for ages in God who created all things; so that through the church the wisdom of God in its rich variety might now be made known to the *rulers and authorities in the heavenly places*" (Ephesians 3:9, 10).

In Colossians 1:16, a letter with many similarities to Ephesians, we read about Jesus Christ: "He is the image of the invisible God, the firstborn of all creation; for in him all things in heaven and on earth were created, things visible and invisible, whether *thrones or dominions or rulers or powers*—all things have been created through him and for him." These forces which are above and beyond those of ordinary human life ("flesh and blood") are still part of the created order and most importantly are under the authority of Christ—"All authority in heaven and on earth has been given to me..."(Matthew 28:18)—even though the "heavenly authorities" or at least some of them may not recognize the ultimate authority of Jesus Christ. Thus the "principalities and powers" are part of God's creation and can be good, neutral, or bad in their influence. They are; however, particularly open to being instrumental for the Opposition to effect large numbers of people.

Wink (1989 [1984]: 99-102) makes a number of important points about the language of power in the New Testament. He states:

> The language of power in the New Testament is extremely imprecise, liquid, interchangeable, and unsystematic, yet [d]espite all this imprecision and interchangeability, certain clear patterns of usage emerge. We found ourselves to be dealing not with analytically precise categories used consistently from one passage to another but with terms that cluster and swarm around the reality they describe, as if by heaping up synonymous phrases and parallel constructions an intuitive sense of the reality described might emerge. (Wink 1989 [1984]: 100).

He goes on to state "Because these terms are to a degree interchangeable, one or a pair or a series can be made to represent them all." For our purposes in this book it is especially important to note Wink's fifth and sixth points about the powers: "These Powers are both heavenly and earthly, divine and human, spiritual and political, invisible and structural. These Powers are also both good and evil" (Wink 1989 [1984]: 100). Wink's description of the Powers should remind anyone familiar with the social sciences of what the sciences have discovered about human life. We should say "discovered for the second time" because the writers of the Bible and many religious believers through the ages have been conscious of powers outside of the individual that impinge on human life. In Biblical times there was no specific language to express what we know today as "socio-cultural forces," but the social scientific terms of "culture" and "social forces" can be used to refer to important aspects of the supra-individual realities of human life (recognized in the Bible) that influence all individuals from "above and beyond them." I will use the combined term "socio-cultural forces" as representing exactly the kind of reality that almost seems to be "hanging in the air," but is constantly impinging on our lives "from above" so to speak. The language used in the Bible shows a very clear understanding, similar to that of the social sciences, that human life is under the strong influence of forces that are beyond the material world and beyond the lives of individuals and, yet, in fact, powerfully affect the lives of individuals and the material world in which they live. Once again, they can be good, bad, or indifferent. What I would like to propose here is the invisible, yet very powerful forces of "culture" and "society" named and investigated in the social sciences refer at least in part to what the Bible recognizes as super material powers in the world, the "principalities and powers." The Bible is freer, of course, in connecting the "principalities and powers" to the supernatural realm of creation than can be done by science, but the socio-cultural forces of the world may certainly be regarded as instrumental to the higher powers.

I use the term "socio-cultural forces" in this book because I want to recognize what Hunter (2010:6-31) has written that is critical of common views of "culture" along with "worldview" that fail to recognize the social network, organizational, and institutional aspects of culture. The term "culture" as used by many people is seen too much as belonging only to human values and customs carried in the mind. In his discussion of personhood, Smith (2010:317-383) agreeing with Hunter, writes in detail of the inevitable participation of humans in the social structural aspects of human life. The powerful forces that impinge on human life are far more than the collected views, values, and customs of people, but include the many social structures that carry these views, values, and customs and give concrete support to them.

The social sciences were initiated in the nineteenth century and became a major project in the twentieth century, yet many individuals in the modern world still seem to be unconscious of the power exerted by socio-cultural forces. Or having learned the concept of "culture" they mistakenly assume that culture can be changed simply by changing individual's ideas or worldviews (Hunter 2010). Those who live in homogeneous societies and cultures are likely to be the least conscious of the socio-cultural forces that surround them and that they take for granted as being "natural." This is also true of people who are clinging to social institutions and a culture or "way of life" that they feel is threatened.

The power of socio-cultural forces originates beyond individual humans, even though they are human creations—group or corporate creations. In fact, as just noted, part of the power of socio-cultural forces is that many people are largely unconscious of them and assume that what they think and do in their group is simply part of the natural world and the natural way of doing things, certainly the way that "makes the most sense." Such people, particularly in the West, typically think of reality primarily in terms of themselves as autonomous individuals surrounded by a material world which they are free to manipulate according to ideas that originated with them. Paradoxically, thinking as an autonomous and distinct individual is a relatively modern way of thinking, but this "individualism" itself has become an ideology affecting large numbers of people. In the pre-modern world people typically thought of themselves as part of a *group* living in a material world. Even after all the years of work by social scientists, many people are still largely unconscious of the distinct culture in which they live like fish in water. Nevertheless, both modern and pre-modern people may be or have been conscious of other groups, usually thought of as "those other people" (a derogatory name is often used), who are different from themselves and who act in different, but inferior ways.

Wink recognizes the link of his studies to the social sciences, but it is at this point that I partly disagree with him. First, he (1989 [1984]: 101-02) notes that the "methodological atheism" of the sociologist, Peter Berger (1967: 100), "brackets out what is (for New Testament writers at least) the most central aspect of reality: belief in the existence of God." I agree with Wink that "methodological agnosticism" is a better term for the scientific method than "methodological atheism" because the scientific method "brackets out" reference to God as a cause, but this does not rule out belief in God by a scientist. (I prefer the term "secular methodology," which actually has broader use than just in the sciences.) The individual scientist must make the personal choice to believe in God. For that matter, any other belief or opinion should be left out in the work of developing scientific theory. Scientific theory is subject to open examination in order to take out the influence of opinion. Nevertheless, science can study beliefs, views, values, attitudes, and opinions as realities with real effects. They may not be directly observable, but they have empirical effects. What people believe may not be true, but those beliefs will have real effects. However, the fact that scientific theory by definition can not refer to God's action or causative power and because many social scientists do not believe in God may well have prevented some sociologists from examining more carefully theological language for the social realities presented by it.

The part where I disagree with Wink is that the major difference between theological and social scientific language and methodology is not, as Wink seems to say, that the secular social scientific approach only deals with the outward and material whereas theology deals with both outer and inner, both material and spiritual realities. I believe that because socio-cultural forces have many inner aspects that are closely related to various external manifestations, the social sciences can and must include many human inner factors in their theories. These inner factors include, for example, motivations and attitudes on the individual level, and values, ideology, and ethos on the group level. The expressions of faith itself can be observed and studied by the "agnostic method." Culture itself includes values and moods, as well as beliefs and opinions that are held in common by individuals through their many social relationships and social institutions. Wink (1989 [1984]:104-113) wants especially to recognize these inner aspects of human life and chooses to designate them primarily with the term, "spirituality." He does not think that the social sciences can deal with this "inner aspect of material or tangible manifestations of power." However, I believe he is mistaken. What the social sciences cannot do, in contrast to theology, is *relate* the outer and inner aspects of human life to God and to supernatural forces. However, the social sciences can and should examine and theorize about what Wink calls the "spiritual" that belongs to the inner aspects of societies and individuals. Nevertheless, only theology can express the redemptive work of God that affects both the inner and outer aspects of human life. In this sense the Biblical view of reality (theological thought) is more comprehensive than the social scientific view. For this reason, it is important that theologians seek to incorporate insights gained from the social sciences, while the social sciences cannot incorporate theological views, except as data.

The social sciences are particularly helpful because they have introduced terminology, such as "culture" and "social forces," that were not available at the time of the writing of the Bible and produced theories on how human life is affected by such realities. They also use a whole host of other concepts, such as attitudes, values, motivations, emotions, and beliefs related to human inner life, all of which are highly subject to influence from social networks, organizations, and institutions. This terminology is useful in understanding how "the powers," identified by Wink, work in the world to affect large numbers of people. The Biblical view of human reality is actually rather close to the social scientific in terms of recognizing that there are great powers existing "above and beyond" the individual that influence human life. On the other hand, the Biblical view of reality is rather far from the social scientific view in terms of relating all of life, including the supra-individual forces, to the work of God in history. Also, the supra-individual forces that exist in human life may come under the power of evil (the Opposition) and hence may be extremely dangerous and destructive.

From a theological perspective there is no "secular" realm

because everything in life is related to God. God is at work in both churches and governments, indeed throughout all human relationships and organized life. But so is evil in the form of Opposition to God. The Apostle Paul in his sermon to the Gentile Athenians quoted approvingly the saying, "In him [God] we live and move and have our being" (Acts 17:28). Also, he wrote referring to Christ, "He himself is before all things, and in him all things hold together" (Colossians 1:17). The "secular" was a term introduced as a tool or a useful device by Christians for distinguishing different types of *religious* work. Clergy not bound by monastic vows, but serving in parishes, were considered "secular," whereas clergy bound by such vows were considered "religious." However, the concept of the "secular" proved to be an even more useful tool later in at least two other places. The first useful tool for the "secular" is in the field of government, in which government is separated from organized religion. This may be (and has been) extended to other public realms, such as education, welfare, recreation, and medical practice in what Smith (2003) calls "the secular revolution." Along with the application of the concept of the secular to government and public life, I believe an important application is to the realm of intellectual investigation. In particular, the field of science through its secular methodology has produced enormous amounts of knowledge, which have proven useful in understanding and using the world. At the same time, false ideas about the world held by religious people, based on their interpretation of the Bible, were shown to be false.

When we look at the realms of thought and government, we see that the "secular" method, both in science and in politics, acts as a control and correction to the many incorrect human views, opinions, and ideologies that have harmed human life. These views, opinions and ideologies include theology or religious thought. Even though theology, unlike the social sciences, makes reference to God and revelation, it is, after all, human thought and therefore subject to error. The Church can and should be looked at theologically, but it can also be looked at social scientifically as a human institution. Human institutions have their failings. Even more so, if a government is only seen theologically or through religious eyes, it may assume all kinds of religious prerogatives, and, in fact, seek to control religions.

Socio-cultural forces can be looked at religiously, as the "powers" in the Bible and also as containing "spiritualities" as in Wink's writings. However, if we also examine them in a social scientific manner, then we will be able to understand further how we come under their influence and consequently how we may avoid their damaging and destructive effects. Of course, we still need additional spiritual resources for resistance and self-correction known only in theology and through faith. In the next chapter, I plan to look at the "powers" through historical and social scientific glasses, as well as with theological glasses.

This long section represents an attempt to look at how both the Bible and the social sciences regard reality and where their understanding clearly overlaps. In the remaining part of this chapter, I will review what the Bible says about the corporate or macro nature of the "Opposition" to Christ in the New Age that Christ introduced and in which we live.

EVIL ON THE CORPORATE LEVEL

In considering the Opposition, as noted in the first of this chapter, it is important to make a distinction between evil or sin operating on the individual level and on the corporate level. The Bible is very clear that all individuals, although created in the image of God, have distorted that image and are therefore sinful. It follows that opposition to Christ is an individual activity of which all people are capable and do carry out. However, this is not the whole story and if sin and evil are only seen as individual matters we will miss an important reality about the Opposition to Christ. Biblical teaching regarding the Opposition to Christ's rule is primarily about evil working through socio-cultural forces that come to dominate *groups* of people. It is about sin and evil on a corporate or macro level more than it is about sin on the individual micro level, although, of course, individuals come under the influence of macro forces. Sin under macro level forces is harder to detect because "everybody is doing it" or "my friends think the same way." People under the domination of the Opposition to Christ are not necessarily bad people. In fact they may be and often are good people, who are also believers in Jesus Christ.

An important early example of the power of the Opposition over groups, which appears only as an individual sin, is found when Peter opposes Christ taking the way to the cross. The passage says, *"But turning and looking at his disciples* [italics mine], he [Jesus] rebuked Peter and said, 'Get behind me Satan! For you are setting your mind not on divine things but on human things'"* (Mark 8:33). Yes, Peter was committing sin as an individual, but he was speaking impulsively not only for himself. He was representing the contemporary dominating perspective of what a Messiah should be like and was a spokesman for the disciples, who agreed with him. It was part of the contemporary *religious socio- cultural* view of what the Messiah should be like. The disciples thought exactly the same way as Peter and that is why Jesus wanted them to hear his condemnation of the conventional thought expressed by both Peter and them. These views were thoroughly supported by the social institutions of the time.

Socio-cultural forces can become and often are focused in and represented by individuals, usually networks of individuals, who provide leadership for groups of people, some of which are quite large, including whole nations. Human life ordinarily becomes organized and requires leadership, but the leadership of individuals and their networks must not distract us from the major fact that large numbers of people can periodically come under the influence of socio-cultural forces that can be highly damaging and destructive and are clearly opposed to Jesus Christ. This is why homogeneity in a society, including a church, can be dangerous.

There is another important characteristic of the Opposition that will become clear in the review of Biblical passages and the history of the Church. The Opposition focuses on seeking to mislead and dominate the People of God. Of course, there is opposition to God from and through the non-believing world. Sometimes this may take the form of fierce persecution. A clear example is the persecution by Rome described so clearly in the Book of Revelation. However, what is often missed by readers of the Book of Revelation is that more dangerous than Rome, which in any case is doomed, are the failings of the seven churches described in the first three chapters of Revelation. The Opposition would rather mislead Christians since they are to be the source of the witness to the gospel of Jesus Christ. It is also true that in later history up to the present persecution and opposition to Christians from the non-believing world often has been based on perceptions of wrong doing (or association with wrong doing) by Christians. No, the major work of the Opposition is in and through Christians. That is where the Opposition finds the work of God to oppose.

There is a tendency for Christians to think of sin and evil only in individual terms. The "seven deadly sins" in Christian tradition is an example of this largely individualistic viewpoint. A traditional list is: pride, lust, envy, sloth, greed, gluttony, and wrath. These mostly "sins of the flesh" are serious matters, but they primarily represent self-destructive attitudes and behaviors, which are evil primarily because of the harm caused to others. An example would be alcohol and drug abuse. Another would be some sexual obsession. They truly bring spiritual death to individuals, but the evil at their core is that these sins are a lack of love for others bringing great harm to those who usually have some relationship to the individuals. These sins provide a distraction so that the Opposition can gain influence over groups of people without being noticed. People focus upon these obvious sins while ignoring the sins of omission and the cruelties brought on by the taken-for-granted socio-cultural forces. The people who led in rejecting Christ were conscious of being highly moral people and were so in many respects, just as many people today who participate in culturally harmful practices may be individually moral people in terms of the "sins of the flesh." Individual moral behavior is important and can be a great struggle to carry out for many, but the broad effects of individual immorality tend to be limited because they are highly self-destructive and harmful primarily to those related to individuals. Others, even apart from any faith, may take self-corrective measures when they realize these self-destructive effects. The Opposition has the greatest effect on large numbers of people through gaining influence over socio-cultural forces that people, often good people, usually unconsciously accept. The result of this broad influence is often death and destruction for many people and their natural and social environment, as we shall see.

CONCLUSION

This chapter has dealt primarily with understanding the Opposition in the light of the Bible and the social sciences. The Bible and the social sciences are remarkably similar in understanding that human life is highly influenced by forces that are outside of individuals. These forces continue over time before and after individual lives and seem to impinge on individuals "from above." They can be good, bad, or neutral in their influence, but they are integral to human life and what it means to be human. The social sciences consider these forces, viewed as "socio-cultural forces," as they appear in natural human life. However, the Bible sees these forces as both instrumental to God and also the means by which the supernatural part of creation affects humans. This supernatural part includes Supportive forces created by God, but also the Opposition or evil forces that are opposed to God's will and harmful to humans. "Principalities and powers" is a term that incorporates both the biblical and the social scientific views. The former view incorporates both the supernatural and the natural supra individual forces and the latter view incorporates these forces as they appear in the natural world of human life. In either case, the forces are supra individual, typically affecting large numbers of people. We turn now to the Opposition as dealt with by God according to the Bible.

CHAPTER 5

THE OPPOSITION
DEALT WITH BY GOD

THE OPPOSITION LEADING UP TO
ITS GREAT DEFEAT BY JESUS CHRIST

Following the general background to understanding the presence and
operation of the Opposition to God's work in the world, we turn now
to a consideration of how the Opposition is dealt with in the Bible. The
Bible is the story of God's work of redemption for all humanity. After
making clear that humans are God's creation in need of redemption
(Genesis 1-11), the story of redemption begins with God's work
with Israel as the People of God and climaxes in the life, death, and
resurrection of Christ followed by the founding of the Church through
the Holy Spirit. The Bible then begins the story of the extension of
the work of redemption to the whole world. From the beginning of
the story and throughout its telling it is made clear that God views all
humanity, indeed the whole of creation as the object of redemption.
With this understanding of the goal of redemption, it should be
understood that the Opposition is the work that seeks to stop or hinder
God's work of redemption, primarily through distorting the human
witness to Jesus Christ, which is God's chosen means of redemption.
How does God deal with the Opposition to the work of redemption?
Interestingly, God does not typically deal directly with the Opposition,
which often seems to be a great disappointment to God's people. That

is, God does not seem to "zap" the Opposition directly and destroy it, as believers would like. What is emphasized in the Bible is that God chooses to work through the faith of human beings, as imperfect as it is. This takes time so that having faith usually means waiting and trusting that God will fulfill the promises made to God's people, but at the same time seeking to give a faithful witness to Jesus Christ. In the meantime, the Bible is very open in reporting how from the call of Abraham, God's people have in a variety of ways shown faithlessness and disobedience. In spite of this, people did respond with faith from the Patriarchs, through the Exodus and Wilderness, to their establishment in the land. The greatest hindrance to the People of Israel becoming an expression of the Kingdom of God on earth was their ongoing tendency to adopt the ways of those around them who worshipped other gods and neglected care and concern for others. The God of Israel specifically made clear through the prophets that worship and the practice of righteousness and justice went together, whereas the religions of the surrounding peoples were primarily aimed at winning the favor of their gods through various ceremonies and thereby neglecting the issues of justice and mercy. The witness of the prophets has meant that the emphasis on seeking social justice has remained one of the great contributions of the Jewish people to societies. However, the major tactic of the Opposition was (and is) to separate worship from right dealing with others, which Christians often have done. For Christians, of course, witness to Jesus Christ should mean walking in his Way of right dealing with others.

Without going into detail in the history of Israel, it is sufficient to recognize that even as late as the period before the destruction of Jerusalem and the Temple by the Babylonians, the people of Israel mixed the worship of God with the worship of idols. The prophets of the ninth and eighth centuries were very clear in condemning the worship of the people that was mixed with injustice and oppression of others. It could be said in the most general way, but sufficient for our purposes here, that the Opposition was successful in bringing the religious socio-cultural forces of surrounding peoples to be highly influential over the People of Israel. Even some social aspects of culture that were relatively neutral, such as the establishment of a kingship in Israel, brought with it new opportunities for wrong practices that led to the division of the Kingdom, religious syncretism, and various injustices condemned by the prophets. As a matter of fact, a clear warning from the Prophet Samuel is recorded in I Samuel 8 about the dangers of having a king like other nations, who would misuse his power to oppress the people, but in the end, on instructions from the Lord, Samuel relented. As we know, a king (David) became in some sense a model for the Messiah, who was to be his descendent. However, the interpretation of what the Messiah should be (like an exalted earthly king) became a stumbling block to recognizing the work of Jesus, as seen in the comment of Peter (Matthew 16: 22, 23) already noted. All of this shows how even morally neutral cultural features (having a king) can become an instrument for distorting the understanding of God's work.

The destruction of Jerusalem and the Temple in 587 B.C.E., foretold by the prophets, marked a major turning point in which Israel was virtually purified of idolatry. After the return to their land under the Persians, there followed a period when Israel sought to establish its distinctiveness and separation from the surrounding peoples since imitation of these people had caused the downfall of Israel. This gave the Opposition a new opportunity to hinder the work of God of bringing redemption to humanity. The distinction from others based on faith and righteous deeds was to be a means of holding up the Light of God for all peoples, of being "a light to the nations (Gentiles or peoples)" (Isaiah 42:6). However, the emphasis on distinction from others brought with it a new emphasis on the law. Then, obedience to the law, instead of being seen as an expression of gratitude for God's mercy, was made into criteria for gaining God's approval and for the separation of God's people from foreigners. Once again, the Opposition had gained a strong influence over people through the subtle means of appearing to support the precious tradition of the God-given law. Along with making the law into criteria for gaining God's mercy and of maintaining a distinction from others, there grew a focus on establishing, presumably re-establishing, an earthly kingdom like other kingdoms. This would require independence from any foreign power and even domination and supremacy over other peoples. Jesus Christ came into this socio-cultural context of obsession with the tradition of the law and with political power.

The New Testament presents the life, death, and resurrection of Jesus Christ as having been accomplished in spite of the Opposition and as specifically rendering a fatal defeat to the Opposition. Jesus cast out demons that were harming people, but otherwise he did not directly and physically destroy the Opposition, which in any case was not a physical and earthly power (as we saw in the last chapter.) Jesus even allowed those under the influence of the Opposition to crucify him, which was an apparent victory of the Opposition. His resurrection is then made apparent to his followers, but not to those who crucified him. Surprisingly, this *seemingly* passive approach to dealing with the Opposition is declared to be a victory over the instruments and tactics of the Opposition. Colossians 2:15 declares, "He disarmed the rulers and authorities and made a public example of them, triumphing over them in it [the cross]." This does not mean that the Opposition is destroyed or ceases activity, much less the People of God cease their failures, as is clear in the accounts of the early church.

Nevertheless, the Opposition has been rendered helpless to stop the work of redemption and believers can participate in this victory of Christ over the Opposition. The fact that there is an ongoing struggle is clear in I Corinthians 15:24, 25: "Then comes the end, when he hands over the kingdom to God the Father, after he has destroyed every ruler and every authority and power. For he must reign until he has put all his enemies under his feet." It is important to remember these are not earthly rulers or governments, but the powers that dominate all of life through the socio-cultural forces. The defeat of the Opposition may be compared to D-Day in World War II. Toward the end of the war, European countries, for example, were still occupied by the Germans, but the people knew Germany was defeated and the time of domination was limited. The destruction of the weapons or instrumentalities of the Opposition will continue until final victory at the end of history, but we know that they are already defeated. This is done, not through direct destruction since the authorities and powers are not evil themselves, but only used by evil or the Opposition. The means of subduing the instrumentalities of the Opposition is exposing them to the truth. Many, if not most of the failures in the Old Testament have been and are being repeated by the Christian Church, but now on a worldwide basis. The means of defeating the Opposition remain the same, as we shall see.

In case the "rulers and authorities" be thought of as earthly rulers, authority, and power, we are told that in his temptation at the beginning of his ministry and throughout his life, Jesus Christ refused to use his power to establish the kind of kingdom that people, including his own disciples, wanted and expected the Messiah to establish. Instead, Jesus established a non-territorial Kingdom, the New Age of the last days, based on faith and living in right relationship with others, exactly what God has always intended for the People of God. Christ suffered death because he challenged the religious socio-cultural forces that were characterized by self-righteousness, exclusion of others, and political ambition and that wanted a direct challenge to Roman power. Although Christ won the victory once for all, realization of and participation in that victory remains the ongoing challenge for his followers to this day. This will become apparent in the remainder of the book.

DEALING WITH THE OPPOSITION IN SPECIFIC BIBLE PASSAGES

It is important to remember that the doctrine of the Opposition should not be taken primarily from apocalyptic literature, but rather should be based on the Biblical view of total reality and the whole story of redemption beginning with Abraham and climaxing in Jesus Christ. Apocalyptic language has its roots in ancient concepts, going back at least to the time of Zoroaster, of the struggle between good and evil that takes place on a cosmic level and affects humans. John Hall (2009) discusses the apocalyptic tradition from its earliest days to the present, although it is particularly manifested in the religions of Judaism, Christianity, and Islam. Apocalyptic literature should be regarded only as a highly symbolic means of giving some insights into God's work in history, especially affirming God's victory over evil. However, there are impressions and influences that can be gained from the descriptions of war and destruction in apocalyptic writings that are not helpful for Christian or simply for human thought and action. Apocalyptic language has sadly periodically given Christians excuses for using violence against their "evil enemies." Apocalyptic literature can be used as long as it is remembered that the major basis for the understanding of the Opposition should be taken from non-apocalyptic writing and the total teaching of the Bible.

The subject of the Opposition to Jesus Christ and the New Age has been very much neglected, even though it is specifically discussed in several places in the New Testament. The neglect is probably because the doctrine or teaching of Opposition to Christ has been very much misused, just as has the doctrine of the "last days" with which it is connected. The specific teaching that is most misused regards "the antichrist," which is the Opposition to Christ that is manifested in history, although the term "antichrist" is only used in the Letters of I and II John. Too many favorite targets of Christian groups, usually some individual, have been identified as "*the* antichrist." Few thoughtful Christians want to be identified with such name-calling and speculation. Actually, the term "anti" is misleading since in modern language it has the sense of "being against." This concept was strengthened in literature and popular thought in depicting the "anti-Christ" as a figure, almost on an equal level with Christ—a kind of opposing figure or opposite being. Instead, "anti" in the New Testament is closer in meaning to "substitute" or something "in place of" Christ. The great danger for Christians is choosing greed, power, unkindness or some other hurtful way in place of the way of Christ that is the way of salvation. Nevertheless, there are specific passages, which I will take up next, that refer to the Opposition. As long as these passages are linked to the larger perspective of the Bible already discussed, these passages are important background to understanding basic characteristics of the Opposition.

THESSALONIANS

The letters to the Thessalonians are probably the earliest literature in the New Testament, with the possible exception of the letter to the Galatians. The early Christians in Thessalonica were excited about the imminent coming again of Christ. Some were so excited that they stopped working in order to wait for Christ's coming, not the last time

Christians would exhibit this behavior! However, Paul told them in II *Thessalonians* 2:1-10:

> As to the coming of our Lord Jesus Christ and our being gathered together to him, we beg you, brothers and sisters, not to be quickly shaken in mind or alarmed, either by spirit or by word or by letter, as though from us, to the effect that the day of the Lord is already here. Let no one deceive you in any way; for that day will not come unless the rebellion comes first and the lawless one is revealed, the one destined for destruction. He opposes and exalts himself above every so-called god or object of worship, so that he takes his seat in the temple of God, declaring himself to be God. Do you not remember that I told you these things when I was still with you: And you know what is now restraining him, so that he may be revealed when his time comes. For the mystery of lawlessness is already at work, but only until the one who now restrains it is removed. And then the lawless one will be revealed, who the Lord Jesus will destroy with the breath of his mouth, annihilating him by the manifestation of his coming. The coming of the lawless one is apparent in the working of Satan, who uses all power, signs, lying wonders, and every kind of wicked deception for those who are perishing, because they refuse to love the truth and so be saved.

There are several important points to be noted in this passage. The term "antichrist" is not used, but the passage fits into the general apocalyptic teaching about antichrist or Opposition to Christ arising in the last period of history introduced by Christ. Even though there is a reference to an individual, "the lawless one," there is also a reference to "the rebellion," the action of a group, but even more important, there is a reference to "the mystery of lawlessness," which "is already at work." The "mystery of lawlessness" is a term for the recurring way in which human socio-cultural forces manifest non-conformity to the will of God. It is a process already underway, in fact is continuous, but is yet to come to a climax. Of course, this Opposition will be defeated when it does come into the open, but note that it is defeated by "the breath of his mouth." This is not a physical force, but represents the revelation of the truth with the Spirit, namely the presentation of the gospel through the Word and Spirit. Since deception is the major weapon of evil, it is defeated by the truth.

A theme appears here that is seen in other apocalyptic writing: first evil is defeated, but then later released temporarily. The "lawless one" is presently being restrained, but later the restraints will be removed and the "lawless one" will be revealed. At this point, note again, he will be "destroyed" by the breath of Jesus (not by any army or by force), which is the same as being "annihilated" by the manifestation of Jesus (II Thessalonians 2:6-8). This is a warning to Christians not to be surprised when after a period of advance of the gospel, there appears an outbreak of evil. It is also a warning against thinking of war as a means of defeating evil: the Opposition will be defeated by the truth of the gospel of Jesus Christ, not by any human earthly force. There will be more on this in Chapter 6.

It should also be noted that "the lawless one" is spoken of as taking "his seat in the temple of God, declaring himself to be God." This phraseology connects this passage to the apocalyptic literature of Daniel and *The Synoptic Gospels*. This literature originally is very much related to the attempt by Antiochus Epiphanes (175-163 BCE) to Hellenize Jewish worship and who defiled the temple at Jerusalem with an idol in 167 B.C.E. Apocalyptic literature is responsible for much of the wording of the teaching about the Opposition or antichrist. It is important to make this point because of the symbolic nature of apocalyptic writing, which unfortunately many Christians do not recognize. The clear point here is that the Opposition to Christ is religious in nature and misrepresents itself as good and worthy of the praise and honor that should belong to God alone.

THE SYNOPTIC GOSPELS

Matthew, Mark, and Luke each contain "little apocalypses" (Matthew 24:15-28; Mark 13:9-27; Luke 21:20-24). Although again the term, "antichrist," is not used, a contribution to the teaching about the antichrist or Opposition to Christ's kingdom is made in several places. The references in Matthew 24:15 and Mark 13:14 to "the desolating sacrilege" are based directly on the apocalyptic writing in Daniel (e.g. 8:13; 9:26, 27). This language is consistent with the passage in Thessalonians about the "lawless one" taking "a seat in the temple." As just noted this refers to the acts of Antiochus Epiphanies (175-163 B.C.E) of Syria. In his Hellenization program he went into the temple and deliberately established the sacrifice of pigs on the altar. This provides the basis for the apocalyptic language that describes how the Opposition to God seeks to set itself up at the center of worship. Also, these passages in the "little apocalypses" say that many will claim to be the Messiah (Matthew 24:23, 24; Mark 13:21, 22), which could easily mean having religious leadership or influence. The Opposition to God (the antichrist) clearly comes in a religious guise, as an "angel of light" and the ministers or angels as "ministers of righteousness" as spoken of in II Corinthians 11:14, 15. The power of evil is not in its obvious manifestation, but in its ability to masquerade as good, even as being religious. This alone is an important message from the Bible that the major concern of God's people should be with purifying themselves, not pointing to the obvious sins of the world.

Speaking of the influence of the Book of Daniel on New Testament eschatology, it should be noted that Jesus' favorite name for himself, "Son of Man," comes from Daniel (7:13). A sentence used by Jesus in his trial, "From now on you will see the Son of Man seated at the right hand of Power and coming on the clouds of glory" is based on the Daniel passage. In the Daniel passage, the "son of man" is redeemed Israel, showing that Jesus identified himself with Israel or the redeemed of God. This also shows that his statement at his trial is not only a statement about himself as being the representative human being (in the image of God,) but an invitation to others to join him in "coming in clouds of glory" as the redeemed people of God, a truly audacious invitation. This would constitute the "revelation of the children of God" (Romans 8:19), something that has already begun.

THE APOCALYPSE (REVELATION)

Consistent with the passage in II Thessalonians above referring to the future coming of the "lawless one" after which he is defeated by the truth of the gospel, the Book of Revelation speaks of Satan being released for a little while after a thousand years of being bound (Revelation 20:1-3). Again, let us recognize that the Book of Revelation as apocalyptic literature clearly uses symbolic language and so great care should be used in its interpretation. What I believe this passage refers to is that there is an initial victory of Christ (Satan "bound") that lasts for a long period symbolized by 1000 years. This phrase is certainly not meant to be taken literally. The constant literalizing of apocalyptic language is truly an immature approach to interpreting the Bible.

After a long period of time, Satan is then released for a time, but is finally defeated when Christ returns. It is important to recognize that in the Bible "Satan" is the accuser or the "prosecutor of our sins before God." However, because of Christ's death and resurrection, when we arrive before God, the accuser is gone and is replaced by Christ and the Spirit, who is our Advocate. Satan is nowhere to be seen because no counting of sins is allowed any longer. The passage regarding the binding of Satan (his disenabling) and then release points to the important principle that evil has a way of reappearing after a period of advance and growth of the gospel. Throughout the history of Christianity, Christians have fallen back into legalism or allowed the Accuser to "count their sins." This means making the Christian life and Church life into a set of duties about which to feel guilty before the Accuser when not fulfilling one's duties. In other words, the vibrant life of the Spirit becomes muted. This "reappearing" of the Accuser should be expected so that believers will not be taken by surprise. Nevertheless, Christ will be victorious in the end over the Accuser, but it is important to remember the means of victory. Christ's victory will not be by some physical war between armies as some imagine. In that regard and also consistent with the passage in Thessalonians, Revelation affirms that evil is defeated by the sword that comes from the mouth (Revelation 1:16; 19:21), namely by the truth, the Word of God, not by violence, as violent as the language in Revelation may sound. It is the gospel of God's grace in Christ that will triumph. Sadly, Christians who concentrate on making pronouncements based on their interpretations of apocalyptic literature often manifest a tendency toward predicting and even advocating wars and violent destruction, another example of an immature and harmful approach to interpreting the Bible. It is an interpretation that ignores the power of the gospel of God's grace in Christ.

THE LETTERS OF JOHN

Only in the letters of I and II John is the term "antichrist" used, but the teaching attached to this term has many parallels to the passages already mentioned and also goes beyond them. An important point to make at first is that there is not simply one antichrist that is yet to come: "As you have heard that antichrist is coming, so now many *antichrists* have come" (I John 2:18) "and now it is already in the world (I John 4:3). This is consistent with the statement that "the mystery of lawlessness is already at work" (II Thessalonians 2:7). We see again that the antichrist is not some opposite being to Christ, but rather an evil influence that repeatedly seeks to substitute itself for Christ. Rather than being a figure standing opposite to and attacking Christ directly, the antichrist may appear as a very mild, but subtle (Genesis 3:1) spirit of apathy toward the sufferings of others, even a kind of self-seeking "spirituality" that looks only at self improvement (Genesis 3:6). The self is substituted for Christ, which means following the spirit of antichrist.

The appearance of the Opposition to Christ or the antichrist, which became clear with the appearance of Christ, is evidence that the last days had begun with the coming of Christ. The writer says, "Children, it is the last hour!" and we know this "because *many* antichrists have come" (I John 2:18). Just as the coming of Christ marks the beginning of the last period of history, the Opposition to Christ is a parallel indicator of our being in the last period of history. It is also very plausible to think that as Christ's Kingdom spreads, the Opposition to it will grow stronger and at the same time also more subtle and dangerous.

John affirms one of the most important, yet elusive, points about the antichrist. II John 7 says, "Many deceivers [the mark of evil] have gone out into the world, those who do not confess that Jesus

Christ has come in the flesh; any such person is the deceiver and the antichrist." I John 4:2, 3 also stress the importance of recognizing the humanity of Christ: "By this you know the Spirit of God: every spirit that confesses that Jesus Christ has come in the flesh is from God, and every spirit that does not confess Jesus is not from God. And this is the spirit of antichrist, of which you have heard that it is coming and now it is already in the world."

Note that there is a "spirit of antichrist" which points to its immaterial nature. This is very similar to the concept of "ethos," a socio-cultural reality that influences the minds and behavior of groups of people. One of the early heresies to appear, known as Docetism, denied that Jesus was truly human. Rather, he was seen as God masquerading as a human as opposed to being fully human. This was related to the belief that the material or physical was inherently evil, which is clearly contrary to the Bible. Therefore, Jesus Christ had to be essentially spiritual and not physical or material. Note that the Gentile concept of celibacy as somehow more holy and "spiritual" than married life entered Christianity quite early (I Timothy 4:3). The Jewish people, who believe in the goodness of creation, never practiced celibacy as a religious act.

Many Christians still overemphasize the divinity of Christ as over against his humanity, often wanting to oppose strongly those whom they accuse of being followers of "secular humanism" or just "humanism." Christ is human, as well as divine, and although secular humanism is a truncated philosophy, there is a "Christian humanism" that is based on the humanity of Christ himself. Calvin, for example, may be considered a Christian humanist because of his high regard for human nature as a creation of God. He also did not hesitate to see good in the writings of pagan writers. In their opposition to humanism, many Christians do not recognize that an overemphasis on the divinity of Christ helps to deemphasize the involvement of Christ in the suffering of the world. In an analogous way there can be such a Docetic emphasis on the "spirituality of the Church" or simply "spirituality" that leads churches and Christians generally to be unconcerned and uninvolved in relieving suffering in the world or particularly doing anything to deal with the sources of injustice. There is a notable lack of concern for social justice among many fundamentalist Christians based on their Docetic theological emphasis.

Basically, the Bible presents evil as very subtle (Genesis 3:1) and having great powers of deception, including using a religious or "spiritual" covering. The only escape is to focus on and follow Jesus Christ. Notice again that the spirit of antichrist is overcome by "the breath" of Christ's mouth. These verses mean that the antichrist is defeated, not by force, but by truth from the Word of God. These teachings emphasize the importance of first, expecting evil to appear in the guise of good, even after much progress in the New Age under Christ has been made. Second, the Opposition to Christ is defeated when Christians continually lift up and witness to the *whole* Word of God by their words and deeds. As the gospel is made clearer and clearer in the world, we can expect increasing Opposition to it. However, we are promised that Christ has won the victory over evil and will win the victory in the end.

DISCUSSION OF THE TEACHINGS
ON THE OPPOSITION TO JESUS CHRIST

In many places the Bible affirms the sinfulness of every individual and hence the opposition of every individual to Christ and his Kingdom is an ongoing reality. Peter certainly showed his tendency to oppose Christ and his Kingdom in his seeking to turn Christ from the cross (Mark 8:33), in his denial of Christ (Mark 14:33-72), in his resistance to the command to eat "unclean food" (Acts 10:14), and in his withdrawal from fellowship with Gentiles (Galatians 2:11-14). If Peter could so oppose the gospel and also Paul confess to his struggle with sin (Romans 7), we can be sure that there is an "antichrist" within each one of us in the sense that there is a natural opposition within each of us to God's will, an opposition that we spend a lifetime seeking to overcome.

However, notice that in each of the cases of Peter and Paul mentioned, the individual is yielding in some way to outside pressure, much of which can be characterized as socio-cultural in origin. Thus, our individual opposition is typically a yielding to a larger Opposition to Jesus Christ that "mysteriously" uses and is even embedded in human socio-cultural forces. Socio-cultural forces are human creations that at the same time exercise power over humans through dominant modes of thinking and through social institutions that support human ideologies. Just as humans are connected to the supernatural through their souls or spirits, so human socio-cultural forces have a connection to the supernatural, in which there is both Opposition to God's will and Support for the right and good.

The teaching about the Opposition to Christ in the passages discussed above is about an aspect of sin and evil that transcends the individual. Most of the teaching is through obviously symbolic language as in the apocalyptic passages, but then in a broad sense all language is symbolic pointing to a reality beyond words. Most interpreters do not link the Opposition spoken of in the apocalyptic passages with the New Testament teaching regarding "the powers" with which we wrestle (Ephesians 6:11). Recognizing that "the powers" are supra-individual forces represented in modern language by socio-cultural forces prepares us also to see that the Opposition to

Christ spoken of in the apocalyptic passages employs socio-cultural forces that gain influence and control over individuals. These forces are much more subtle and powerful than any individual who might be identified as "the antichrist." The focus on individual sins only is even a distraction that serves the forces of evil, which become part of "taken-for-granted" human thinking.

Finally, there is a danger, often unrecognized, in claiming to identify exactly what is good and evil. This danger is expressed in the deep theology in Genesis 2 and 3 that warns against eating of the fruit of the tree of *the knowledge of good and evil.* I take this to mean that we are not to seek to become "experts" in knowing good and evil or continually to be making judgments about good and evil. Nevertheless, it is helpful to us as individuals and to the Church as a whole to use the teaching about the Opposition to Jesus Christ to discern warning signs of being led astray, particularly in participating in corporate evil or yielding to socio-cultural influences that advance harm and suffering to others, typically our "sins of omission." The teaching about the Opposition to Christ applies particularly to evil on a corporate or macro level, where we may not have much consciousness of what is taking place. We can use the principles in the teaching about the Opposition to Christ together with insights from the social sciences to examine ourselves and to look at the history of the Church and thereby build a Christian philosophy of history that will help us be prepared to face and turn from evil that continually arises in new forms within Christianity or a Christian context.

It is important to note that the teaching about the Opposition and antichrist does not refer to the opposition (small "o") of those who have not heard and believed the good news of Jesus Christ and the New Age. The Opposition discussed in the New Testament is manifested primarily *among* those who have heard and begun to believe and are subsequently misled by strong socio-cultural forces. In other words, it is Opposition to God and the Kingdom of God that arises primarily from within the Christian context. Once arisen, however, the Opposition may move outside the Christian context and gain power over large numbers of people in general. This will be clarified in the historical examples used in the next chapter. At any rate, Christians should look primarily at themselves, not the non-believing world, for providing opportunities to the Opposition to gain domination. As stated in I Peter 4:17: "For the time has come for judgment to begin with the household of God." Furthermore, the Opposition I am talking about is not so much the opposition (small "o") of individuals, since according to the Bible, it can be assumed that individual opposition to God is found in all people, including all Christians. Individual sin tends to be highly self-destructive and therefore less dangerous to groups of people than corporate sin, much of which is unconscious.

The teaching about the Opposition that is of concern here is expressed in the teaching in the Bible about resistance to Christ's way that arises among believers at a macro level. This is a resistance that is a result of corporate or society-wide influences, which are beyond the individual although individuals easily yield themselves to these influences. Because of an individualistic outlook many people are not accustomed to thinking of evil and sin on a corporate basis. They will object to expressions of corporate sin typically used in the "Confession of Sin" in worship services. These expressions often refer to sins to which we as individual Christians may yield ourselves to unconsciously. Sometimes they are referred to as "sins of omission," which are both subtle and powerful affecting groups of people.

Even though the Bible does not have the language of the modern social sciences, it does contain language, particularly in the writings of the Apostle Paul when he speaks of "principalities and powers" that is very consistent with social realities investigated in the modern social sciences. It is important, therefore, to keep in mind the supra-individual nature of the Opposition, including "the antichrist." It is true that I John 2:18-24 and II John 7 speak of antichrist as coming in many individuals, but even here a careful reading shows that the antichrist in individuals is an effect of a larger force. I should also add that since there are "many antichrists" (I John 2:18), the Opposition to Christ comes in many forms simultaneously. This does not take responsibility away from individuals for yielding to any particular Opposition, but it is important to understand the nature of the force that is larger than any individual and how to resist it.

The first and most important fact to remember about evil in whatever forms it appears, individual or society-wide is that it is extremely subtle. Its major weapon is deception and the power to masquerade as good. This is made clear in the earliest pages of the Bible in the story of Adam and Eve where the snake (the tempter) is spoken of as the "most subtle" or "crafty" of all God's creatures (Genesis 3). Also, the snake promises something good and uses God's word. This is seen again in the Temptations of Jesus. Deception and lies are the major weapons of evil powers.

Even though the language in Genesis could be called "primitive" because of its ancient origins and anthropomorphic images of God, it is extremely sophisticated and full of deep theology. It expresses an understanding of sin and evil that is much deeper than most thought about human morality and ethics. The human Fall in Genesis 3 did not involve Adam and Eve doing anything obviously "bad." That came later. The Fall was basically a theological issue – a failure of faith or trust in God. This means that evil is basically theological and must be understood theologically. Good likewise is to be understood basically theologically. Non-theological discussions of ethics are possible and do have a place in many walks of life, but do not speak to the sources of evil or how to resist it other than to "not do it."

When people talk about good and evil they are usually talking about the outcome, not the source of evil. That is why it is possible to talk about good and evil or right and wrong on a secular level without reference to God. This level is simply called "ethics" as in "business ethics," "medical ethics," "political ethics," etc. and is available to all people to discuss. Such discussions can be very useful in giving guidance, but they do not deal with root causes or provide the energy to choose the right. Christians must go beyond and encompass discussions of ethics in order to deal with the cause or source of hatred, fear, greed, unkindness, apathy, jealousy and all the other expressions of the "flesh" or the sinful heart. Sexual sins are also an expression of the sinful heart, but are not as close to the source as the ones named, namely the attitude sins. Christ came to deal with the source of sin and thereby replace the harmful outcomes with good outcomes.

We turn now to consider the Opposition as it has appeared in history, primarily Christian history.

CHAPTER 6

THE OPPOSITION IN HISTORY

INTERPRETING THE BIBLE WITH THE HELP OF HISTORY

In the last two chapters, we took up the complex and often misunderstood and misused teachings of the Bible regarding the Opposition to God's work of redemption in the world, specifically to Christ and his New Age, the term that I am using for his Kingdom. This Opposition is also referred to as "antichrist" (plural as well as singular), but only in the letters of John.

In this chapter I want to apply the teachings regarding the Opposition to the New Age of Christ by discussing in more detail specific examples of the manifestation of this Opposition in history. This likely will be the most controversial part of this book because of its selection of specific historical examples which may be interpreted differently by different people. My trepidation expressed at the first of Chapter 4 continues. My purpose is to help people be alert to the signs of Opposition to Christ's rule with the aid of both the Bible and the use of social scientific tools for viewing human history. In this combined approach a Christian view or philosophy of history is developed.

Interpretation of the Bible, which when systematized or organized in some way is equivalent to Christian theology. It should take account of the history, language, society, and culture and all the contemporary conditions of the writers of the Bible. However, in addition to reporting long past and then more recent events that are the basis for human salvation, the Bible projects a particular view of subsequent history. Much of this projection into the future is in symbolic language, making its interpretation difficult. This leads to the observation that the Bible should also be interpreted in the light of what actually took place from Bible times to the present. This does not mean that the original projections were wrong, but that their meaning has been unfolding over time. Even though almost (only!) 2000 years have passed since the New Testament was written, this is enough time to see how some of the projections of the Bible have been fulfilled. At least in the last 2000 years some of the principles for interpreting God's work in the world (and the Opposition to it) as taught in the Bible can begin to be understood. I believe such an understanding of biblical interpretation is warranted, even required, by the words of Christ in John 16:12: "I still have many things to say to you, but you cannot bear them now. When the Spirit of truth comes, he will guide you into all the truth; for he will not speak on his own, but will speak whatever he hears, and he will declare to you the things that are to come."

A few illustrations help to show how God has continued to unfold the meaning of his will according to what God has already revealed in Jesus Christ. For example, the Bible never condemns slavery, but there are practically no Christians in the world today who would say that the practice of slavery is God's will for any society or individuals. The same could be said for racial segregation, only very recently outlawed in the United States and in South Africa. Human rights are not specifically set forth in the Bible, but most Christians of the world would agree that all human beings are due certain rights on the basis of their humanity, namely as creatures of God. Democracy is not specifically set forth in the Bible, but most Christians of the world would agree that some form of democracy is what God wills for the societies of the world. At the same time, very few if any Christians would declare that a dictatorship is God's will for any society. The institutions of modern medicine and universal education have brought blessings to countless people. Most Christians would agree that these modern institutions are part of the expression of God's care and concern for all people, yet these institutions were not directed in the Bible to be set up. All of these examples show that the will of God has continually been revealed throughout history based on God's original revelation in Jesus Christ, but in ways that were not envisioned originally or specifically mentioned in the Bible.

The spread of the gospel of Christ has had an effect on all of the developments mentioned. At the same time, evil that I am calling "the Opposition" has often blocked these and other blessings, as well as brought terrible suffering and destruction to many people on a periodic, but irregular, and scattered basis. Furthermore to the great dismay of many Christians and others, the Opposition has arisen from within a Christian context. Also, it must be admitted that Christians were involved in seeking to block a number of the important historical developments that have benefited humanity, including the elimination of slavery and racial segregation, the extension of human rights, the elevation of the status of women, and the development of democracy. Not only have blessings for humanity often been blocked by Christians; if the wars and persecutions (particularly the Holocaust) of the twentieth century are considered, Christians have participated in, certainly assented to bringing about evil activities and conditions. It even seems that evil has had more powerful and destructive manifestations affecting ever more people as time has passed, particularly in light of the last century with its two World Wars.

To understand the nature of the Opposition, it is important to note that the blocking of positive developments for humanity has typically been through socio-cultural forces, not simply individuals that opposed these developments. Individuals and networks of individuals certainly emerged to provide leadership for the Opposition, but socio-cultural conditions provided the context and stimulus for their emergence. Furthermore, the individuals that provided leadership blocking positive developments for humanity were (are) not always "bad people." Sometimes they were (are) quite "good" in many respects. This is important to understand and, I believe, is especially consistent with the Biblical teaching about the Opposition in the form of "principalities and powers" that deceive and come to dominate whole societies and groups, often through appearing as "good." I will consider historical developments in more detail below and particularly how I believe the Opposition affected them.

THE CHURCH SURRENDERS TO THE STATE

For three hundred years the Christian message spread in the Roman Empire through faithful, but diverse witnesses. During this time the voluntary spirit in the Church was strong. There were disagreements about what to believe and do as Christians, but no outside coercion could settle the disputes. However, in the fourth century an important change took place in the position of Christianity in relation to the government of the Empire. This change has been heralded as "the conquest of the Roman Empire" by many people. It has typically been seen as a great moment of triumph rather than for what it was, a time of great defeat. In fact, in the fourth century the Church fell for the temptation that Jesus rejected in the wilderness. It accepted the power and prestige of state approval and sponsorship instead of relying purely on the power of its message and the Spirit of God to make that message effective. Instead of being persecuted as before, the Church became the persecutor of both internal and external people deemed to be wrong in their beliefs. The Church went the way of almost all religions by allowing itself to be co-opted by the state. In effect, the Church became an arm of the state and the state came to be conceived of as a religious or spiritual entity, a typical conception in the pre-Christian world. This was the Opposition at work in the Church in the guise of good. The Opposition was unbound!

The "fall" of the Church spread its effects as Christianity spread northward in the second great expansion of Christianity. In spite of the distortion given to the gospel, faithful believers carried it to the numerous tribal people to the north. This took place, contrary to what is usually believed, without domination from Rome since Roman power had collapsed in the fifth century. Nevertheless, as European tribal leaders came to accept the Christian Faith they too adopted the "Constantinian" or "Holy Roman Empire" model and became little Constantines. Even the Reformation churches, which broke with the monopolistic Roman Catholic Church many centuries later, still accepted the state church pattern as the norm for themselves. The creation of the state church which became typical in the so-called Christendom of the West, may be considered the first large scale manifestation of the Opposition to Christ. Needless to say, it has produced much oppression, destruction, and death, as well as very tragically, resistance to the gospel of Christ internally in Europe and externally in the world at large. A major regression of the Church, often overlooked by historians, was the disenfranchisement of women in the churches that took place as the Church conformed to the patriarchal pattern of Roman and subsequent European societies. The recognition that women had gained in the Church was lost. The early recognition of women is evident in the ministry of Jesus and in the New Testament Church, for example, in the list of those greeted by Paul in the church in Rome (Romans 16:1-16), as well as in the centuries of growth before the fourth century (Stark 1997:95-128).

As the Church became closely allied with the state, it began to rely on state power to create conformity. As a result, the Church was no more pervaded by the voluntary spirit of the first three hundred years. The territorial concept of the Church became normative and has lasted in Western and Eastern Europe down to the present day. It was on this basis that the great misunderstanding of Christianity was established in which it came to be thought of both by its followers and others as a "Western" religion. Particular nations in the West were then considered "Christian" nations. Many Christians still make this a political goal, namely to have the nation as such considered "Christian" and as creating a kind of quasi church having appropriate Christian signs, rituals, and mottos. Creating a "Christian nation" has become a kind of sub-cultural force working in many Christians, even in the United States where church and state are formally separated. The misunderstanding that the West or the United States is "Christian" has had an extremely negative effect on the spread of Christianity to non-Western lands. Only recently, particularly since the collapse of colonialism, has this misunderstanding begun to be overcome.

It is important to see the alliance of church and state in light of the historic relationship of religion with political power. This was discussed in Chapter 3. Many believers in monotheism do not recognize that the emergence of monotheism that lifted up "one true God" and designated all other gods as false actually offered political leaders a new tool for authoritarian rule in which they could impose a single religion on their subjects. However, a "hidden card" in monotheism is that the God who approves may also disapprove, as illustrated in the prophetic tradition in the Hebrew Scriptures. An analogy to this may be found in the "Mandate of Heaven" tradition in China, although "Heaven" in China did not have the personal qualities and the direct involvement in human history of the biblical God. At any rate, the dual possibilities of monotheism, a tool for tyrannical rule or for resistance to that rule, provided a basis for both types of phenomena in Western history. This tension created the "revolutionary" history of the West in which numerous opposition movements were spawned. The dual possibilities can also be seen at work in the Muslim world. Secular democracy provides deliverance from both tyrannical rule and revolution.

Philip Jenkins (2010) in his *Jesus Wars* gives a horrendous picture of how the ability of church leaders to wield political power combined with a socio-cultural understanding of religion as an ideology for unifying societies produced enormous suffering and seriously injured the witness to Jesus Christ. Given the importance of doctrine in Christian thought, it was inevitable that there would be vigorous doctrinal disputes, just as there have been down to the present. However, the struggles that today would have resulted in Christian denominations produced major political struggles with cruel violence constantly used. In the end, large "denominations" were actually formed (Orthodox, Monophysite, Nestorian – the Arians had already been formed) after the Council of Calcedon in 451. However, it is important to note that these "denominations" followed ethnic and national lines even though the disputes were over understandings of the incarnation and the Trinity. These disputes were often primarily over the use of correct terms in doctrinal statements, terms that could have different connotations in different languages. Of course, the use of violence between Christians and the tendency for Christianity (like other religions) to follow socio-cultural lines continued until the introduction of the modern secular state that separated the power of the church from governmental power. Nevertheless, the ongoing influences from the past are still very much present. Even in the United States, where organized religion is formally separated from the state, Christians have politicized issues producing struggles for political power, as shown very clearly by Hunter (2010). Some Christians, as noted above, want to make the United States a "Christian nation" thus identifying Christianity with the coercive power of the government.

One of the early tragedies to come out of the close alliance of Christianity with the state and the identification of Christianity with "Western culture" was the building up of enmity between the Byzantine Empire, a "Christian Empire" that lasted some 1000 years, and the peoples to the East. In many respects it can be argued that the rise of Islam was greatly stimulated by the existence of state Christianity, which had dominated many of the lands, often cruelly, that were later liberated by Islam. Of course, Islam likewise combined religion with state power and replaced one form of domination with another, a historic pattern of "liberators." Would the course of history have been different if the contact of Arabs had been only with individual Christians living in vital Christian congregations instead of with a "Christian Empire?" I believe it would.

The creation of enmity between the West and the Middle East has been responsible for great destruction and the loss of many lives in the recurring conflicts that have taken place over the centuries, the Crusades being perhaps the most infamous conflict. The application of "holy war" or complete destruction of Muslims by Christians, though not successful, was certainly the work of the Opposition. The "Crusades" also resulted in terrible persecutions of "heretic" Christians and of Jews, which included the slaughter of many Cathars in France and Jews in Europe as the Crusaders traveled toward the Middle East. Later, "heretic" Constantinople was sacked. The enmity and the destructive conflicts with the Middle East continue to this day. One of the great lessons of the Church's close alliance with state power is that Christianity like all religions is very much subject to becoming identified with particular cultures and ethnic groups. When this begins to take place it is a good time for Christians to take note and take preventative measures to keep the faith from identification with one culture or one ethnic group. The argument here is that the acceptance of state sponsorship and the identification of Christianity with particular cultures and ethnic groups is an example of the work of the antichrist or Opposition to the New Age of Christ.

If this argument is granted, it does not mean that everyone in state churches is evil or that God ceased to work through people of faith in state churches. It simply means that a distortion was introduced by the Opposition into Christianity that hindered and continues to hinder the spread of the gospel of Jesus Christ. At the same time, death and destruction, a hallmark of the work of the Opposition, was brought to many people. Under God's providence a separation of church and state was forced in North America in an "accident of history" by the mixing of many religious groups. However, tendencies for Christian people to lean toward assuming political power are still present. Sadly, the formal separation of churches from political power actually opened the way to an *unrecognized* surrender of churches to socio-cultural domination—another action of the Opposition. The contention of this book is that the first great manifestation of the Opposition to Christ, a "release" of evil if you will, was the alliance of Christianity in the fourth century with the coercive power of government. This came after the successful spread of Christianity throughout the Empire. The effects of this alliance have lasted to the present day. I will consider some of them below as further manifestations of the work of the Opposition.

COLONIALISM

Beginning about 1500 Western nations began exploring the non-Western world. The state Christianity that they carried with them perpetuated and spread the "great misunderstanding" initiated in the fourth century. This created tremendous opposition to Christianity throughout the world, especially in the ancient civilizations that were explored and dominated whenever possible by Western "Christian" nations.

An example of the harm created by "state Christianity" has been mentioned in the case of the rise and opposition of Islam to Christianity. Another example of the harm caused by "state Christianity" is the strong opposition of Japan to Christianity beginning in the seventeenth century and lasting to the present. This took place after there was great success initially in the spread of the gospel in Japan, showing that there is no inherent opposition of Japanese or Japanese culture to the gospel. Japanese leaders became aware of the conquest of the Philippines in connection with the spread of Christianity and did not want a similar event in their own land. Many other societies, such as, India, China, the lands of Southeast Asia, African societies, and Islamic lands have been quite resistant to Christianity because of its association with intrusion and domination. The hindrance of colonialism to the spread of Christianity was revealed by what happened after World War II. It was not until the end of World War II that colonialism in the old form finally collapsed. Just as the prophets pointed to God's use of Assyria and Babylon to bring judgment on Israel, so it may be said that God used Japan to break the power of British, French, American, and Dutch colonialism in Asia. Of course, just as Assyria and Babylon fell, Japanese colonialism was also brought to an end. Also, the weakening of European power by internal wars greatly helped to break colonialism in Africa, as well as in Asia. The result of the collapse of Western colonialism has been an unprecedented growth of Christianity in the world, most particularly in Africa and China. (Korea, a colony of Japan and not of a Western power, had previously welcomed Christianity in the twentieth century.) Thus colonialism and its association with missions, was an extension of the Opposition to Christ and the New Age that took place in the fourth century when Christianity became closely allied with the state.

In spite of the Opposition working through colonialism to hinder the spread of the gospel, God still worked to bring about good even through evil, as I have pointed out before. Important research was carried out by Robert Woodberry (2012) on how the effects of missionary efforts that often accompanied colonialism. These efforts stimulated the spread of stable democracies around the world, which were supported by religious liberty, mass education, mass printing, newspapers, voluntary organizations, and colonial reforms. In addition, it should also be said that while the major old civilizations of the world were resistant to the Christianity that accompanied colonialism and imperialism, numerous minority peoples, particularly in Asia, together with Pacific Island peoples welcomed the gospel. For them, the gospel affirmed their distinctive identities as people loved by God, even when looked down upon by majority peoples, not unlike the effect of the gospel on the European tribes.

SLAVERY

Opposition to Christ and the New Age arose in the form of the slave trade that grew out of imperialism and colonialism and became part of Western culture, most notably in the United States, the "land of the free." This could be considered an example of a "release" of "the lawless one" (II Thessalonians 2:3) or "the beast" (Revelation 20:7). On the one hand, Christianity enjoyed great success in the centuries leading up to the settlement of the New World. The gospel had spread throughout Europe so that many immigrants who came to North America brought their faith with them. Churches, schools, and land development took place, benefiting the lives of many people, but the land development came at a great cost. White settlers overran and displaced Native Americans, often at a terrible cost in lives. Then, in addition the slave trade was initiated to provide laborers for the land development in the New World. (Native Americans were found not "suitable" as workers for the large scale agriculture that was developing.) Once again, culture, as well as ethnicity, both supported by social institutions, came into play as "cover" to justify the evils of the slave trade and conquest.

A distinctive religious culture was formed in the slave states in which the Church abdicated its responsibility to promote justice for all people and, in fact, supported racism. An example of this religious social culture is seen in the articulation of a theology of the Church that emphasized "the spirituality of the Church." James Henry Thornwell (1812-1862), who otherwise was a brilliant theologian, gave special emphasis to this doctrine. It was part of his and others' providing a cover for slavery. The concept of the "spirituality of the Church" allowed slave owners and traders to ignore the injustice of their actions. This particular emphasis from the theology of Thornwell and many other church leaders became normative in the society and culture of much of Evangelical Christianity in the South. What is especially significant for our examination of the Opposition to Christ and his New Age is that this justification for not opposing slavery and later for legalizing segregation is related to what the Bible associates with the antichrist, that is, a de-emphasis on the physical aspect of the incarnation along with the physical ministry of Jesus to suffering people.

The Docetic pattern of thought, mentioned in the previous chapter under the teachings from the Letters of John, is spoken of as characteristic of the antichrist. The doctrine of the "spirituality of the Church" enabled people to regard the Church as separated from human life and above concern for suffering humanity. It should not be missed that the socio-cultural forces supporting slavery eventually led to great destruction and death on a very large scale in the Civil War of the United States. In addition terrible suffering was inflicted on the slaves, both in their transportation from Africa and their labor in the New World. One hundred years after the emancipation of the slaves, people in the former slave states, many earnest Christians, were still defending their society and culture as "our way of life," which "outside agitators" were trying to change. Church actions to pave the way for desegregation were considered "meddling in social affairs" and "forsaking the spirituality of the Church." Beating and lynching was another form of suffering and killing inflicted on many that was considered "normal." Both previously in the Civil War and in the Civil Rights struggle of the last century the attempt to preserve "the Southern way of life" led to suffering and death of untold numbers of people.

It is important to make clear that the Opposition to Christ and the New Age by its capture of socio-cultural forces was able to dominate large numbers of people. However, it is also important in understanding the work of the Opposition to note that individual people under the influence of evil socio-cultural forces, who were socialized to accept and support these forces, may not have been bad or evil people, but were good people personally. Certainly, James Henry Thornwell, who supported slavery was not an evil person. Also, most famously, Robert E. Lee, who led military forces supporting the slave system, was even a model character in many ways, an icon for the "southern gentleman." I can personally testify to knowing earnest Christians who were personally kind and gracious, but who supported racial segregation that injured the lives of countless people, not to speak of causing many "little ones" to stumble (Mark 9:42). The ability of the Opposition to deceive and dominate large numbers of people through socio-cultural forces ("principalities and powers") is clearly demonstrated in what took place under both colonialism and the slave system. The result was both a distortion of the gospel and death and destruction brought to many people.

Again, in spite of the evils of slavery, God worked through some Christians to bring the gospel to the slaves and their descendants. Many of the slaves heard how God saved the slaves from Egypt and applied that message to themselves. They also identified with the suffering of Jesus and then his resurrection to new life. In the end, the Opposition, for all of its destructive force, was defeated by God through the weak and the "low and despised" (I Corinthians 1:26-31).

SECULARIZATION AND SECULARISM

The earthly authority and power of Christianity were eventually challenged successfully by forces from within the Christian context itself. The historical process by which Christianity lost and is still losing the coercive power it gained in the fourth century (a coercive power never claimed by Jesus Christ, but specifically rejected) has been given the name "secularization." This is my short definition (loss of coercive power) of a complex process that is much debated. Christians and scholars in general are divided with some seeing secularization in a very negative light as decreasing the influence of Christianity (many non Christian have seen this as a positive development), while other Christians, joined particularly by many American scholars, see secularization as a liberating process producing more vital faith.

It is true that many anti-Christians joined in the work of "dethroning the Church," but at the same time many Christians worked hard to make a clear distinction between the power of the gospel and coercive earthly powers. This has been especially true in the United States where the "great accident" of history took place in which people of diverse religious groups landed on the same soil and where agreement was reached that no single religious group should have the power of the government behind it. Of course, from a Christian perspective this was God working in history.

Secularism is one of the unfortunate byproducts of the secularization movement. Secularism is an ideology developed within the secularization process, which has been adopted by many who were (are) opposed to the authority and power of the Church, particularly when they were used coercively. Unfortunately, this opposition has blinded many people to the true authority and power of the Church, which is based on the death and resurrection of Jesus Christ. Secularism, the ideology, produces a lifestyle that ignores religion and considers God irrelevant to life. On the other hand, "the secular" as opposed to "secularism" can be seen as a useful tool or instrument to protect humans from bad religion or bad religious ideas. Actually, since God made all things there is no truly secular. In other words, the secular belongs to God. Individual humans may be involved in the secular (eating, sleeping, working) and be simultaneously praying and thinking of God and God's will. Thus, the secular is most useful as a methodology or an approach in which humans deal with God's creation, but without introducing religious language or rationalization outwardly. This does not mean that they do not think about God or pray about what they are doing. Rather using a secular methodology is a way to reduce the effects of wrong or even evil religion. An important reason for the outward setting aside of religious thought and language (even though internally religious motives continue to be important) is that religious thought and activity are fallible and are often misused. The clearest examples of the secular as methodology are in science and in government. That is, in science God is deliberately not introduced as a causative factor. This eliminates the possibility for religious people to introduce their wrong ideas about the world. Likewise, in a secular democracy, God's name is not to be used by the government as a justification for its policies and programs, eliminating bad policies introduced in the name of religion. Justice and fairness alone should be the basis and goal of government policies and actions. Actually, the secular alone (Christians remembering that God creates and works in the secular) can be of benefit to humans as in the arts, in all kinds of technology, and in various areas of daily living. By recognizing the secular as an approach or methodology, which does not introduce religious language and rationalizations, humans are prevented from taking God's name in vain. At the same time, it is important that Christians wrestle with what God may be doing in and through the secular, even though reference is not made to God. In all of life, both religious and secular, Christians are to be motivated to give glory to God. In this way, the secular is made sacred to Christians and becomes a means for benefiting humanity.

I believe secularism could be said to be one of the works of the Opposition affecting individuals, but it should not be seen as the central work of the Opposition to Christ as some Christians tend to see it, especially those who are attracted to political power and influence, perhaps out of nostalgia for the past when the Church was more openly influential in society. These Christians tend to see Christianity under attack from "secular humanism" as already noted. I believe this is an unfounded fear and ignores the importance of Christian humanism, as seen for example, in John Calvin and in many Christian leaders and thinkers. The secular lifestyle can certainly lead to self-destructive behavior by individuals, but secularism has the basic weakness of not providing the highly rewarding meaning to life desired by individual persons. Secularism fails to produce wonder or a sense of the holy, which may help to account for the attraction of many people to the occult as a substitute for the flat life of secularism.

The most dangerous effects of the Opposition affecting large numbers of people are through socio-cultural forces that are overtly religious, not secular. Secularism in an extreme form revealed its weakness in the twentieth century, when it, like historic religions, including Christianity, was able to achieve political power through Communism. Its excess was to establish a system that made atheism an official policy. It is true and it should be noted by religious people that the secular approach in science and government, as well as in much of public life (Smith 2003) places a special burden on the Church and on Christian families for transmitting the Christian faith. But this is where responsibility should be and not with public institutions. The greatest public need for the Church and Christians is for freedom of life and expression, not a "religious atmosphere" created by people who are "generally religious" and want to impose their religious views on others.

COMMUNISM

Communism is secularism gone mad. Extreme secularists or followers of secularism may go beyond believing that religion is irrelevant to believing that it is dangerous and needs to be eliminated by force. It is important to believe that even this form of extreme secularism is not the Opposition itself, but nevertheless was produced by socio-cultural forces influenced by the Opposition that created a reaction against both religion and free government. Communism with its enforced atheism arose from a Christian context where many people were suffering injustices associated with the industrial revolution. Christians misused their freedom and the prosperity they gained with it. These were conditions that never would have existed if Christians had behaved as they should have and not allowed the effects of industrialization to be so harmful to so many people. Christian neglect of justice continues to stimulate secularism and an anti-Christian spirit in those who see prosperous Christians ignoring poverty in their midst.

Communism developed political parties in Europe and the parties were strongest in the parts of Europe where the state church was the strongest and most authoritarian and the people the poorest. In the end Communism was not able to gain control of a single Western European nation. However, in Russia on the eastern edge of Europe, where state Christianity and the Docetic doctrine of the "spiritual" Church were quite strong, Communism did succeed in gaining power. Considering another area of some success where the Church and governments were quite authoritarian was in Latin America, but in the end, Communism gained power only in Cuba. Outside of Russia and Cuba (countries with strong Christian presence), the main success of Communism has been outside of the West where it could become identified with nationalism in lands that suffered under Western domination, as in China, Vietnam, and North Korea. It thus became a tool to oppose Western domination, one evil opposing another evil, a common occurrence in history and a way in which the Opposition loses influence.

I am not trying to identify Communism itself as the Opposition to Jesus Christ or as the antichrist. Rather I am saying that the lack of concern of Christians for justice in human life, hidden behind a doctrine of "the spirituality of the Church," together with the lack of democratic institutions laid the groundwork for the development of atheistic Communism and for its triumph as a political force. It was not Communism per se, but rather the socio-cultural forces justifying inaction for justice and the non-recognition of human rights that represented the spirit of antichrist or Opposition to the Christ of the New Age. Communism did not originate in a non-Christian context, but it found greatest acceptance where people were not accustomed to the tradition of human rights and democracy that had developed in the West and also where people suffered from Western domination.

The Opposition to Jesus Christ used Communism to elevate atheism to a point where it became the official policy of governments. The rise of Communism was also accompanied by large-scale destruction of human life and the loss of freedom, including freedom of religion. This proved to be a great hindrance, at least for a time, to the spread of the gospel of Christ. An instructive fact is that the project of Communism in the Soviet Union to eliminate religion was a colossal failure, although its influence remains. *In The Plot to Kill God*, Paul Froese (2008) has written very perceptively how Communism over extended itself in its goal to eliminate traditional religions. Its extremism led to a miscalculation. If the Communists had co-opted and used religion instead of trying to eliminate it, they would have been more successful in their aims to weaken religion. It is an example repeatedly seen in history, including the crucifixion of Christ itself: Evil over plays its hand, but also founders on the rocks of what God has built into human nature, namely a desire for God. The same foundering may be seen in the modifications made in the Communist system by in China, Vietnam, and Cuba.

GERMANY AND HITLER

A similar overplaying of its hand may be seen in the Opposition's employment of fascism, especially in Germany. One of the most often used examples of the antichrist is the person of Hitler in Germany. As a person Hitler perhaps comes as close as anyone in human history to embodying the spirit of antichrist and Opposition to the New Age of Christ. This is reflected both in his ability to use religion to his advantage and in the large scale destruction he caused. However, it is not Hitler as an individual person who was the antichrist. He was supported by networks of people in Germany. It was the socio-cultural forces created by the victors in World War I that paved the way for Hitler and created support for his policies from otherwise good German people that represents the Opposition to Christ or the antichrist. This fact is not sufficiently understood and emphasized. Hitler would not have appeared unless certain socio-cultural forces had not paved the way for him and encouraged the support he received. Some of these forces originated in the victorious Allied nations that sought to punish Germany for World War I. Other forces were found in Germany itself in the racial and cultural pride of the German people. Hitler and those with him were human agents in exploiting these socio-cultural forces and bringing about terrible destruction of human life. Germany as a society and culture, otherwise so beautiful, was turned into a force for evil.

As an example of how socio-cultural forces linked with religion prepared the way for Hitler, Diarmaid MacCullough (2010:941) points out the sense of betrayal felt in Germany at the 1918 defeat and the proclamation of the Weimar Republic:

> It has been estimated that when the Weimar Republic came into existence in 1919, 80 percent of its Protestant clergy sympathized with its enemies, and were monarchist and angrily nationalist. This was not a good basis for mounting a critique of Nazism, which drew on the same anger and turned it to its own uses.

According to the teachings regarding the Opposition or the antichrist, the gospel first has great success before evil is "released." We have already seen this effect in the fourth century Roman Empire. The Christian gospel made even greater advances among the German people than in the Roman Empire, beginning after the decline of the Roman Empire. However, an early sign of a poison in the culture was the persecution of Jews seen particularly at the time of the Crusades (Stark 2003). Still Christianity, later in the form of the Reformation, was very successful in much of Germany. The Bible was translated into the language of the people. Beautiful churches were built. The culture flowered with music, literature, philosophy, and science. Then after so many successes of Christianity and its attendant social institutions and cultural productions, Hitler appeared bringing great destruction and causing the Holocaust in which some 6 million Jews and others were killed. Satan was unbound! As usual, this reappearance of evil came in the guise of good, reviving the ancient folk culture of Germany and bringing unity and prosperity to the nation. Many in the church followed Hitler or simply remained quiet. Only a few spoke out or opposed him openly, which came at great personal sacrifice. Hitler is famous for having said, "I am not concerned about dogmas, but I don't tolerate a cleric who gets involved in earthly matters" (Busch 2010:1). Once again we see the signs of antichrist: evil masquerading as good, the employment of socio-cultural and ethnic values to appeal to large numbers of people, an emphasis on the "spirituality of the Church," meaning avoidance of "meddling" in political and social affairs, and finally great destruction and death brought to large numbers of people. We may add another important point about the Opposition to Christ: Hitler and many of the people who carried out his policies may be regarded as bad or evil people, but vast numbers of people who "went along" with Hitler's policies were certainly not bad or evil people in the ordinary sense of these words. The Opposition to Christ or the spirit of antichrist comes to dominate many good people on a broad national and ethnic level, namely a socio-cultural level. The Biblical references to the release of evil for a time can now be understood.

ETHNICITY AND NATIONALISM

One of the most notable characteristics of religions is that they often tend to follow ethnic and national lines. Christianity has not been immune from this characteristic. This was noted in the terrible struggles among Christians after they attained political power in the fourth century (Jenkins 2010). The connection of Christianity to ethnicity and nationalism is also seen in the terrible wars in the sixteenth and seventeenth centuries over which version of Christianity would become the official religion of a given nation or territory. I would even argue that the Christian gospel did much to encourage ethnic pride and the spirit of nationalism, with their good and bad effects, that developed in the West. As evidence of this, consider the Euro-Asian land mass. Ancient civilizations existed to the east and south with empires dominating large numbers of people. In contrast, in Europe, where Western civilization developed with and after the introduction of the Christian gospel, numerous ethnicities developed a sense of their own distinctive identities and self-esteem. Numerous nations came into existence resulting in the birth of modern nationalism. In fact, the spirit of nationalism has been carried by Western nations around the world and has become strong among numerous people creating a sense of identity and pride. The same could be said about movements of indigenous people throughout the world to express their distinctive identities as minority peoples.

The major difficulty which I would address here is that the Opposition has taken what is inherently good, namely the sense of identity and self-esteem among peoples and the spirit of nationalism that takes pride in the creative accomplishments of a society, and used these socio-cultural forces for highly destructive purposes. The warlike history of Europe is a good example of how the Opposition was able to use good for evil affecting numerous peoples. The "good," of course, includes different versions of Christianity, which were combined with ethnic and nationalistic spirit and goals showing a beautiful diversity within the Kingdom of God, but became a motivation for numerous wars based on ethnicity and nationalism.

In Africa, Christianity contributed to the development of nationalism. Specifically, Lamin Sanneh (1991) points to how the translation of the Bible simulated the spirit of nationalism, just as it had in Europe, even if it was an unintended effect. The translations created self-esteem based on the knowledge that God spoke the local language. However, in recent years, we can see ethnic identity being used by the Opposition in Africa to terrible effect, just as in Europe. After the collapse of colonialism in the wake of World War II that greatly weakened the European powers, there was a tremendous growth of Christianity in Africa. The majority of the populations of many of the new nations became Christian. The small nation of Rwanda became the nation in Africa with the highest proportion of Christians in the population. Yet this was a country where ethnic rivalry led to a time of terrible bloodshed for a large number of people.

Thus Rwanda is another illustration of how "the powers and principalities" of the Bible, namely socio-cultural forces, which may be good or at least a morally neutral influence, can come under the power of the spirit of antichrist or Opposition to Christ and the New Age. Ethnicity is not evil in itself, but it represents a very powerful influence on human life. It can overwhelm and dominate religion so that religion becomes a badge for ethnicity. When religion becomes identified with an ethnic group and its distinctive culture, then it joins the typical ethnocentrism of ethnic groups that supports hatred toward outsiders and often violent action to "defend one's own group," typically described as protecting "our way of life."

Christians have often been overpowered by the forces that drive mutual ethnic hatred. This is clearly demonstrated in European history, in the United States, as well as in modern African nations. Ethnic and national distinctions and the feelings that go with them certainly have been a major tool for the Opposition to Christ. They have been a source of major destruction of human life. This leads to a deeper consideration of violence itself.

THE SOCIO-CULTURAL FORCE OF PERCEIVED REDEMPTIVE VIOLENCE

One of the most useful contributions of the work of Walter Wink (1992:13) is his drawing attention to the on-going and pervasive socio-cultural force of the belief in redemptive violence with supporting organizations and institutions. It is worth considering his analysis in some detail in this section. He describes the influence of views of violence:

> Violence is the ethos of our times. It is the spirituality of the modern world. It has been accorded the status of a religion, demanding from its devotees an absolute obedience to death. Its followers are not aware, however, that the devotion they pay to violence is a form of religious piety. Violence is so successful as a myth precisely because it does not seem to be mythic in the least. Violence simply appears to be the nature of things. It is what works. It is inevitable, the last and, often, the first resort in conflicts. It is embraced with equal alacrity by people on the left and on

the right, by religious liberals as well as religious conservatives. The threat of violence, it is believed, is alone able to deter aggressors. It secured us forty-five years of a balance of terror. We learned to trust the Bomb to grant us peace.

Wink's identification of "ethos" with "spirituality" at the first of the paragraph fits my view that what he calls "spirituality" is a phenomenon subject to social scientific study like other inward human characteristics. At the same time, of course, he is right that "spirituality," "ethos," "values," "attitudes," "motivations" are all areas of life that in religious thinking are related directly to God. The inward life thus has a dual quality of being able to be examined in a social scientific manner (with a secular methodology) and also theologically (from the perspective of faith based on perceived revelation.)

Wink (1992:13-17) traces the ethos of violence to the ancient religion of Babylon in which creation takes place through the violence of the gods and this myth of creation is reenacted in recurring rituals used by rulers to justify their domination through violence. Drawing on the thought of Paul Ricoeur (1967), Wink (1992:16) describes the usefulness to rulers of the belief in redemptive violence:

> The ultimate outcome of this type of myth, remarks Ricoeur, is a theology of war founded on the identification of the enemy with the powers that the god has vanquished and continues to vanquish in the drama of creation. Every coherent theology of holy war ultimately reverts to this basic mythological type. The relation of King versus Enemy becomes the political relation par excellence. According to this theology, the Enemy is evil and war is her punishment. Unlike the biblical myth, which sees

evil as an intrusion into a good creation and war as
a consequence of the Fall, this myth regards war as
present from the beginning.

Wink (1992:17-31) shows the perseverance of the religion of redemptive
violence by moving from ancient Babylon to modern popular culture
with its cartoons and movies and then to the culture that supports the
national security state. The ethos of violence hides under the cover
of nationalism and patriotism, both of which can be constructive and
destructive.

It is not surprising that people should use religious language
to help them endure the terrible violence of war. Jon Pahl (2010)
emphasizes especially how the religious concept of sacrifice is used
in supporting violence. War and other kinds of dangerous activity,
such as required of the police and firefighters, certainly does require
sacrifice by those who participate and by the families who stand
behind them. Nevertheless, while the sacrificial motives of those who
suffer are very admirable, as well as much appreciated by survivors,
Christians and others should remember that the use of the concept of
sacrifice itself does not mean that the violence carried out, especially
in war, was right or wise. In fact, the concept of sacrifice may well be
misused by those who make decisions for wars that bring suffering
and death to so many.

In many respects the ethos of violence, seen as a redemptive force
and able to solve the problems of society, underlies almost all of the
"outbreaks" of the antichrist or Opposition to Christ and the New
Age. This is seen in each of the historic examples already given. It
becomes clearer and clearer that the outbreak of Opposition to Christ
(the loosening of the antichrist from its bonds) takes place when
socio-cultural forces ("the principalities and powers") in their benign

and constructive aspects become infused with the powerful socio-cultural force in which violence is seen as a necessary redemptive action. Death and destruction on a large scale then take place.

THE STATE AND VIOLENCE

It is important to understand the relationship of the state to violence. A working definition of the state is given by William L. Kolb (1964:690):

> The term *state* denotes a body of people living in a defined territory organized in such a way that a designated few of their own number can expect to control, directly or indirectly, by means of appeal to real or imputed group values or by force if necessary, a more or less restricted range of activities of the body of people.

Notice that the state reserves the right to use force or controlled violence if necessary. Max Weber (1967 [1946]:77-78), who wrote extensively on the state, pointed out that a state can carry out a multiplicity of tasks, but he stated:

> Ultimately, one can define the modern state sociologically only in terms of the specific means peculiar to it, as to every political association, namely, the use of physical force…Today the relation between the state and violence is an especially intimate one. In the past, the most varied institutions–beginning with the sib [the set of siblings and their families]–have known the use of physical force as quite normal. Today, however, we have to say that a state is a human community that (successfully) claims the monopoly of the legitimate use of physical force within a given territory.

It is difficult to imagine any government that does not have the power of coercion. However, the difference between power and authority is important to understand in relation to the state. Power may be exercised with or without authority. For example, a state may establish and maintain itself through the exercise of raw power, but this is quite expensive and also risky for the long term. This is why states seek authority, which grants the legitimate use of coercive power or the right to use such power. As already mentioned, this tells us why governments have traditionally allied themselves with or even become fused with religion. Religions supposedly have access to the highest authority, God, and governments want to gain the approval of God from religions. Religions in turn look to governments for protection and even sponsorship. Typically, they will ask the government for a monopolistic position that will eliminate religious rivals.

As Wink (1992: 13-104) points out, the history of states going back to the earliest civilizations has been a history of "the domination system." The evidence is difficult to obtain from pre-literate societies, but there is evidence that many if not most of the earliest societies were considerably less violent than they became after the rise of the city-states and early empires. Whatever the case, as populations increased, "[t]he new capacity for expansion and enrichment through conquest created a situation of anarchy in which no one could choose that the struggle for dominance should cease"(Wink 1992:40). War became incessant as rulers sought to dominate their people and lead their societies in domination of other societies. "The source of war is not physiological (aggression) nor philosophical (ideas) nor psychological (competition), but structural – the contest for domination means that everyone is forced to become involved" (Wink 1992:41). Let us give up the idea that "culture" is simply views, values, and worldviews as encouraged by Hunter (2010) to do. The domination system became an important part of socio-cultural systems and the justification of violence, seeing it as redemptive and participating in it, became an important part of culture, including religious culture, and its institutional structures.

Since it is impossible to think of the state without at the same time thinking of its possible and even necessary occasional use of violence, what is the realistic alternative to recognizing the inevitability of violence or coercion in human life? There probably is none. The problem appearing throughout history is the overuse of violence and the idealization of violence as "redemptive," namely as a major means of solving social problems instead of simply limiting evil. In other words, force cannot solve problems; it can only temporarily limit evil in some of its outward aspects. A corrective that has accompanied the history of states from the earliest days has been their recurring failure or their fall after a period of rule through force. The greater the violence on which states are built and the more violence is used to establish the power of states, the more inevitable is their eventual failure. Unfortunately, the time may seem long for those under the domination of such violence.

The search of states for authority or legitimacy on which to base their power is evidence of at least the minimal understanding of humans that raw violence is an insufficient basis on which to establish a lasting and healthy society. It also explains why states so often seek religious support for their authority. Violence may be necessary to limit violence, but it is not a solution to changing the causes of violence. It certainly cannot create strong and lasting states or strong and lasting interstate relationships. The concern of this book is that the Opposition uses the legitimate need for controlled violence in societies to create violence prone governments and violence prone people. This is especially possible through employing the myth of redemptive violence, as described in the previous section.

IS HISTORY GETTING BETTER OR WORSE?

From both the teaching regarding the Opposition and the review of historical examples of the Opposition in this chapter, history appears to move in both good and bad directions. History contains numerous improvements for the life of humanity, many if not most of which have had some connection with or been influenced by the spread of the gospel of Jesus Christ, even though Christians have often participated in blocking these improvements. Non-Christians and even anti-Christians have often recognized the value of advancements, such as democracy, science, medicine, and public education, and joined or led Christians in their promotion. At the same time, there are outbreaks or rather sudden and unexpected appearances of evil occurrences that bring death and destruction to large numbers of people. Technological improvements that have brought better conditions of living to many people often also become means for bringing misery to many. An example of the two-fold effect of technological advancements is that developments to improve military capabilities also may be used to improve living conditions. The development of the computer and communication during World War II became useful in subsequent civilian life. Advances in treating wounds in war also helped to advance the use of antibiotics. History is complex, but Christians believe that God often turns the results of evil actions to some good purpose.

Christians disagree about the possibilities of eliminating wars, particularly large-scale wars. The Bible says, "And you will hear of wars and rumors of wars; see that you are not alarmed: for this must take place, but the end is not yet" (Matthew 24:6). Because of this verse, many Christians believe that wars are inevitable, in fact, are a prelude to the end of history. But they forget the phrase, "but the end is not yet." Wars are not a predictor of the end as many people think. There is no reason from the Bible that wars may not be severely limited some day by the nations of the world. Wars are certainly one of the major causes of terrible suffering in the world, and the century that is just past saw the most destructive wars of human history. International cooperative efforts, the United Nations in particular, are often criticized and attacked, surprisingly, by Christians along with others. The earlier League of Nations was also blocked in the United States by good people for patriotic reasons, thus slowing the development of international cooperation. International cooperation is actually seen by some as an instrument of the Opposition to Christ's kingdom and the means of evil gaining control over the nations. International cooperation is depicted as "world government" that takes away "our freedoms and sovereignty." Nevertheless, the next period in world history may see the increasing recognition that wars do not solve basic human problems and should be eliminated. If I project that wars may be eliminated in the future and international cooperation increased, including the strengthening of the United Nations, does that mean that I am siding with those who say the world will see only improvements and social progress? I believe the elimination of war or certainly its reduction is possible, but this will not eliminate evil in the form of the "principalities and powers" (socio-cultural forces) that oppose Christ. In fact, evil may simply become more subtle and hidden. The Opposition to Christ will continue to be "unbound" (Revelation 20:3) causing harm and destruction in new ways. This may mean Christians falling back into more legalistic and routine religion and becoming more apathetic toward those who suffer. A great victory of the Opposition is to make Christians apathetic toward and uncaring for others.

It is very difficult to make predictions, but based on the history of socio-cultural characteristics that become a basis for harmful action,

I will hazard a prediction. One of the socio-cultural characteristics of the modern world and especially of the United States that has contributed greatly to the advance of political freedom and democratic governments has been the elevation of the individual and individual rights. The spirit of Individualism has been a "principality and power" that has brought good, but it has also brought evil. There is a negative side to the socio-cultural expression of individualism when it is carried to an extreme expression. Extreme individualism has already caused much suffering, as it did in the nineteenth and twentieth centuries in the form of laissez faire government and economics. The culture of hyper-individualism has had great influence in the United States and could increase in influence. The socio-cultural expression of unbridled accumulation of wealth contributed to the economic difficulties that have recently engulfed the world, beginning primarily in the United States, the world's so-called superpower. Individualism also has encouraged a destructive and wasteful approach to the environment that has caused great harm to many people. While extreme individualism may lead some into a quiet and isolated life, it seems to lead others into violent actions against the supposed "governing forces" that "threaten to take over society" and "take away our liberties." The great rise in radical hate groups is testimony to the increasing fear by many hyper-individualists. Fear has always been a major weapon of the Opposition. My prediction is that one of the great effects of the Opposition in the future, which is already seen, will be apathy toward poverty and the many people who suffer want in the midst of plenty.

The interesting and encouraging fact is that the gospel of Jesus Christ directly undercuts the socio-cultural expressions of exaggerated individualism. This is the "sword from the mouth of Jesus" (Revelation 1:16). There are already movements afoot to block or correct anti-environmental actions as harmful to all life. Some are also seeing that apathy toward poverty in the midst of plenty is harmful for all. Like the other manifestations of evil in history, the socio-cultural expression of hyper-individualism demonstrates the basic self-destructive effect of sin. The Opposition is following its historic tendency to exaggerate its power and reveal its basic negative effect on life.

CONCLUSION

"Principalities and powers" or socio-cultural forces will always exist, but they must always be wrestled with. Readers may not agree with my selection of historical examples of the appearance and work of the Opposition to Jesus Christ and the New Age. Many other examples may be found, but the examples certainly make clear that in the last two thousand years, as the message of Jesus Christ has spread around the world, there also have been major appearances of destructive forces arising from *within Christian contexts and with support by Christians.* The Bible depicts the Opposition as arising in the guise of good and not as something easily recognized as evil. The destructive forces of the Opposition clearly have been counter to what we know of Jesus Christ and his Kingdom, which he established at the beginning of "the last days" that he inaugurated. Yet the Kingdom or the New Age has not been stopped and the destructive forces, though increasing in effect, have repeatedly failed and faded. As apocalyptic literature indicates, the forces of evil and the destruction brought by them will always be temporary, as terrible and as long lasting they may seem to those affected by them. At the same time, another important principle to keep in mind is that of "release" of evil after its apparent subjection. That is, evil with its destructive force has a way of "reappearing," often in more virulent and more subtle forms than before. Simply apathy toward others encouraged by the Opposition through extreme individualism may actually be highly destructive. This is why Christians need to exercise special discernment and be on constant guard (Ephesians 6:13).

CHAPTER 7

RECOGNIZING AND DEFENDING AGAINST THE OPPOSITION

AN ALREADY DEFEATED OPPOSITION

There is no mention of *defeating* the Opposition to Christ in the title of this chapter because a severe defeat to the Opposition has already taken place and final defeat of the Opposition will take place on the Final Day. However, enough has been written in previous chapters to show that the Opposition definitely is still at work. Nevertheless, it is comforting to know that the deathblow has already been delivered to the Opposition. This is stated very clearly in the New Testament. Examples are:

> He disarmed the rulers and authorities and made a public example of them, triumphing over them in it [in the cross] (Colossians 2:15).

> God put this power to work in Christ when he raised him from the dead and seated him at his right hand in the heavenly places, far above all rule and authority and power and dominion, and above every name that is named, not only in this age but also in the age to come (Ephesians1:20-23).

> "Now is the judgment of this world; now the ruler of this world will be driven out. And I, when I am lifted

up from the earth, will draw all people to myself." He said this to indicate the kind of death he was to die (John 12:31, 32, 33)

Jesus answered them …"I have said this to you so that you may have peace. In the world you face persecution. But take courage, I have conquered the world!" (John 16:31a, 33).

And Jesus came and said to them, "All authority in heaven and on earth has been given unto me…" (Matthew 28:18a)

While Christians do not affirm enough that the Opposition has been defeated and that the authority of Christ has been established, this may be because it is rather obvious that a struggle continues with the Opposition that is still capable of causing much harm to human beings. Furthermore, the authority of Christ has not been fully recognized and received in all aspects of the life of Christians leaving people open to the influence of the Opposition, the Opposition which originally led to the crucifixion of Christ. Thus we have to place alongside the above words of victory such statements as, "We know that we are God's children, and that the whole world lies under the power of the evil one" (I John 5:19) and "Like a roaring lion your adversary the devil prowls around, looking for someone to devour" (I Peter 5:8). Still, the word is "Resist him, steadfast in the faith" (I Peter 5:9). Resistance can be successful exactly because Christ is much more powerful than the evil one and, in fact, has already defeated the powers of evil. An effective defensive action begins with being able to recognize the major strategies and tactics of the enemy. Therefore I begin this chapter with a description of some of the main characteristics of the Opposition to the New Age initiated by Christ.

RECOGNIZING THE OPPOSITION

I draw on two sources for help in recognizing the Opposition. One is the Bible, including apocalyptic passages, but primarily the whole New Testament. The other source is from the history of Christianity, since there have been many examples of the influence of the Opposition, especially among those who claim to follow Christ. This is where the Opposition is able to create the greatest harm since it is "opposition from within" or what was called the "fifth column" in World War II. Furthermore, by affecting Christians the witness to Christ is directly affected, which is the main purpose of the Opposition.

Recognizing the Opposition to Christ and the New Age is made difficult by the fact that although present on earth and active among humans, the Opposition specializes in not being obvious. It works particularly through the inner life of people. However, the inner life of individuals is highly affected from the outside by the on-going collective forms of human life that we call "society" and "culture." The most powerful part of society and culture is more than their outward aspects seen in customs and practices of groups of people and the organizations and institutions to which people belong. Rather, it is the invisible inner part of socio-cultural forces found in collective beliefs, views, values, and attitudes into which people are socialized and tend to take for granted. These forces form the dominating ideologies of organizations, institutions, and even whole societies that injure and sometimes destroy people, often large numbers of people. The invisible part of socio-cultural forces is the major influence affecting how people act, but the invisible forces gain much of their power from supporting social institutions and other structures. Of course people can break from the influence of the inherited views and values of the social groups to which they belong, but this usually requires an inward struggle to "not be conformed to this world" (Romans 12:2). In a real sense all Christians are called to be counter cultural and critical of their social groups in some respects, but disagreements among Christians are to be expected on what aspects of socio-cultural forces to reject, as well as how to counter their harmful influences. Both the inwardness of the struggle and the dominating outside sources of influence on the inner life are expressed by the words, "For our struggle is not against enemies of blood and flesh, but against the rulers, against the authorities, against the cosmic powers of this present darkness, against the spiritual forces of evil in the heavenly places" (Ephesians 6:12). Lest we should think that "rulers" and "authorities" are merely human governments, we are soon corrected by the words, "cosmic powers" and "spiritual forces of evil in the heavenly places." On the one hand, these are theological categories and terms, but, as I argue in this book, these forces also work through the invisible and visible forces that have been recognized by the social sciences as the powerful socio-cultural forces affecting all people. These forces are both external to individual humans and yet exist within humans and human societies. That is, they are experienced as coming from outside of us as individuals, but they become part of the inner experience of individuals living in societies, even if the societies are relatively small groups. In fact, individuals become agents in expressing and maintaining these forces, usually thinking of them as "natural" or "common sense" or simply "our way of life." Our powers always and clearly to recognize the Opposition are limited, but there is some guidance, as mentioned, both from the Bible and from Christian history that can help us.

LOOK AT THE CHRISTIAN CONTEXT

As already noted, the primary Opposition to Christ in the New Age comes from within the context of the Biblical faith rather than from a context in which that faith has little influence or acceptance. That is why the Opposition or antichrist did not appear until the revelation of God's self in history, first in Israel, and then specifically in the life and work of Jesus Christ. This does not mean that evil is not at work among other humans, but only that it is from within the Christian context that God's work of redemption is most easily opposed. The message of the New Age had to begin its spread before the Opposition or antichrist appeared, but it did not have to spread very far or for very long. In fact, the Opposition to Christ already appeared among the early followers of Christ, for example, as already noted, in the Apostle Peter's opposition to Christ going to the cross (Matthew 16:22), but also in the mutual rivalry among the disciples (Mark 9:33-37;Matthew 20:20-27). In the New Testament letters we read that "the mystery of lawlessness is *already* at work" (II Thessalonians 2:17), "now many antichrists have come" (I John 2:18), and "many deceivers have gone out into the world" (II John 7). Nevertheless, it is made clear that worse days were to come when the Opposition would be "released." A major point in this book is the first great "release" of the Opposition affecting the most people took place in the fourth century as the Church made its alliance with coercive governmental power.

One of the greatest protections against the Opposition is diversity among the people of God. We can now see that the diversity in the Christian Community in the first 300 years largely prevented *domination* of large portions of the Church by the Opposition to Christ. Close to diversity in importance is the lack of governmental coercive power exercised by some Christians over other Christians. This allowed the inherent power of the gospel of Christ to work. As just noted, the Opposition to Christ or "antichrist" did not gain a *dominant* position until after Christianity had spread throughout the Roman Empire and was legitimated and then made a state religion.

Until then there was no dominating society and culture that could claim to be Christian. The truth was advanced through proclamation and persuasion. There were many false or half-false versions of the faith, but they were dealt with primarily through the cooperative work of Christians and the positive witness to the faith. Christianity was not threatened as much by the various heresies of the first three centuries, which tended to wear out by themselves, as it was later when the church became closely identified with the state and also with particular ethnic groupings.

Although the Opposition to Christ works in every believing individual the most dangerous Opposition to the New Age of Jesus Christ is the Opposition that develops in the Christian context and especially from what is considered an "official Christian society and culture." In this way, the Opposition comes to dominate large numbers of people and particular groups of people. Therefore, the major focus of Christians in discerning the Opposition to Christ should not be on individuals or on groups and societies of unbelieving people, but on the major socio-cultural forces that appear where Christianity is prevalent. In this sense, Christians are following the attention of God, as expressed in I Peter 4:17, "For the time has come for judgment to begin with the household of God." This is consistent with the words of the Prophet Amos, "You *only* have I known of all the families of the earth; therefore I will punish you for all your iniquities" (Amos 3:2). If it is God's purpose to win the world through the witness of believers, then it makes sense that the dangerous Opposition to the rule of Christ would be found most often in what harms and distorts the witness of groups of Christians, even whole societies that are known to be predominantly Christian, especially when they are considered to be "Christian" by both Christians and non-Christians.

LOOK AT THE SUPPOSEDLY GOOD AND SPIRITUAL

The Opposition masquerades as good and often as religious, especially if it can have Christian trappings. It would have little success if the Opposition came out as clearly opposed to Christ and his rule. Its power and success are based on its ability to deceive. (Note Genesis 3:1 regarding the subtly of sin.) This is why it is of little use to look for the Opposition in the context of the "sins of the flesh" or the "dens of iniquity." These obvious sins of the world are largely self-destructive, as already noted. Sadly, individuals get caught in them and bring suffering to themselves and others, but the major Opposition to Christ affecting large numbers of people, which is the major concern here, comes in the guise of good and even as being religious. People who come under the influence of the Opposition to Christ may even be good people personally. This fact is important because the Opposition to Christ often uses truly good people, who are believers in Christ. This is counter to what most Christians think, but it is important to recognize.

The characteristic of the Opposition to hide behind the good and the religious leads to the observation that the Opposition to Christ has been typically Docetic. That is, it has been dualistic in emphasizing "the spiritual" over against the physical. An emphasis on the "spiritual" is used by the Opposition to lead people to avoid responsibility for the physical and material conditions of suffering people. The protection and care of nature and ministration to the physical suffering of people, tends to be ignored when the Opposition is influential. The term "justice" is even considered a dangerous "liberal" term by some Christians because of its association with advocacy for social changes they do not want. The religious aspect of life is thus compartmentalized to the realm of the "spiritual" and believers are urged to leave physical and material concerns to the "earthly authorities" and "experts," who can "take care of these things." This was a typical emphasis of the Opposition in the twentieth century in Germany and also in the United States during the Civil Rights struggle when churches were urged to stick to "spiritual affairs" and not "meddle in social concerns." The thought of Hitler when he said, "I am not concerned about dogmas, but I won't tolerate a cleric who gets involved in earthly matters" (Busch 2010:1) was often echoed by supporters of racial segregation in the American South.

Paradoxically, while the forces of the Opposition urge Christians to "stick to spiritual affairs," they also contain a materialistic emphasis ("enjoy the world while you can") for many people, but most ominously, they encourage developing a culture with an underlying violent streak. In that regard, the Opposition makes use of apocalyptic literature with its violent images in order to create an atmosphere that encourages warfare. The materialistic emphasis of the Opposition also includes raising expectations of an earthly kingdom ruled by Christ based in Jerusalem. This is very different from the Kingdom of God or the real New Age brought by Christ, the Prince of Peace that has been breaking into human history for the last 2000 years.

LOOK AT SOURCES OF VIOLENCE

In regard to violence and warfare, the work of the Opposition to the New Age of Christ typically results in death and destruction on a large scale. One of the basic characteristics of the Opposition is that it elevates violence and the causing of death as a means of accomplishing goals and even of bringing about peace and good. This is the belief in "redemptive violence" identified by Wink (1989:13-31) as a current religion that dates back to the earliest civilizations and continues under the surface in modern American society.

Again, this Opposition to Jesus Christ in the New Age is a socio-cultural force that seeks to capture large numbers of people. It does this through the neutral and even good aspects of cultures. The "folk" or "down home" aspect of culture is celebrated, as Hitler liked to do. It draws distinctions between "us" and "them" and between "those like us" and "those who do not follow our way of life" or "the foreigners." The divisions of culture, and particularly ethnicity, are made very sharp by the Opposition. Those who are not of "our way" are given a lower status, even a sub-human status. Again, the characteristic of the Opposition to lead people to view other people as sub-human was very obvious in the twentieth century in World War II and also since then in areas where "ethnic cleansing" was and is practiced. Both personal and systemic racism are expressions of the Opposition to Christ. Systemic racism refers to how a society is organized or structured to create disadvantages to particular ethnic groups. This kind of racism is practiced unconsciously or almost unconsciously and is often accompanied by violence.

LOOK AT CHRISTIAN "SUCCESSES"

Since the Opposition is most dangerous in a Christian context, it is understandable, as the Bible emphasizes, that the Opposition will often appear after the apparent and even real success of the Christian message in spreading to a particular people. After many people accept the message and many positive benefits are produced within a culture, people may be least likely to expect the rise of a force that will capture the minds of large numbers of people and lead them and others down a path of destruction. Historical examples abound to warn Christians to stay alert, especially after the success of the gospel in producing much fruit in a socio-cultural group. The success of the gospel in spreading to large numbers of people often gives people a sense of superiority and invulnerability with the expectation that God owes them special protection, including victory over their enemies. They may take their prosperity as a sign that God favors them above other people and will also protect them from their enemies because of their faith. The prophets spoke to this delusion in ancient Israel. An important goal of the Opposition is accomplished when it is able to distort the gospel by associating it with a proud and dominating people, who look down on others.

NO CHRISTIAN CLASSES

The characteristics of the Opposition listed above should help believers in Christ in the New Age at least to be alert to how the Opposition may appear. Nevertheless, the power of deception by the Opposition should not be underestimated and the discernment of believers, even so-called strong believers, should not be overestimated. I personally do not like the term, "strong believer" or "strong Christian." Too many "strong believers" have particular weaknesses, one of them being a tendency to be judgmental and dominant over others. More appropriate terms may be "active Christian" and "thoughtful Christian." Once again, what is needed in the Christian community is diversity of gifts that includes diversity of views and opinions and a willingness to learn from others of different views and opinions. Certainly, there should be a willingness to work with others, especially in areas of service to those in need.

It is important to emphasize that the Christian faith and community are not divided by "spiritual classes," with some more holy or stronger than others. Rather, the Christian community is divided by functions, gifts, and emphases at both individual and group levels. It is wiser and safer to regard oneself as an average believer (as I remember Otto Piper of Princeton Seminary recommending) and one's Christian community as one among many being used by God. As we have learned, "some are last who will be first, and some are first who will be last" (Luke 13:30).

One of the clearest indications of the influence of the Opposition is when one particular style or expression of faith is considered superior to all others and made normative in a coercive way for a particular group of people. A coercive approach is typical of state churches and churches identified with particular ethnic groups. In these socio-cultural conditions the social pressures to conform are very strong. A coercive approach can also be used in religious movements in which expressions of disagreement are not allowed and diversity is frowned upon. Divisions among diverse Christians and Christian groups have been a major means of the Opposition to distort the gospel for those who see how Christians do not get along with each other. This brings us to look at the defenses we need against the Opposition.

DEFENDING AGAINST THE OPPOSITION

The Ephesian passage (6:10-13) regarding putting on the whole armor of God recommends a defensive stance. We are to "stand firm." I say this to avoid claiming that it is our responsibility to defeat the Opposition to Christ, but also to take away any sense of panic or of impending doom. The defeat of the Opposition to Christ in the New Age is sure and may even be said to be simple *if* we follow the directions given to us. As Martin Luther said in his hymn, "One little word shall fell him." He goes on to say, "That word above all earthly powers, no thanks to them abideth," but concludes his verse on a sober, but triumphant note, "The body they may kill, God's truth abideth still, his kingdom is forever." Many Christians who have strong opinions about what they regard as the truth, do not seem to have the faith that what they believe will "abide forever" even if they are in a minority. Instead, they prefer to separate themselves from other Christians with whom they disagree. Much separation of Christians from other Christians is based on weakness of faith and unwillingness to let their witness stand on its own power.

It is highly important to dismiss fear from becoming a dominating attitude ("they are going to destroy our religion and culture" or "they are going to change our way of life") because fear makes even good people mean. With the confidence that a victory has already been won, that a post-victory clean up is going on, and that a final victory will take place in God's time, how are we to deal with the Opposition that though defeated still rises from time to time to surprise us with its strength?

The emphasis of the New Testament is that the Opposition is defeated by the "breath of his [Jesus Christ's] mouth" (II Thessalonians 2:8) and by a sword coming from the mouth of Jesus Christ (Revelation 1:16; 19:21). These are indications that it is the Word and the Spirit of God that defeats the Opposition to the New Age, as Luther wrote.

When the Seventy disciples returned from the Mission on which they were sent, they had great joy at the power over demons they were able to have. Jesus said to them:

> I watched Satan fall from heaven like a flash of lightening. See, I have given you authority to tread on snakes and scorpions, and over all the power of the enemy; and nothing will hurt you. Nevertheless, do not rejoice at this, that the spirits submit to you, but rejoice that your names are written in heaven" (Luke 10:17-20).

It is clear that in the choosing and training of disciples and in the Great Commission (Matthew 28:18-20) given to them that Jesus Christ intended to spread the gospel of the New Age *through* the work of his followers. At the same time, he warned them to do their work with appropriate humility, always looking to and tending to their own spiritual weaknesses.

The Apostle Paul expressed this humility well in II Corinthians 4:7-12:

> But we have this treasure in clay jars, so that it may be made clear that this extraordinary power belongs to God and does not come from us. We are afflicted in every way, but not crushed; perplexed, but not driven to despair; persecuted, but not forsaken; struck down, but not destroyed; always carrying in the body the death of Jesus, so that the life of Jesus may also be made visible in our bodies. For while we live, we are always being given up to death for Jesus sake, so that the life of Jesus may be made visible in our mortal flesh. So death is at work in us, but life in you.

What is our only defense against the Opposition? It is the Word and the Spirit, both sent from God. The Word comes to us as living on earth (Jesus Christ) and as written, read, and proclaimed from the Bible. I have always been struck that the Westminster Shorter Catechism in answer to Question 86, "How is the Word made effectual to salvation?" answers, "The Spirit of God maketh the reading, but especially the preaching of the Word an effectual means of convincing and converting sinners and of building them up in holiness and comfort, through faith unto salvation." It is a privilege of followers to witness to Christ by speaking about him, but always to back up the message with love. That is why everything must be accompanied by the work of the Holy Spirit to be effective.

In the passage from Ephesians (6:10-17) that speaks of putting on the "whole armor of God" in order "to withstand on that evil day, and having done everything, to stand firm" there is a strong emphasis on the protective power of truth, which in the New Testament is personalized in Jesus Christ. There is the "belt of truth," "shoes" to make one ready "to proclaim the gospel of peace," "the shield of faith," and the "sword of the Spirit, which is the word of God." Other pieces of armor are "righteousness" and "salvation," both of which, with the other pieces are seen in the New Testament as found in a relationship with Jesus Christ, who revealed God personally in his life, death, resurrection, and on-going presence.

We come now to a great conundrum. How can we be sure that our witness is true to the word of God, that it is the truth with which Christ defeats his Opposition? How can we be sure that we have the truth and represent the truth and way of Christ to the world and in the face of the Opposition?

The Apostle Paul in his great Chapter on Love (I Corinthians 13) made it clear that even if we said all the right words and spoke them with great eloquence, if our lives did not convey love, our words would be useless in conveying the truth of God. The verbal truth is important, but it is conveyed primarily by how people are treated, namely loved, by the followers of Christ. In other words, we are to witness to Christ himself, who is the Way, the Truth, and the Life (John 14:6), by acting, as he would act. But it will always be partial, as the Apostle said, "We know only in part and we prophesy only in part" (I Corinthians 13:9). Nevertheless, we have to conclude that Christ has chosen to defeat his Opposition through our partial witness to the truth in representing the love of Jesus Christ to the world. It is the partial witness of many Christians, which together conveys a more complete witness to Jesus Christ than any individual can give.

However, as already pointed out, the effectiveness of even the mixed witness of Christians was blocked for many centuries by the

Opposition by identifying Christianity with coercive and dominating power backed by governments. Historically, the followers of Christ adopted the power of governments to enforce conformity to a particular version of verbal truth. This applies to all three major divisions of Christianity: Orthodox, Roman Catholic, and Protestant. All three versions of the Christian faith have come under the influence of the Opposition through the state church, the ethnic church, or the territorial church. All three major versions of Christianity (Orthodox, Roman Catholic, and Protestant) through the coercive use of power helped to prepare people to follow militant atheism or simply apathetic passivism (more dangerous than militant atheism) as a reaction against both authoritarianism and injustice. The irreligion movement may be seen as primarily a reaction against authoritarian Christianity associated with authoritarian governments and with the injustices existing under these so-called Christian governments (Montgomery 2012:293-341).

Through providential historic circumstances and the rise of secular forces the ability of the various versions of Christianity to use the power of the state has been greatly diminished. In the United States, where state and religion have been formally separated, freedom of religion has led to the religious diversity of the denominational system with its varied expressions of faith. However, even the formal separation of church and state did not prevent the triumph of culture over faith in which churches were captured by American local and regional "ways of life." "They are trying to change our way of life," became the cry of defiance by those opposed to the elimination of racial segregation. The formal separation of church and state, strongly supported by the Baptist and Presbyterian churches as minority religions in the United States, for example, seems to have blinded these and other churches and many Christians to their capture by a racist culture. In other words, the official separation of church and state did not separate church and culture, but even allowed the culture to invisibly capture the churches and Christian thinking.

Still, freedom of religion and religious diversity, which were accompanied by great socio-cultural diversity, contributed greatly to the self-corrective forces in American society and to vitality in religious expression. These forces were able to work to bring the society out of the darkness of slavery and legalized segregation. Even most recently, the self-correction of political pluralism has helped to restrain the use of military force. Thus diversity in society, including both religious and political diversity, has proven to be very useful in exposing the truth about human behavior and enabling society to make self-corrections. Because the truth is multi-faceted, the truth, so important for defeating the "Opposition" requires a context of freedom and diversity of expression, especially freedom to be critical of those with power.

Religious diversity expressed in the denominational system in Christianity has become the prevailing system for witnessing to Jesus Christ, the living Word, under the power of the Holy Spirit's gift of love. However, even the denominational system with its good effect of representing diverse aspects of the Kingdom of God, has had a bad effect of providing an easy excuse for people to separate themselves from other Christians in order "to preserve the truth" or form a more "spiritual fellowship." This may be considered a Docetic disregard and lack of love for the physical and visible catholic (universal) Church. Where does this leave the prayer of Christ for unity among his followers (John 17) and the plea for unity by the Apostle (Ephesians 4:1-16)? How much diversity can Christianity stand and still be a witness to the one Jesus Christ? The answer to this question is still not clear. One thing is clear: there has been diversity and conflict among the followers of Jesus Christ from the beginning as witnessed to in the Gospels, the Book of Acts, and the Epistles. On the other hand, the effort to bring about conformity of faith by force has proven to be a ready tool of the Opposition to Jesus Christ. Freedom needs truth ("you will know the truth and the truth will make you free"— John 8:32), but it is also a fact that the spread of the truth is aided by freedom. That is, it is difficult for people to learn the truth unless there is freedom to express the truth and to consider the various aspects of it. The Christian Faith allies itself with freedom so that it can be heard. This means that with freedom of expression and freedom of religion there will always be various versions of the Christian faith because the response to the faith will always be partial. Since this is true, then one of the major tasks of Christian denominations, groups, and individuals, in addition to proclaiming the Word, namely verbally witnessing to Christ, is to listen to each other and then make changes and corrections when this will improve the witness to Christ. To some extent this has been taking place more or less unconsciously in the United States for the last few hundred years as various religious groups "rubbed up against" and competed with each other, as well as organized cooperative groups and efforts. However, Christians could do a much better job of learning from each other by actively seeking to interact with Christians who are different from themselves. As noted, individuals and groups of Christians still find it too easy to separate themselves from other Christians in order to establish "more spiritual" or "more orthodox" groups and churches and to maintain the truth "once for all delivered to the saints" (Jude 1:3). Many Protestants forget that the Reformers would have preferred to stay in the Roman Catholic Church, but were physically forced to leave.

Homogeneity in society and in religion lends itself to being led in wrong and possibly evil ways. (Note the homogeneity of Germany and Japan before World War II.) Given the human tendency to dislike and even hate and persecute those who are different, diversity is often difficult to tolerate. Homogeneity in the European state churches led to a deadening effect on the life of the churches. Orders within the Roman Catholic Church proved to be one way to preserve some diversity and vitality. In many respects Protestant denominations function as "Protestant orders" (each with their own rules), but sadly relationships between them can be quite hostile and reflect an "adolescent" stage in the great movement toward being the mature Church in Christ (Ephesians 4:15, 16). It is wise that Christians learn to tolerate diversity under the guidance of God's Word and Spirit. This will increase the likelihood that the Word and Spirit of God will affect many people and not be blocked by Christians themselves.

Since the Opposition to Christ gets its wide influence through the "principalities and powers," which I argue in this book are found in the powerful influence of socio-cultural forces, then it is up to believers to create their own counter societies and cultures. It is not necessary to be different just to be different, but if one thinks and behaves by the standard of Jesus Christ as known through the Bible and the Holy Spirit, then one will not be dominated by any single current social structure or culture, including a single Christian society or culture. The different Christian societies and cultures that are represented in various congregations and denominations influence each other and help to correct one another's faults and failures.

Probably one of the best recent examples of the interaction for good of diverse societies and cultures among Christians is when first many of the congregations and denominations in the Southern United States allowed themselves to become captured and dominated by segregated Southern culture, which was expressing the Opposition to Christ. However, churches in other parts of the country were not as dominated as the Southern churches by the socio-cultural forces that aimed at preserving segregation. (Of course, racism existed and still exists throughout the nation, often in hidden ways through social systems.) Representing social, as well as religious diversity, the secular government of the nation, under pressure from the Civil Rights Movement, made laws that required Southern culture to change in certain basic ways. Furthermore, American socio-cultural life as a whole was affected by this internal interaction of sub-cultures in ways that reduced racism. Some speak of the "decline of morals" since the 1960s, but they forget that the elimination of legal segregation and some aspects of racism have brought a great improvement in justice in society. The way in which this improvement took place with the help of government action is an example of how God works through both religious (non-violent movements) and secular (governmental) actions.

Actually, the Opposition against Christ in the New Age tends typically to overextend itself (as it did from the time of Christ), not understanding that it is opposed not only to God's Word or revelation, but it is also opposed to God's whole creation in human nature and the rest of creation in both their natural and supernatural existences. As the Apostle Paul writes:

> For the creation waits with eager longing for the revealing of the children of God; for the creation was subjected to futility, not of its own will but by the will of the one who subjected it, in hope that the creation itself will be set free from its bondage to decay and will obtain the freedom of the glory of the children of God. (Romans 8:19-21)

There is great mystery in this statement, but I take it to mean that nature and super-nature, which were created by God, are waiting for God's re-creation of all things. My (Montgomery 2012) own study of the world's religions and of the spread of the missionary religions leads me to conclude that all human beings long for access to God, the very access that God has provided in Jesus Christ. Defending against the Opposition through the Word and Spirit is greatly aided by the fact that nature itself, including human nature, though affected by human sin, is made of "redeemable material" that can be and wants to be healed and restored and that will be re-created in a new heaven and a new earth. In the meantime, the natural creation has built-in powers that are opposed to evil and that are to a great extent self-corrective. The Opposition is an enemy of nature and nature an enemy of the Opposition. This is reflected in some of the popular literature of C. S. Lewis and of J. R. R. Tolkien, in which nature comes to the aid of the forces for good.

One of the pieces of evidence that nature is against the Opposition to Jesus Christ is to consider how the highest spiritual gifts through Christ named as faith, hope, and love are goals for ordinary human life in the secular world. All humans need these qualities if they want to flourish in life. Consider faith. Ordinary human relationships need mutual trust in order to be strong. The secular economies of the world depend on credit, another word for faith or trust. Banks often use the word "trust" in their titles. The comedian, Steve Martin, has noted that no bank uses the name "Ace Bank" or "Acme Bank" for obvious reasons; they do not convey a sense of trust. Consider hope. The ability to look to the future and plan for a desirable outcome is a distinctive and needed human characteristic. Early humans exhibited hope when they planned hunting and gathering forays, planning to meet at certain places, and bring home the garnered food. The opposite of hope or hopelessness is the darkest of human despairs. Finally, consider love. Humans know that love that is not permanent is not true love. A romantic song entitled, "I'll Be Loving You for the Next Few Years" would be a joke because the heart wants to hear, "I'll Be Loving You Always." Also, it is "Our Love is Here to Stay" though "the Rockies may crumble and Gibraltar may tumble," rather than "Our Love is Here for Awhile." Yes, thankfully, certain forces have been written-in to human nature that with the Word and Spirit recognize the truth of Jesus Christ as meeting the need for faith, hope and love and these built-in needs and desires check the power of the Opposition to Christ.

Perhaps the greatest force in defending against the Opposition is the elimination of fear, an almost impossible task for humans. It is fear that makes even good people do mean things—fear of losing their "way of life" or fear of losing a distinctive identity of which people are proud or fear of being dominated by others. Such fears fed by leaders, usually seeking power for themselves, led to the terrible epidemic of death and destruction in the American Civil War, World Wars I and II, the persecutions of supposed "security risks" in the eras of the two World Wars and of the Cold War, and many ongoing racial and ethnic conflicts. Unfortunately, fear is also used in domestic political struggles. The usefulness of fear in the hands of the Opposition is being currently demonstrated in the death and destruction caused in the "war on terror." Christians should remember that faith is the opposite of fear.

SOME CURRENT CHALLENGES FROM THE OPPOSITION

I close this chapter by calling attention to a number of current socio-cultural instruments of the Opposition in the United States. They represent how good aspects of the socio-cultural heritage can be carried to extremes, even by good people. The challenges are found not so much in outside effects on the nation, but more in *reactions* to outside effects or to internal problems. The challenges of the Opposition are not so much the problems themselves, such as the major social problem of poverty in the midst of plenty, which is also associated with hunger and homelessness and harm, especially to women and children. These are great social problems in themselves, but the Opposition has a way of causing people to use inherited values that are good or morally neutral to cause or exacerbate social problems and to block attempts to alleviate them. What is most harmful and the first goal of the Opposition is distortion of the gospel of Jesus Christ. A close second goal is to cause as much human suffering and death as possible.

REACTION TO TERRORISM

Remembering that the aim of the Opposition is to distort the witness to Jesus Christ, a current challenge of the Opposition has been to use the horrendous event of 9/11/2001 and other attacks since then to lead Christians to distort the witness to Jesus Christ, particularly as that witness needs to be made to Muslims. In addition, it is to cause as much suffering and death as possible. There is nothing wrong with defense by the state against attacks, but many Christians have gone far beyond that in their thinking and actions.

Christianity and Islam have been in touch with each other for many centuries and the relationship has not been one that has given a clear witness to Muslims of Jesus Christ, even though there have been some important exceptions in peaceful and non-intrusive missionary work. The present period should actually be looked upon by Christians as an opportunity to correct many of the distortions in the Christian witness to Christ given to Muslims. At the same time, the Opposition has been given the opportunity to dominate the attitude of many Christians with hatred or disdain towards Muslims. The present situation gives an important clue to how the Opposition works. Whenever the socio-cultural forces are pushing in the direction of creating negative attitudes towards a large group of people, the Opposition can be recognized to be at work within these socio-cultural forces. Remembering that a major goal of the Opposition is to cause suffering and death to large numbers of people, one of the most important ways this is done is by creating hatred towards those who are to be destroyed.

First, it is important for Christians to recognize that the Opposition is not "those other people," especially those who consider themselves "our enemies." The Opposition is not the radical Muslims who are carrying out attacks. This is not to condone the attacks or to say that no defenses should be taken against them. What is happening is that the Opposition is making use of the attacks to create hateful attitudes in Christians that will cause them to distort the witness to Jesus Christ in the world and especially to Muslims. These attitudes can lead to negative actions and even to the destruction of large numbers of Muslims and others, including those sent to fight against terrorists. The Opposition has already had some success in bringing about death to large numbers of both civilians and military. One of the major restraints on American Christians has been the diversity in American religious culture, which makes it possible to see that the large majority of Muslims are not "our enemies" and are loyal citizens

In the first place, the attackers are very distinct from Muslims as a whole. The attackers consider themselves enemies of the West, but this is not true for Muslims as a whole. Most Muslim governments are moderate and are threatened themselves by the radical Muslims. When it comes to the attackers themselves, Jesus gives very clear directions in his words and especially in his life on how to relate to those who consider themselves our enemies. The outcome of the current challenge by the Opposition is still not clear. There is still much to be done to generate and maintain the Christian attitude of love towards Muslims and all people.

THE RETURN TO "THE HOLY LAND"

There is another issue that I believe has become a weapon of the Opposition. This weapon has enabled the Opposition to influence many Christians. I am speaking of the application of a literal interpretation of the Old Testament promises to *the last days in which we now live* regarding the land on which the ancient Israelites lived. I dealt in detail with this misinterpretation of the Bible in the second chapter, but many are influenced simply by reading the stories of the Old Testament to think that the State of Israel is the "natural territory of Jewish people." The "natural territory" for God's people, both Jewish and Christian is really the world, which is for all the meek! In the first place, the prediction of return to the land was already fulfilled when the Israelites returned with the help of the Emperor Cyrus. Once again dwelling on the land and rebuilding the temple, in and of itself, did not create a purified and representative People of God, who could turn the Gentiles to God. Once again it was demonstrated that the sign of being God's people was not to be possession of a given territory. Then came Jesus Christ, who made no claim to any territory nor did he claim that he or the people of Israel would rebuild the temple in Jerusalem, which would then become the center of his earthly kingdom. John's gospel (2:19-22) makes it clear that Jesus used the earthly temple as a metaphor for his body. In his conversation with the Samaritan woman he also showed no interest in the location of worship (John 4:21-23). The apostles in Acts and in the epistles showed absolutely no interest in the establishment of an earthly kingdom based in Jerusalem. The problem with the present focus of some Christians on the coming of Christ to establish an earthly kingdom based in Jerusalem is that these Christians often become quite war-like, looking forward to a final physical battle between God and evil in the form of "the antichrist." The wars in the Middle East are seen in a positive light as signs that the End of history or the last phase of history (after believers have been raptured out of the world) is at hand. The destructive and warring imagery of apocalyptic literature, especially in the Book of Revelation only intensifies the warlike attitudes of these Christians. Many Christians have also adopted a view of God in which God is very authoritarian and punishing. They forget that God is represented by the way Jesus Christ lived, died, and rose again and that victory comes through the proclamation of the truth in love, not through any physical warfare. Remembering that the Opposition is opposed to human life and seeks to bring about death and destruction on a large scale, it can be seen that the Opposition is able to use the misinterpretations of the Bible and of the nature of God for its purposes. Christians must be on their guard!

There is nothing wrong in itself of establishing a state and the Jewish people have made wonderful contributions to every society, as well as whole areas and civilizations in which they have lived. At the same time, is it possible to make a religion, any religion, to be compatible with exercising the coercive powers necessary for the state? This is a sensitive issue that applies to the three biblical religions of Judaism, Christianity, and Islam, as well as to all other religions. (Christianity, of course, began its association with the coercive powers of the state in the fourth century with tragic results.) This issue is yet to be settled in the course of human history.

APOCALYPTIC ACTION

An important book by John R. Hall (2009), *Apocalypse: From Antiquity to the Empire of Modernity*, brings fresh light on how humans are seduced by the Opposition to adopt violent action to attain the supposed defeat of evil and the bringing in of a supposed new age or utopia. The concept of the apocalypse rises from the ancient perception of a struggle between good and evil that can be traced back beyond the first millennium before Christ, particularly to Zoroaster. "Apocalypse," of course, means "revelation" not the common assigned meaning of "destruction." It acquired the meaning of "destruction" because of the depictions of war, death, and destruction found in apocalyptic literature. Examples of this literature are found in the Hebrew Scriptures (Old Testament,) particularly Ezekiel and Daniel, but also in all three Synoptic Gospels ("little apocalypses") and most clearly throughout the Book of Revelation ("The Apocalypse"). Hall (2009) shows how throughout Western history to as recently as "9/11" and its aftermath, apocalyptic language has been used in connection with the use of violence. In the first place, Hall's study is a very strong repudiation of the views of many scholars that modernity has meant the elimination of religion and religious language. What the continuing presence of apocalyptic language has meant is that often violence is justified by one group against another, as the struggle of good against evil. The declaration of the "Holy War" in the Crusades is an example. As already noted, many Christians insist on not recognizing the symbolic nature of apocalyptic language. Most ominous currently is the use of apocalyptic language by extremists in the West and in Islam against one another and even by political leaders to gain support for their policies. "Evil Empire" and "Axis of Evil" are examples of apocalyptic terms that may foster violence. This is where "the cleansing power of the secular" as God's creation is needed so that religious rationalization and language will not be used. In other words, use of religiously charged language by political leaders can be and has been dangerous.

THE CULTURE OF VIOLENCE IN THE UNITED STATES

After the review of the culture of redemptive violence and the relation of violence to the state in the previous chapter, I note that the cases listed just above represent a continuation of the struggle with the culture of violence as promoted by the Opposition to Christ. The Second World War elevated the United States to the premier world power, but also helped to elevate the strain in American culture that idealizes violence because the Axis enemies had been brought down by violence. As Wink (1992) points out, the "religion of violence" exists in American popular culture. Of course, this is only one aspect of American culture, but it is part of or an aspect of the "principalities and powers" that can have great influence over many people. This has recently been brought to the attention of the American people by the murders of large numbers of people by "home-grown terrorists." There has also been an increase in the number of domestic "hate groups," most of which advocate violence.

Since World War II there have been at least two major occasions when the United States was led into needlessly destructive wars in which the culture of violence exercised considerable influence. These were the Vietnam War and the Gulf Wars, or at least the Second Gulf War consisting mainly of the invasion of Iraq. After the "9-11" destruction of the World Trade Towers, the American public was extremely angry and the cry for revenge was very strong. It was deemed a time for "kicking butt." The United States government used this spirit to gain support and to recruit soldiers for a war against Iraq, a country that had not participated in the attack on the World Trade Towers and the Pentagon.

The thesis of this book is that the "principalities and powers" of the New Testament can be understood today as socio-cultural forces, which can be constructive, destructive, or neutral. The Opposition to Christ's New Age or the spirit of antichrist represents the rise of a force within culture and society that results in distorting the gospel and in needless suffering and death. I am not saying that any individual or individuals are antichrist (remember that good people come under its influence), but rather that a strain or element within socio-cultural forces can gain great influence over a large number of people resulting in much suffering and death. I believe this took place in the United States after the destruction of the World Trade Towers and led to a needless war. However, the United States is blessed with a diverse society and culture (varied aspects of the "principalities and powers"). Because of this the "cowboy syndrome" was checked. The American people saw the futility of violence, at least in the specific case of the war in Iraq, and the basic inability of military force to solve problems in interstate relationships or political and social problems. The checks on governmental power worked and the government was changed in November 2008. Nothing could better demonstrate the importance of limiting the power of government through periodic change of leaders and placing civilian leadership over military leadership. In fact, many military leaders are stressing the importance, not simply of defeating their enemies, but of "winning the support of the people" and of creating "political solutions." This was not part of the language of World War II or of most previous wars, although the Marshall Plan after World War II reflected this spirit.

Sadly, monotheism itself, can be used to justify violence if the one true God is seen as an authoritarian and punishing God, as shown in studies of *the kind of God* in which people believe. It is only one step from believing in such a God for people to believe that God is using them to "punish the wicked," whether it is a family member or some outside group. This is another example of how the Opposition can use a truth, especially a half-truth, to turn people away from God and cause harm, death, and destruction. It is also an example of how Christianity is about believing in and following Jesus Christ (in his Way) rather than simply believing in the existence of God or promoting a public recognition of God.

EXTREME INDIVIDUALISM

It has already been noted that one of the most powerful ideologies in the United States is individualism. The ideology has its roots in the Bible with its emphasis on the value of each person and the importance of individual responsibility for faith and moral action. The good side of individualism is its contribution to the development of the concept of human rights, a concept absent from many societies, but now spreading around the world, as witness the "Arab Spring." Protestantism, with its emphasis on the importance of individual faith contributed to the development of the ideology of individualism, especially in the United States, and tends to support extreme individualism. This development was greatly aided by the large land and the many opportunities that lay before people to advance themselves. However, many American Protestants forget that the Bible emphasizes throughout that the individual believer also belongs to the Community of God and has sacred responsibilities to care for others, especially the weak, the needy, and strangers, as well as for the natural environment. Under the influence of individualism people tend to blame the poor for their condition and to take personal credit for material success. The help of inherited wealth and opportunity are often forgotten. The ideology of individualism is an excellent example of how something good is employed by the Opposition for evil with many harmful results.

EXTREME NATIONALISM

A very strong and growing socio-cultural force over the last 500 years has been the spirit of nationalism. As already noted, if one considers the European side of the Euro-Asian land mass, it will be noticed that there are numerous nations on the European side in contrast to the relatively few nations on the Asian side of the land mass. This is because the gospel came to the European tribes before they developed Western civilization, whereas in ancient or pre-Christian times civilizations with their great Empires developed in the East. Under the influence of Christianity in Europe, ethnic groups developed a distinctive consciousness of their identities and also the desire to be free from outside control. There were attempts at the formation of empires, "Holy Roman" and Napoleonic, but these failed. They crashed on the rocks of nationalism. Nationalism became an important part of Western civilization and contributed greatly to its dynamism as the various nations competed, but also unfortunately fought with each other. Then Western colonialism helped to spread nationalism around the world so that it has become a strong socio-cultural force within globalization, namely "glocalization." "Glocalization" is the assertion of the distinctive identities and cultures of people on the local level.

The need for cooperation among the nations has become increasingly evident, but also very difficult to accomplish because of nationalism. A major effort after World War I to develop cooperation among the nations through the League of Nations failed largely due to the efforts of extreme nationalism within the United States. The United Nations was finally formed after World War II, but it has not become a strong body in many respects even though it has carried out many good works. Also, there are important efforts to establish international cooperation in the areas of law and justice and economic development in the United Nations and elsewhere, such as the

International Court in the Hague.

As the world becomes increasingly small through globalization and the "leveling of the nations" continues, the need for international cooperation in numerous areas will only increase. The need is already very evident in the area of environmental protection. An excessive nationalistic spirit can easily become a major tool for the Opposition to block international cooperation. Again, fear is a major weapon of the Opposition in creating resistance to international cooperation. Europe, the seedbed of nationalism and the area in which excessive nationalism caused terrible damage and death to millions, is slowly and painfully learning the lessons of international cooperation. The rest of the world needs to learn from the European struggles, but the Opposition may be able to increase its use of nationalism in the United States as a force against international cooperation, especially since the United States is such a powerful nation.

It is the desire of many Christians in the United States to create a "nation under God" or actually a "Christian nation." This could be called the movement of "Christian nationalism." As in the Old Testament and in the time of Christ, the Opposition is leading people to focus on outward religious trappings, especially religious language and symbolism in the public sphere. There is a concern to create and enforce religious, particularly Christian, morality with the help of the coercive powers of government. As a result the weightier matters of the law, justice, mercy, and compassion for the weak, are neglected. The cultural ethos created by the Opposition through the human desire for security gives people the sense that with the proper religious language and "traditional" morality made official, God will be pleased and will grant protection and prosperity for themselves, of course. Ominously, this is exactly the movement that took place within Israel before it was destroyed, first by Assyria and then by Babylon. Thus "Christian nationalism" becomes an instrument of the Opposition to lead people away from the "weightier matters of the law," just as happened in ancient Israel.

Extreme nationalism combined with extreme individualism remains a potent force within American society and culture. This force may assert itself repeatedly and bring harm to many. In the future, extreme nationalism may become a major obstacle to bringing peace to much of the world. It would be well for Americans to remember the dictum of Samuel Johnson: "Patriotism is the last refuge of a scoundrel." Of course, as Johnson knew and as with so much that has been mentioned already, there is good and bad patriotism. Nevertheless, patriotism and nationalism are examples of good values that can become useful tools for the Opposition to the New Age of Christ.

EXTREME CAPITALISM

Extreme capitalism or extreme free enterprise, which may sound better, is linked to extreme individualism and extreme nationalism. Extreme capitalism is another example of how the Opposition tends to go to extremes before it is checked by sensible people, not necessarily Christians. In fact, Christians and good people generally have often supported the extremes with their harmful results. (Extreme emphasis on morality or legalism is another example from the New Testament of evil overreaching itself.) The United States began checking extreme capitalism in the late nineteenth century with Theodore Roosevelt's "trust busting." Again, it was checked after the "roaring 1920s" during the 1930s and with government spending (unfortunately it was on a war) in the 1940s. There continues to be a vigorous debate as to how much it should be checked in the late twentieth century and up to the present.

Marxism and Communism were the extreme reactions to the abuses of capitalism in the nineteenth century. They appealed to some people in the United States in the 1930s Depression. Communism has been repudiated for its failings, after bringing suffering to millions, even though Marxism has some insights which can be used, although very carefully. For example, Marx saw that people's ideas or their ideologies were very much affected by their social and material circumstances—an early insight in the sociology of knowledge. I found a source for insights from a Marxist, Antonio Gramsci, in a book by Willie Baptist and Jan Rehman (2011). They expanded and applied his analysis to the perpetuation of poverty. As I interpret it, capitalism, like individualism and nationalism, builds on some important values, in particular freedom for business and industrial innovation and policies that have contributed to improving the life of many. A result has been the development of a large middle class in the United States and other capitalist societies. With the middle class, as Gramsci recognized in the 1920s in Italy, came a very active "public sector" in which people felt free to interact outside of government control. This worked, at least initially, until the Fascist gained control in Italy and Germany through building on fear—fear of Communism in particular. Then the public sector collapsed. However, when there is a large middle class, as there has been in the United States, living comfortably, the members may find it easy to adopt and maintain an ideology that is oppressive of those who are in poverty and, surprisingly, as well an ideology that is against their own interests. The power of the Opposition, as we have emphasized is that it is able to take what is good, even what is more dangerous, the perception of what is good, and use it destructively. Today, it is the fear of Socialism or of "losing freedom" that is being used to cause those in more or less comfortable circumstances in the middle class to avoid dealing with the problem of poverty in the midst of plenty. What is weakening the argument, however, is that the middle class itself is being reduced.

This has brought the United States to where it must face the question of limiting capitalism as it has before. While the United States is struggling with this issue, extreme capitalism is now extending its influence over much of the world through globalization and is doing so partly by enabling parts of populations to advance economically, while suppressing the poor or simply leaving them behind.

Societies, including the United States, need government and private business and industry to work together. At the same time, the powers of both government and the private sphere need to be limited. Christians need to be wise in their study of the insights gained from historians and social scientists, some of whom were (are) anti-Christian or anti-religious (including Marx as a pioneer social scientist). Nevertheless, Christians need to recognize that good people may be swept up by the socio-cultural forces from the right because of the freedoms enjoyed by both individuals and corporations to accumulate wealth. The less regulations and taxes that exist the more wealth can be accumulated while others are impoverished or kept in poverty. This is the danger of extreme capitalism.

EXTREME POLITICIZATION

Democracy is one of the prizes of the American people, not only as citizens, but also in public life, which includes religious life. In fact, a strong case can be made that democracy grew out of the democratic processes at work in Christianity, particularly in the development of democratic church life. By its nature democracy creates partisans, in the United States and Great Britain it has meant two parties, but almost all democratic countries develop "liberal" and "conservative" or "left" and "right" groups vying for power. In a democracy, differences are to be resolved by debate followed by a vote to determine the will of the majority. An agreed upon political process is followed. There are winners and losers; some gain power while others lose power. Clearly, in such an environment that focuses on power there are numerous opportunities for the work of the Opposition. Once again, the Opposition is able to use something good to bring harm. At least we can be thankful that armed conflict has not broken out in the United States as it did in the nineteenth century Civil War. Nevertheless, in the country, strong feelings of antipathy between followers of the two political parties have been created, roughly following liberal and conservative lines. Some activists issue threats of violence. What is particularly serious for Christians is that the witness to Christ has been clouded by the conflict between liberal and conservative Christians that continues to cause numerous divisions in the churches. The question for Christians is whether they can see issues, especially justice issues, other than in terms of power and domination.

More than any other scholar, Hunter (1991, 2010) has draw attention to the culture wars within America. He has shown that turning almost all social issues into political issues has sharpened the conflict among Americans. He (2010:108, 109) writes, "It is my contention that Nietzche was mostly right; that while the will to power has always been present, American democracy increasingly operates within a political culture – that is, a framework of meaning – that sanctions a will to domination. This, in turn, is fueled by a political psychology of fear, anger, negation, and revenge over perceived wrongs." As important as political participation is for Christian citizens, extreme politicization has caused many Americans, including Christians, to act with extreme fear and anger and seek to use political power to impose their religious and moral views on others.

CONCLUSION

The Opposition to Jesus Christ and to the New Age or the "antichrist" has been defeated and bound. This means that the gospel of Jesus Christ cannot be stopped and that it will continue to spread around the world. At the same time, the Opposition continues to writhe in defeat like a snake that has been killed, but still moves. As such it is able to cause much damage. We are also told that evil will be "unbound" (II Thessalonians 2:7, 8; Revelation 20:7). I take these passages as symbolic of the uneven or irregular appearance of evil in history. After periods of success in the spread of the gospel, evil reappears in new and characteristic subtle forms, not all violent as often depicted. In the meantime, in the last days in which we live there are many antichrists (I John 2:18; 4:3; II John 7) that hinder the witness to the gospel. The collapse of colonialism with and after World War II was a major defeat for the Opposition and since then the demonstration of the futility of violence and international domination has continued that defeat. However, there are still effects of colonialism in the current period as the rise of radical Islam in opposition demonstrates. Again, the Opposition to Christ is not so much in radical Islam, but works most effectively in the response of fear to radical Islam.

It should be recognized by Christians that the creation of global socio-cultural forces through globalization gives an opportunity for the Opposition to extend its influence and effects of its destructive work over large segments of the world's population. Globalization as a socio-cultural force can be benign, good, or bad, just as the counter forces it has created can be benign, good, or bad. Christians must work with the good in both globalization and "glocalization" (the affirmation of local identities and values.) "Glocalization" in the form of nationalism has been a positive force for the advancement of peoples, but excessive nationalism has already shown itself to be a force that can block international cooperation that is needed to avoid conflict and benefit many lives. The positive and negative effects of nationalism have become especially evident in the last century with the two World Wars and collapse of colonialism. At present, the negative effects of extreme capitalism are seen in the shrinking of the middle class in the United States along with the problem of continuing poverty in the midst of plenty. At the same time, poverty on the international level has become a major problem. A major work of the Opposition is to encourage apathy toward the suffering of others, possibly one of its major effects into the future, all the worst because of its hidden nature —"I'm not hurting anybody."

Thankfully, in a real sense, the world does not belong to non-faith, but to faith. The Opposition to Jesus Christ and the New Age is out of place in the world and does not have real possession of it. It is to the children of God that the world belongs, beginning with the diversities of faith in Christ, as the Apostle spoke: "For all things are yours, whether Paul or Apollos or Cephas or the world or life or death or the present or the future—all belong to you, and you belong to Christ, and Christ belongs to God" (I Corinthians 3:21-23). The world belongs to God and God is working in it, so "If God is for us, who is against us?...We are more than conquerors through him who loved us…Neither death, nor life, nor angels, nor rulers, nor things present, nor things to come, nor powers, nor height, nor depth, nor anything in all creation, will be able to separate us from the love of God in Christ Jesus our Lord" (Romans 8:31, 37, 38, 39).

CHAPTER 8

BEYOND DEFENSE -
LIVING IN THE NEW AGE
AS A DISCIPLE

MAKING SENSE OF JESUS CHRIST

Although a defensive position is the proper position to take against the Opposition to Jesus Christ in the New Age, we are to be more than simply defensive in our stance of faith. When it comes to the whole life of faith, we can and should respond positively as individuals in local Christian communities, in the Great Community of God, the Church Universal, and in God's world as a whole to the call of Jesus Christ to live with him and under his authority in his New Age. I have tried to draw attention in the previous two chapters to some of the subtle ways in which the Opposition works. The work of the social sciences developing the concepts of culture and social forces reaffirms realities recognized in the Bible. However, even today we continue to be largely unconscious of these powerful forces that so easily become the instruments of the Opposition. Nevertheless, we should not focus on the Opposition or become obsessed with discerning where the Opposition may be working, but rather we should focus on the Triune God through Jesus Christ. The detection of the Opposition will always be beyond us even though we should be aware of some of the major techniques of the Opposition to dominate large numbers of people, particularly Christians through *non-obvious* means.

The focus on God through Jesus requires the recognition, first of all, that the coming of Jesus Christ marks the turning point of our individual lives and also of all human history. If history is simply the on-going flow of events, and what happened 2000 years ago with the coming of Jesus Christ is simply another short series of events in a long flow of events in human history, then there can be no sense that we are living in a special New Age introduced by Jesus Christ. Everything in our own lives hinges on recognizing Jesus Christ as having been sent by God to carry out the special plan of redemption for humanity. This plan involves the bringing together of all things in Christ and through Christ we are made part of the carrying out of this plan (Ephesians 1:9, 10).

There is no outward proof of this. It is necessary to rely on the inner testimony of the Holy Spirit that was revealed through those who prophesied before Christ and those who personally knew Christ, as explained in Hebrews 1:1, 2: "Long ago God spoke to our ancestors in many and various ways by the prophets, but in these last days he has spoken to us by a Son." A supporting comment is I John 1-4:

> We declare to you what was from the beginning, what we have heard, what we have seen with our eyes, what we have looked at and touched with our hands, concerning the word of life—this life was revealed, and we have seen it and testify to it, and declare to you the eternal life that was with the Father and was revealed to us—we declare to you what we have seen and heard so that you also may have fellowship with us; and truly our fellowship is with the Father and with his Son Jesus Christ. We are writing these things so that our joy may be complete.

In addition to the witness of the writers of the Old and New Testaments, we have the testimony of all those in the great mixed multitude of believing people, amounting to millions of people, over the last 2000 years who reported believing in Jesus Christ and lived in many or some respects like Jesus Christ. Of course, as we have noted, Christ was not seen in many who claimed to be Christian. Nevertheless, most of us have come to faith through personal connect with persons of faith. For me it was my parents plus many people in the larger Community of Faith.

It would be very helpful for our faith and a strong argument for the reality of the New Age of Jesus Christ if everyone who said that they believed in Jesus exhibited the same character, with the same compassion and the same kind of spiritual power that Jesus exhibited. As we know, this is not the case. At the same time, it is possible to argue that some remarkable changes have taken place in history that would not have taken place except for the coming of Christ and his influence through his followers. Furthermore, there has been a gradual speeding up of changes over the last two thousand years, an acceleration that has become especially noticeable in the last few centuries and even now in the last few decades.

The sociology of history is a discipline that specifically undertakes to develop theory about history or, in other words, explanation of historical changes. Max Weber (1964 [1922]; 1958; 1967 [1964] 1967), one of the founders of the discipline of the social sciences, sought to explain the rise of the West or at least the distinctive nature of Western history by linking aspects of that history to particular versions of Christianity and to the witness of the ancient Israelite prophets. Arend Th. van Leeuwen (1964) was a more recent social historian and missiologist who linked Western history very convincingly to Christianity. He speaks of the "revolutionary West" with good reason. Certainly Western history would not have taken place as it did without Christianity. However, although there is much in Western history that has benefited humanity, there also has been much that has been very harmful to humanity.

Recently, Stark (2001, 2003, 2007) has taken up the task of showing how religion in the form of monotheism and Christianity in particular has influenced human history. He links the Protestant Reformation and also the rise of science very specifically to Christianity. In addition, he shows how Christianity contributed substantially to the abolition of slavery. However, in addition to these positive contributions, Stark describes the terrible witch-hunts and persecutions, particularly of the Jews, carried out by Christians. In the end, whatever good is pointed to as coming from Christianity, some can easily point at particular evils arising from Christians or at least where Christians formed a majority of the population. At the very least, Christianity introduced a dynamic element to world history that has brought about many changes that are continually accelerating, but it is not possible to argue that those who claim to be followers of Jesus Christ have always made positive contributions to world history. In fact, this book has shown that the terrible Opposition to Jesus Christ has arisen *among Christians*.

To name the age since Jesus Christ came to earth as "the New Age" remains primarily an act of faith. People cannot be argued into the New Age or the Kingdom of God. The world continues to be a place where it is possible to live an apparently "normal" life and not believe in God, much less in Jesus Christ as the Savior of the world. God coerces no one so there is no empirically based argument to prove God or the Divine purpose of God in sending Jesus Christ. Any argument about the supposed spiritual or moral superiority of Christianity or of Christians is rather easily shattered by a few choice examples of Christians involved in wrong doing, as well as examples of exemplary non-Christians. This book's recognition of the Opposition to Jesus Christ and his New Age is intended to help in the understanding of why evil has always been close at hand among Christians and has periodically arisen among Christians to wreck terrible damage on humans and particularly injure the witness to Jesus Christ.

In spite of the discouraging examples of evil forces among Christians, if we turn to God and to Jesus Christ as revealed in the Bible, it is possible to make sense of all that has happened and is still happening. We can see God at work in the Bible and since then in spite of the poor witness of Christians. I use the following argument, which I believe "makes sense." Although there is no empirically or rationally based argument to prove that Jesus Christ introduced a New Age for humanity, there is a rational, reasonable, and plausible argument that can be used to support belief in the triune God, *if certain assumptions are granted as to what a Creator God would be like.* After all, the issue is not simply whether we believe in the existence of God, as it is so often posed, but whether we believe in the actions of God through Jesus Christ for our redemption. It is a circular argument, but it is plausible and reasonable nevertheless. We start with the assumption that God exists and that his creative power initiated and upholds the universe. But believing that alone does not bring about any change in us. In other words, belief in the reality of God is not the issue or is it what God wants from humans. After all, "The devils believe—and shudder" (James 2:19). But granted the reality of God, it is reasonable that the Creator would love what was created, especially the most complex of creations, namely human beings. Furthermore, it is reasonable that the Creator would want to interact and have fellowship with the humanity that was created. Genesis 3:8, 9 presents a picture of such a God walking in the Garden looking for Adam and Eve, namely the humans God created. It is here that a major problem is encountered by God, although it becomes a problem for humans. The problem for God provides a major rationale for believing in Jesus Christ: How can

God interact with human beings without creating fear and dread as we see in Adam and Eve because of their disobedience of God?

It follows that because of the difficulty of repelling humans by creating fear in them based on their sin, God would act toward humans in a way to create hearts of loyalty, gratitude, and love so as to support a true and lasting relationship. This is exactly what we see in the salvation and preservation of Israel and then in what happened in the life, death, and resurrection of Jesus Christ. The whole Jesus Christ episode, preceded by the history of God's dealing with Israel, makes sense in the light of God's problem—the problem of how to connect and remain connected with humans. And God wants to do more than that. God wants to create a new humanity after God's own image (originally spoken of in Genesis 1), the image of the Son or the living Word, Jesus Christ. His life of compassion for suffering people and his loving fellowship with his followers, his death for human sin, his resurrection from the dead, his ascension to a place of authority with God above, and finally, the sending of the Holy Spirit to empower Christ's followers, all makes sense in the light of how an all powerful Creator God would undertake the work of redeeming humanity. It is a great circle of love that starts and ends with God, but in between reaches down and lifts up humans and brings them back to God.

A WORN OUT WELCOME?

However plausible may be the story of redemption found in the Bible, in some respects, Christianity in the Western World has worn out its welcome. At least this seems to be true for many people in the West who are interested in a spiritual life, but prefer not to be related to "organized religion." For many, the failures of Christianity are too obvious and they choose to ignore the successes or the blessings that have come through Christianity, many of which are taken for granted as "natural historical developments." The non-coercive approach of God in creating a world where humans can "get along" and ignore God provides just such an opportunity for many people. It may be that Christianity will need to go out and come back in again from non-Western sources. Of course, there are many Christians in the West who would not trade their experience with Christ and life in his New Age for anything else. I am one of these. I am thankful that I had an opportunity to "go out and come in again" by serving overseas and seeing the joy and excitement of those receiving the gospel for the first time. There are Christians in the West who seem to have lost their confidence that faith in Christ is all that special. Others seem to have dropped off or dropped out more or less quietly. In addition, there is a small but vocal group of out and out opponents of the truth of Christian claims about Jesus Christ. In the United States the opponents of belief in God are much fewer than usually assumed, while active Christians are also a smaller number than usually assumed.

Many individuals feel that they cannot meet the challenges to faith in Jesus Christ. At the same time, there are many rewards that are intrinsic to faith and experienced by believers, but this does not mean gaining them is easy. The fact that the rewards of faith are largely intrinsic means that they remain hidden to many people. How many can see that the reward of faith is faith, the reward of love is love, and the reward of following Christ is following Christ? Only those who have these experiences can know these intrinsic rewards.

Understanding the meaning of Christ's coming as introducing a New Age and as also stirring up Opposition to it can help in facing the challenge of faith in Christ in a world where God does not coerce us to believe and where part of this non-coercion is the possibility of a "normal" life in which God is ignored. In the end, when the call of Christ in the New Testament is examined, we see that we are not asked to understand life, particularly our own lives, but to do simple things that have profound meaning and consequences. I will turn now to the simple steps we need to take to live in the New Age of Jesus Christ. This section of this chapter will seem fairly conventional to many people because it is primarily an application of the biblical narrative to life today. The focus is primarily on the individual believer, but will be broadened in the next chapter to the essential life in the Community of Faith.

FOUR STEPS IN THE NEW AGE

The Christian faith could not be what it is unless it required simple, but profound steps from all people – high and lowly, rich and poor, educated and uneducated. And the later steps of Christian faith cannot be that different from the initial steps because they have a basically similar purpose. Taking these steps is more important than having an intellectual understanding of what is involved. Having a Christian view of history as discussed in this book can be comforting, especially in knowing that God is working in history to accomplish God's aims, but it is most important to take the simple steps of the Christian life. Intellectual understanding has a way of unfolding as we go. This is certainly true in the life of faith. In the end, the best defense against the Opposition, which is really more than simply a defense, is what Thomas Chalmers called in his famous sermon, "The Expulsive Power of a New Affection." It is focusing our lives on Jesus Christ that removes the power of the Opposition to affect us and replaces it with the power of the living God to work in our lives. This is why Jesus Christ came into the world and comes into our lives. The steps to focusing on Jesus Christ are shown to us by the actual experiences we see of the relationship of the first disciples to Jesus Christ.

FOLLOWING

The first and last word of Jesus to his disciples was "follow me." He said this when he called his disciples to come after him (Mark 1:17). And he said this to Peter after the resurrection when Peter was asking what he did not need to know, namely what would happen to his fellow disciple, John (John 21:19). Following Christ means not being distracted by judgments about others or speculation about the return of Christ. Although following Jesus incorporates imitating him, it means much more. It means going where he went and where he continues to go, as he said, "Whoever serves me must follow me, and where I am, there will my servant be also" (John 12:26).

It is highly significant that the New Testament presents Christ as on the move. If we are to follow Jesus Christ it requires that we examine where he went during his ministry and walk in our hearts and minds with the disciples. It is true that people came to Jesus, but Jesus also took the initiative in relating to people. Following Jesus means that we seek to relate to people as Jesus related to people, recognizing their need along with ours and offering friendship and help. It means looking at every individual as a person made in the image of God. This means a radical shift from thinking only of oneself and looking down on others, who, for whatever reasons, we do not like. The shift is so radical that it is compared to a kind of death to self. It does not exclude thinking of the self and one's goals, but it means thinking of the self and one's goals in relationship to Christ and his love for all people. I take this to mean something very similar to what Hunter (2010:261-269) describes as a "faithful presence" and "a covenant relationship with others." It involves active engagement with others and the world in which we live.

Jesus said that for people to follow him meant "denying themselves and taking up a cross" (Mark 8:34). Following Jesus means making choices not in the old way when we make choices simply in the light of what we think and want for ourselves, but in the light of what Jesus wants for us and others. The cross is a symbol of death. If we pay attention to the words of Jesus and of the Apostle Paul, we will see that being a follower of Jesus Christ involves experiencing a death — death to the self. Christianity and Buddhism have some overlap here, but Christianity goes beyond death to one's desire or "thirst for the self" to emphasize new life in which desire is not simply killed but redirected to "knowing Christ" (Philippians 3:10). Paul speaks of baptism, the initiatory rite for Christians as involving death (burial) followed by resurrection (Romans 6:3, 4), but resurrection and death, death and resurrection continue like a revolving experience (Philippians 3:10). Again, speaking of himself, he says, "I have been crucified with Christ; and it is no longer I who live, but it is Christ who lives in me. And the life I now live in the flesh I live by faith in the Son of God, who loved me and gave himself for me" (Galatians 2:19, 20). This obviously is a mysterious experience that is offered to every believer in Christ, an experience which may not sound inviting, but nevertheless contains a joy set before us, as it did for Christ (Hebrews 12:1, 2).

These indicators of an inner death for the Christian are truly daunting, but we cannot forget that Jesus Christ went to the cross and the cross is the central symbol of the Christian faith. Our following of Jesus Christ will never be completed this side of death, but the word, "following," itself indicates that the life of faith is a process. The Apostle Paul spoke of the process when he said, "Not that I have already obtained this [dying and rising with Christ], or have already reached the goal, but I press on to make it my own, because Christ Jesus has made me his own...I press on toward the goal for the prize of the heavenly call of God in Christ Jesus" (Philippians 3:12, 14). The Letter to the Hebrews (12:1, 2) emphasizes the same process when it says:

> Therefore, since we are surrounded by so great a
> cloud of witnesses, let us also lay aside every weight
> and the sin that clings so closely, and let us run with
> perseverance the race that is set before us, looking to
> Jesus the pioneer and perfecter of our faith, who for
> the sake of the joy that was set before him endured
> the cross, disregarding its shame, and has taken his
> seat at the right hand of the throne of God.

Clearly, Christians are to think of their lives as lives of movement—movement in following Jesus Christ toward God. Our physical death at the end of our individual physical lives becomes the completion of our baptism to be followed by our final resurrection, coming after a life of repeated "small resurrections."

The pattern of movement in faith is as old as Abraham following the call of God, the Children of Israel in the wilderness, and certainly the ministry of Christ leading to the cross and resurrection, followed by the sending out of Christ's followers. For many Christians, some physical movement in the world in the service of Jesus Christ is inevitably involved. Jesus told his followers to "Go therefore and make disciples of all nations..." (Matthew 28:19). But even if no major physical movement is a part of a Christian's life, there is a spiritual movement with Jesus Christ for all lives having faith in him—movement away from lives centered on "what's in it for me?" as we see in Genesis 3, to lives centered on God through Jesus Christ. If we are following Jesus Christ, we have begun that movement.

LISTENING

Next to "following," the word "listening" catches up what is important for believers in Christ as they focus on him. In fact, it is a necessary part of following and a major reason for participating in a Christian community where the Word is shared. Early in his ministry, Jesus called on people, "Let anyone with ears to hear listen!" The famous Parable of the Sower illustrates how easy it is *not* to listen or to listen superficially, but how important it is to let the Word of God enter deeply into the heart. The climax to the experience of the Transfiguration, when Christ was transformed before Peter, James, and John was when a voice came from heaven that said, "This is my Son, my chosen; *listen to him!*" (Luke 9:36).

The description of the disciples who were baptized on the Day of Pentecost is simply, "They devoted themselves to the apostles' teaching and fellowship, to the breaking of bread and the prayers" (Acts 2:42). We are saved by God's grace, but how does that grace come to us? This verse tells us that at the forefront is listening to the Word of God, which comes to us through the witness of the apostles, which for us is found in the Scriptures. The "means of grace" are often spoken of as the Word, the Sacraments, Fellowship, and Prayer. These also closely correspond to the "marks of the Church." That is, you recognize the Church by where these things are going on because there people are receiving the grace of God and receivers of God's grace in Christ are what constitute the Church. Good listening requires the right kind of context that includes communication of the Word as known primarily through the Person of Jesus Christ, participation in the Sacraments Christ left us, fellowship with others in Christ, and prayers to God through Christ. These are all experienced in the visible Catholic Church which nourishes us.

Some may desire to hear the audible voice of Jesus or God (or some divine being) and some may claim that they have literally heard such a voice. Some people are rather fond of saying, "The Lord told me such and such." I will not deny that some people may hear an audible voice from God, but there are two simple reasons why Jesus or God does not ordinarily communicate with us audibly. In the first place, if God spoke to us literally, it might literally "scare us to death." However, primarily, if God spoke to us audibly, then we would discount the importance of reading and wrestling with the written Word. We would say, "I don't need the Bible because God speaks to me directly." The whole Bible from Genesis to Revelation needs our study in order for us to be familiar with the ways of God. In other words, if God spoke to us audibly, we would ignore the written and preached Word. In addition, and just as important, if God spoke to us audibly, we would discount the importance of listening to others in the context of the Christian Church. We would say, "I don't need to listen to others because I have my own private line to God." This is a reminder that our listening should be in the context of the fellowship of faith that begins with the present Christian fellowship and extends back in Church history to Christ and to the witnesses to faith found in the whole Bible.

The task of listening means that we are to spend our lives interpreting the revelation of God found in the Bible. Our interpretation is our theology or our version of faith and it will always be partial and to some extent faulty (I Corinthians 13:9). It is important to recognize that first and foremost the revelation of God is Jesus Christ, the living Word of God. We only know about Jesus Christ through the Bible, but the Bible is not identical to or equivalent to Christ. The reason we do not need an additional Bible is that we do not need an additional Savior and for him to die and rise again. Jesus Christ is in the Bible, but he is also above and beyond it. The authority of Jesus Christ (Matthew 28:18) is above that of the Bible and the Bible derives its authority from that of Jesus Christ. Some people are so insecure in their faith and so in need of an absolutely intellectually and verbally clear authority, that they deify the Bible, treating its words in a very mechanical way, as if they were not human words, but only words spoken directly by God, as some Muslims look at the Koran. This is a form of Bibliolatry or worship of the Bible rather than the Triune God of the Bible. It is also an example of how the Opposition uses a good value, recognition of the authority of the Bible, to mislead people, principally by creating an exaggerated emphasis on literal words. "Inerrant" becomes a watchword for the words of the Bible and then become weapons to use against others. People forget the words of the Apostle, "for the letter kills, but the Spirit gives life" (II Corinthians 3:6). The same Holy Spirit who inspired the written Word, helps us to interpret it in a way that is consistent with and expresses the Way, the Truth, and the Life of Jesus Christ. The focus on Christ of the teaching by the Holy Spirit is emphasized in the Gospel of John (John 14:26; 15:26; 16:12-15).

Listening requires the recognition of an authoritative source for our faith. That authoritative source is Jesus Christ himself, as witnessed to by the Bible. It is important to recognize that no individual has exclusive access to that authoritative source. In individualistic societies, such as the United States, people are tempted to think that they have a private pipeline to God and do not need any help in interpreting the Bible. "Just give me the Bible," they say, "I will take it as it is." Instead, listening to Christ should be done in the context of the Church established 2000 years ago by Christ *and* with the aid of the Holy Spirit, who inspired the Bible. To do otherwise is like declaring, "All the work that Christians have done during the last 2000 years to understand and interpret the Bible means nothing to me." This kind of pride has led many Christians and Christian groups into false or distinct interpretations of the Bible, as well as to form separatist groups based on these interpretations.

It is important that believers listen with the help of an historic

Christian tradition and with the help of biblical scholars. It is not necessary and it is not wise to rely on only one Christian tradition and particularly only one biblical scholar or even set of scholars. In understanding Scripture there is some safety in numbers over one particular leader or preacher, not matter how eloquent. Christian humility requires that individual believers listen to Jesus Christ speaking through the Bible in the context of other Christians. This is also the way to receive help from the Holy Spirit because the Spirit was given to the Church, not to isolated individuals. It is better to change, modify, or improve the interpretation of a particular historic tradition with others than to initiate one's own distinctive interpretation of the Bible. The Church represented in a particular historic branch to which one belongs is a secondary authority under the ultimate authority of Jesus Christ. Nevertheless, the authority of the church to which one belongs should be respected and heeded if at all possible, even when one disagrees with it. If one's insights and interpretations of the Bible are different from those of other Christians, it is best to witness to them and then let God establish the truth, perhaps over an extended time. To separate from those with whom we disagree shows a lack of trust in the power of God's truth ultimately to prevail.

Since listening to Christ should not be simply a private activity, listening means that the believer sees himself or herself as part of the historic visible Church that is currently divided into numerous denominations. One cannot lift oneself out of the world and place oneself above and outside of the visible Church. Some attempt to do this because they are tired of "the organized Church" and feel that "being spiritual" makes it unnecessary to have "rules of order," "constitutions," "officers," etc. Such attempts often lead to coming under a single charismatic leader, who makes promises of a "blessed," read "prosperous," life. It may also lead one to follow some leader in forming a "purer" church than the "lax" and "worldly" traditional church that does not provide the entertainment or excitement found in the new church.

In individualistic societies, such as the United States, it has proven relatively easy for Christians to separate themselves from other Christians. However, I believe that in the long run, those Christians, and churches that are willing to listen to each other, will be blessed by God. By listening to each other they demonstrate the unity that is in Christ and the many facets of God's truth that are displayed to the world. Listening to each other is also showing a sense of "the physical family of God's People" and of the catholicity (universality) of the Church. From the time of the Bible itself with its many witnesses, the diversity of the Divine gifts to the Church have been shown and have served to display the Rule of Christ in the world.

RECEIVING

The third word for living in the New Age of Jesus Christ is "receiving." The fact that it has already been used just above under "listening" indicates how the steps in following Christ are overlapping. Before Jesus Christ ascended to heaven, leaving his disciples standing on earth, he said in Acts 1:8:

> It is not for you to know the times or periods that the Father has set by his own authority. But you will receive power when the Holy Spirit has come upon you; and you will be my witnesses in Jerusalem, in all Judea and Samaria, and to the ends of the earth.

The Bible and this book are opposed to speculation about when the New Age introduced by Jesus Christ will be transformed into a "New Heaven and a New Earth." At the same time, we are to observe the "signs of summer" and so know that Christ is near, "at the very gates" (Mark 13:29). What are the primary signs? What has been the most important event, really a process, to take place over the last 2000 years? Already it has been said: it is the spread of the gospel around the world. We too often take this event or process for granted because it has taken place over many lifetimes, but it has been a relatively short time in the tens of thousands of years of human history, which justifies calling it an "event." Furthermore, there has been a recent acceleration in the spread of the gospel. We know that Christ was and is primarily concerned that a faithful witness be given to him throughout the world. We also have seen that the witness over the last 2000 years has been quite flawed at various times and places. The only reason it has been effective at all is because of the Holy Spirit, who was given to the Church at Pentecost.

Believers in Jesus Christ, who seek to follow him and listen to him, must take seriously the promise, spoken by John the Baptist about Christ, "I have baptized you with water, but he will baptize you with the Holy Spirit (Mark 1:8). Matthew (3:12) and Luke (3:16) add "fire." Before leaving his disciples Jesus spoke at length about the work of the Holy Spirit. It is worth listening to these words, which constitute a promise, from John 16:7-15:

> Nevertheless, I tell you in truth: it is to your advantage that I go away, for if I do not go away, the Advocate will not come to you; but if I go, I will send him to you. And when he comes, he will prove the world wrong about sin and righteousness and judgment: about sin because they do not believe in me; about righteousness, because I am going to the Father and you will see me no longer; about judgment, because the ruler of this world has been condemned.

> I still have many things to say to you, but you cannot
> bear them now. When the Spirit of truth comes, he
> will guide you into all the truth; for he will not speak
> on his own, but will speak whatever he hears, and he
> will declare to you the things that are to come. He
> will glorify me, because he will take what is mine
> and declare it to you. All that the Father has is mine.
> For this reason I said that he will take what is mine
> and declare it to you.

This passage tells us about the work of the Holy Spirit in the world—
convincing the world about sin and righteousness—and that there is
an unfolding of the truth of Jesus Christ throughout history because
the truth could not be borne by the disciples nor by any particular
group of followers. This shows that the process of receiving the
Holy Spirit is very close to the processes of following and listening.
The Holy Spirit brings the person of Jesus Christ, representing the
righteousness and the truth of God, to live within us.

When Jesus appeared to the disciples after his resurrection, it
is said in John 20:22, 23: "When he had said this, he breathed on
them and said to them, 'Receive the Holy Spirit. If you forgive the
sins of any, they are forgiven them; if you retain the sins of any, they
are retained.'" These words easily may be misinterpreted, especially
when the sentence about sins being forgiven or being retained is made
dependent on a ritual statement made by a "religious specialist."
For one thing, we do not see such a practice being carried out by
the apostles in the Book of Acts. John 20:22, 23 does not tell the
disciples to make pronouncements of forgiveness or condemnation,
but rather that they have a responsibility to spread the word of the
grace from God through which forgiveness is received. It is also a
warning that not spreading the word of grace is enabling sins to be

retained. This work can only be done as the Holy Spirit is received. These words place a great responsibility on believers to be active in forgiving others along with proclaiming the gospel. It is only the Holy Spirit who can give the power to believers to love and forgive others. Forgiveness is not something generated from within believers. In fact, this is the major work of the Holy Spirit, as the Apostle says, "God's love has been poured into our hearts through the Holy Spirit that has been given to us" (Romans 5:5).

This brings us to the important teaching of what the Holy Spirit does within believers. Since the presence and work of the Holy Spirit is so essential for believers to be able to fulfill their mandate of being witnesses, how can we know if we have the Holy Spirit? What is the evidence that the Holy Spirit has been received and is working in us? In the first place, it is not important for us to try "to show" that we have the Holy Spirit or to present outward signs of the Holy Spirit, which inevitably involves comparing ourselves to others, not an activity for followers of Christ.

There is an important word in the Bible that points us to the evidence of the presence and work of the Holy Spirit. That word is "fruit." The Old Testament prophets emphasized that God was looking for "fruit" from his people. A particularly clear example is "The Song of the Unfruitful Vineyard" in Isaiah 5:1-7. God planted his people like a vineyard and "he expected it to yield grapes, but it yielded wild grapes" (Isaiah 5:2). Jesus also used the illustration of a vine to teach the importance of "abiding in him" in order to "bear much fruit": "Those who abide in me and I in them bear much fruit, because apart from me you can do nothing...My Father is glorified by this, that you bear much fruit and become my disciples" (John 15:5,8). The Christian life and the Church as a whole is disciplined in order to bear fruit: "He [the Father] removes every branch that bears no fruit.

Every branch that bears fruit he prunes to make it bear more fruit"
(John 15:2).

An important word about "fruit" that connects it with what was
said about "death through Christ" in the section above on "Following,"
is what is said in John 12:23-26:

> Very truly, I tell you, unless a grain of wheat falls into
> the earth and dies, it remains just a single grain; but
> if it dies, *it bears much fruit*. Those who love their
> life lose it, and those who hate their life in this world
> will keep it for eternal life. Whoever serves me must
> follow me, and where I am, there will my servant be
> also. Whoever serves me, the Father will honor.

Following, inwardly dying, and bearing fruit are all part of the same
process of living with Jesus under his Holy Spirit in the New Age.

The evidence of the presence and work of the Holy Spirit is the
bearing of fruit in life, not some outward expression, such as speaking
in tongues or showing some other evidence of enthusiasm in worship.
In this regard, it is important to distinguish between gifts (plural) and
the fruit (singular) of the Spirit. There are many and varied gifts that
are given to the Church, the People of God, through the Holy Spirit as
recorded especially in Romans 12:3-8 and I Corinthians 12 and 14. The
varied gifts are important, even necessary, for the Church to function
well. But there are no spiritual levels or classes in the Christian faith
with some people being more holy because of their jobs or the gifts
they use in the Church. The gifts create functional differences within
the Church based on different kinds of service. The gifts of preaching,
teaching, and public praying are important gifts for which people
should strive and which the Church should recognize as it calls those
who are to serve on behalf of the whole Church. However, no matter

how gifted people may be in performing these functions, or any other functions that are important for the Church, if the gifts are not accompanied by the fruit of the Spirit, then the gifts are useless. This is pointed out very clearly and forcefully in the chapter (I Corinthians 13) placed between the two chapters (I Corinthians 12 and 14) that discuss gifts.

I Corinthians 13 makes very clear that the primary fruit of the Spirit or "the more excellent way" than any specialized gift is love, without which the gifts are empty, for example preaching becomes "a noisy gong or a clanging cymbal." Displaying great faith, giving large contributions, and even martyrdom empty of love are nothing. The fruit of the Spirit is singular, as pointed out in Galatians 5:22, but it has *many aspects*: "…the fruit of the Spirit is love, joy, peace, patience, kindness, generosity, faithfulness, gentleness, and self-control." In I Corinthians 13, these characteristics are found in the description of love: "Love is patient; love is kind; love is not envious or boastful or arrogant or rude. It does not insist on its own way; it is not irritable or resentful; it does not rejoice in wrongdoing, but rejoices in the truth. It bears all things, believes all things, hopes all things, endures all things."

Of course, words are inadequate to fully express this "fruit of the Holy Spirit," but it is close to the very nature of God, who is love (I John 4:8). There should not be any argument about what is the major work of the Holy Spirit or what is the evidence of the presence of the Holy Spirit in people's lives. It is not any particular outward sign to which people can point. It is the multiple signs of love in action. This is the power and fire of the Holy Spirit that Christ came to give at baptism and throughout the Christian life. It is what above all else gives credibility to the witness to Jesus Christ that Christians are to bear to the ends of the earth. The "whole creation has been groaning in labor pains" for this revelation of the children of God, just as we ourselves "groan inwardly while we wait for adoption, the redemption of our bodies" (Romans 8:19, 22, 23). There is a great problem created for Christians by the Opposition, which is the separation in thinking of love from the practice of justice. Yet, the overall goal of the Christian life and the force by which Jesus Christ defeats the Opposition through his followers is expressed most fully and clearly by the word love, but love requires and carries out many things.

LOVING

Unfortunately, "love" is not considered a strong term in English and many other languages. It is associated with softness. Some might prefer that I use the phrase, "doing justly," as referring to the needed practice of Christians. However, I am taking the term "loving" as incorporating doing justly, including seeking to establish justice. I am thinking that acting with love includes the kind of work done by Martin Luther King in which he sought the welfare of the oppressed and challenged the prejudiced "way of life" that was enshrined in many local laws, particularly in the South. He even regarded his opponents as being injured by the unjust system of legalized segregation that needed to be changed for their benefit. I am taking acting in love toward others as the second part of the Law that accompanies love toward God. Working for justice, freedom, and human rights in the world, therefore, is a major expression of love. So also is working to improve the environment for people everywhere. So also is sharing the Good News about Jesus Christ and his New Age, as long as it is done humbly as Jesus and the Apostles did it.

Hunter (2010:263) points out: "Love is certainly about the elemental need for intimacy, affection, and the bonds of belonging without which one is left alienated and estranged from others and one's environment. But love is also about grace, mercy, and justice, without which we are left with malice and humiliation, cruelty and coercion, and injury and injustice." He goes on to state using—to emphasize his major theme: *"The practice of faithful presence, then, generates relationships and institutions that are fundamentally covenantal in character; the ends of which are the fostering of meaning, purpose, truth, beauty, belonging, and fairness – not just for Christians but for everyone."* This is love in action.

God sent Jesus out of love for us. Acting in love Jesus challenged the religious authorities, as well taught his followers and brought healing to so many. It took him to the cross for us. The apostles made loving others their aim and the aim for all Christians. This is the love that Jesus left as his commandment to his "friends" (John 15:12-17), that is "poured into our hearts through the Holy Spirit" (Romans 5:5), that fulfills the law (Romans 13:8-10), that is the first part of the fruit of the Spirit (Galatians 5:22), and that is "the more excellent way" (I Corinthians 12:31-13:13), without which everything else that we do even in God's service is of no benefit to us. But let it be remembered as we work for justice for everyone out of love that justice in the Bible is not simply the establishment of a good feeling for everyone, but the establishment of right and just relationships among people. Because people are created in the image of God, then just relationships mean that the weak, suffering, and poor are cared for. In history, this led to the concept of human rights that under girds democracies. Democracies may be considered an outgrowth of love, even if people living in democracies do not exercise love toward others. Actually, the ability to disagree with one another and still work together, so essential in democracies, was first demonstrated in the Church in congregational life in which mutual forgiveness was made central. After this demonstration, it was carried forward in secular government under the concept of "loyal opposition"—parties that disagreed with government policies, but were loyal to the nation.

All the steps listed before, following, listening, and receiving, are expressions of love for God as revealed in Jesus Christ. Their outcome, the most important fruit that God is looking for from those living in the New Age, are loving attitudes that result in loving actions towards others. As Paul says, love is tough. It "bears all things, believes all things, hopes all things, endures all things" (I Corinthians 13:7).

Love makes up and completes the "Great Circle" that starts with God, reaches down to broken humanity, moves through humans to other humans, and returns to the Creator God. God made and continually maintains the Circle through Jesus Christ, who came down for us, and by the Holy Spirit moves in and through us. If we are in this Circle of love, then we are already experiencing eternity because "love never ends" (I Corinthians 13:8) and "God is love" (I John 4: 7,8).

AN INESCAPABLE PARADOX

Living in the New Age brought by Jesus Christ presents an inescapable paradox. On the one hand, the present life is in a universe created by God that is good and beautiful and, even more, Christ brings us a life of joy and excitement with numerous blessings in the present life, sometimes (for some, often) in the midst of hardships. On the other hand, something better is coming – a completely new creation called "a new heaven and a new earth." We honor and serve God by loving and enjoying this life and God's creation, but we are not to cling to this life unnecessarily, certainly not grasp it for ourselves. We have tasks to carry out in this life, the most important being to be a witness to Jesus Christ by word and deed, but at some point both our individual lives and human history itself will come to an end. The paradox of present blessing and future greater blessing after our death as individuals and after the end of history as we know it is inescapable. The Apostle Paul is torn in his desire for both, but prays to be as useful in this life as long as possible (Philippians 1:22-26).

Will the end of history be with flames, destruction, and great suffering? Some Christians seem to enjoy describing this type of ending for the world, the flames being for others, of course. These are often people who see the language of the Book of Revelation in literal terms. Unfortunately, this tends to make many of them rather war-like, as well as uncaring about improving the world and human life in it. It should be remembered that apocalyptic writing from which this destructive description comes is very symbolic writing. Regarding the statements that sound as though the world will end literally by fire (Luke 17:30; II Thessalonians 1:8; II Peter 3:7, 10-13), it should be remembered that the term "fire" is use repeatedly as a synonym for judgment. John the Baptist says that Jesus will baptize with fire (Matthew 3: 11-12) and God, who loves the world, is spoken of as a "consuming fire" (Hebrews 12:29). We may believe that God's judgment is continually purifying the witness to the truth, beginning with the coming of Jesus Christ, but not necessarily with literal fire.

Apocalyptic thought originally comes out of an era before the New Testament when thought about God's Kingdom and the Messiah who would bring it was very materialistic and nationalistic. It took Christ and the New Testament to salvage from the words of the Old Testament, which were never meant to be interpreted only physically or materialistically and nationalistically, what is the real meaning of the rule of God in the world. To say it another way, Christ and the apostles were able to express the real meaning to which the material and nationalistic language of the promises pointed. The real meaning of the promises is in them, but it is hidden when it is seen primarily externally. For example, the real meaning and purpose of the sacrifices and of circumcision are seen in the Hebrew

Scriptures (Psalm 51:16, 17; Deuteronomy 10:16) as having more than physical or ceremonial significance, but this is made especially clear in the New Testament (Hebrews 10:1; Romans 2:29). Christ had to deal with the misconception, even of his disciples, of the meaning of the Messiah and of God's kingdom. Thus, as already emphasized, apocalyptic language should be understood to be highly symbolic. Yes, Christ is depicted as riding on a horse, but it must be remembered that in real life he preferred riding on a donkey. He has a sword, but it is proceeding from his mouth (Revelation 1:16). Finally, he is depicted repeatedly as the "the lamb" and the "lamb that was slain" no less (Revelation 5:6). This language is not usually associated with the traditional royal figure seen in much of the Old Testament regarding the heir to the Davidic throne. Finally, what is usually forgotten about the apocalyptic passages in the gospels and Revelation is that the destruction and suffering described is *before* the end. In fact, it is more or less continuous, though irregular. The fact is that a candid look at history shows that there has been much suffering and many destructive events throughout the time since Jesus Christ. Some events, for example, the American Civil War and the two World Wars in Europe pretty much measure up to the terrible visions in apocalyptic writing. The apocalyptic writings are first a warning to Christians so that they will not be surprised by suffering and disasters, but even more, the writings are to comfort Christians with the assurance that God is in charge and will preserve his people through all the sufferings and disasters of this world, which in any case are temporary. The kingdoms of this world will rise and fall, but God determines the future. This is exactly what has happened over the last two thousand years.

I will be accused by some of being a "post-millennialist," namely someone who believes that the world will get better and better leading up to the return of Christ and his long reign on earth. That is an oversimplification of the paradox of history. We should expect the world to get better as it has in many respects over the centuries and we should work toward that end. I would not like to return to a world without antibiotics or where basic human rights are not recognized, as was the case for many of my ancestors in Europe who suffered under Christian absolute rulers and in terrible wars. Does anyone honestly want to return to the Medieval times or even to the nineteenth century or much of the twentieth century? At the same time, I agree that we should not be surprised by the appearance of evil on a more global scale than ever before in the coming years. One form of global evil, already present in some cultural attitudes among Christians, would be if one part of the world where life has greatly improved should become uncaring of and apathetic toward people in other parts of the world where life is still a difficult struggle. An expression of uncaring on a global scale is the principle of the reappearance of evil after it was "bound." We have already seen that this "unbinding" may be taking place in the rise of the ideologies of extreme individualism, extreme nationalism, and extreme capitalism. The Bible has a very positive attitude toward creation as being good and places responsibility on human beings to care for the world and especially the welfare of all human beings. But the Bible is very realistic about the ability and tendency of humans to inflict suffering on one another.

In thinking how the world and history will come to an end, I believe the Christian is helped by the word "creation" and especially "new creation." The new creation has already begun having been introduced by Jesus Christ. The Apostle states that any person in Christ is "a new creature" (II Corinthians 5:17). Also, speaking to the argument over religious practices, Paul states, "For neither circumcision or uncircumcision is anything; but a new creation is everything! (Galatians 6:15). The important thing for the Christian is that whatever the "new heaven and new earth" will be like, we are to begin experiencing it NOW. The Letter to the Hebrews (12:22-24) states that in coming to Jesus we have come "to Mt. Zion and to the city of the living God, the heavenly Jerusalem" and to much more! Also, do not forget the comment in Ephesians 2:6 that uses the past tense to say that God "raised us up with him in the heavenly places in Christ Jesus." This makes heaven a present experience! Certainly it is to be an experience that begins in this life. To look to the earthly Jerusalem as the center of the rule of Christ is to look down on the heavenly Jerusalem that Christ has brought to us and that we experience now and begin at least to build on earth in every land. This was certainly the vision of William Blake in 1808, who wrote of building Jerusalem "in England's green and pleasant land." I believe Christians are called to envision every place and make every place in some way Jerusalem brought to earth by Christ, that is, a place where God is glorified and served and where the healing of all who come takes place.

For me this is the answer to the paradox: we are given a blessed life now, but an even better life in a new creation in the next life with the return of Christ. At times, we do not want the blessed present life to end, but at times because of difficult and trying circumstances, especially some form of physical suffering and pain that goes with sickness and aging, we are more than ready for the better life to come. The best part of the better life to come is that through a transformation we will be recreated in the image of God, the image shown to us in Jesus Christ. "What we do know is this: when he is revealed, we will be like him, for we will see him as he is" (I John 3:2) The purpose of God in the New Age of Jesus Christ is to let us have some foretaste of that future transformation NOW. "Even though our outer nature is wasting away, our inner nature is being renewed day by day" (II Corinthians 4:16)

CONCLUSION

Living in the New Age brought by Jesus Christ is aided by being "wise as serpents and innocent as doves" (Matthew 10:16). This recommendation by Jesus Christ comes with a warning that at times there may be great suffering by his disciples. This same warning in Mark (13:9-13) and Luke (21:12-17) comes just before apocalyptic passages predicting destruction and suffering, but also the "coming of the Son of Man." I see this "coming" as both continuous in history, but reaching a climax in the future at the end of history. The purpose of Christ is to allay fear and to encourage faithfulness in spreading the gospel. I will be bold enough to describe this as a "passive aggressive" approach. On the one hand, we do not try to do God's job of defeating evil, so we can relax a great deal in dealing directly with evil and concentrate on being innocent ourselves, as Christ was innocent. But on the other hand, we need to be fearless in bearing witness to the revelation of God's love in Jesus Christ. We do not need to defeat the Opposition because it has already been defeated, but we still need to defend against its remaining efforts to hinder as much as possible the spread and acceptance of the good news of Christ's Kingdom. We do this best by living in the Kingdom as children of the New Age with the help of the Holy Spirit as we follow, listen, receive, and love. Many other terms can be used to describe the way of being a disciple of Jesus Christ in his Kingdom. I should add that joyous worship is an important part and outcome of following, listening, receiving, and loving. Worship, a "useless" activity in the eyes of the world, has always been an integral part of the life of the People of God and a source of great joy and empowerment. Note the hymnbook in the middle of the Bible (Book of Psalms) and the importance of the hymnal and other music in the life of the Church.

The concept of being a disciple applies particularly to individuals, but being a disciple has from the beginning meant being part of the Community of God's People, who are disciples together.

CHAPTER 9

BEYOND DEFENSE -
LIVING IN THE NEW AGE
IN COMMUNITY

THE COMMUNITY FOR THE LAST DAYS

It is possible to think of the Christian life primarily if not entirely in individual terms, but that would be a distortion and would certainly not be according to the view of the Christian life or of human life in general in the Bible. American socio-cultural forces, in fact, tend to carry individualism to an extreme and one result is to encourage Christians not to recognize their place in the Christian Community. While individualism has had a positive influence in emphasizing individual human rights leading to the formation of democratic governments, a negative effect has been an overemphasis on rights over responsibilities and a lack of emphasis on individual connectedness with others. As already seen, individualism has even been turned into an ideology that is used to dominate others and keep people in subordinate positions.

By naming "the Community," I am referring to the important fact that every individual Christian, whether conscious of it or not, is part of a worldwide Community of believers. I am emphasizing this here in order to avoid an overly individualistic emphasis that is always possible in the Christian life, especially in the Protestant (my) version, but also because individualism is increasing around the world. Although in modern societies individuals must make many choices, which tends to create a feeling of being an autonomous individual, the process of becoming a Christian is not the apparent one of simply making an individual choice or of making a choice to become a Christian and then joining a fellowship that is a branch of the Church. We may make a choice to join a particular fellowship or congregation, but becoming a Christian and becoming a member of the universal Church is a simultaneous event.

The lack of emphasis on Christian connectedness and also human connectedness is a negative by-product of individualism fostered especially by Protestantism. Everything in life is capable of misuse, especially the best things. The strong need for individuals to make decisions to follow Christ and receive the rich blessings that are experienced by the followers of Christ can very easily lead to a self-centered focus on the self and a disregard on the importance of relating to other Christians and their churches, as well as to other human beings. This could be called the "Protestant sin" and leads to the "adolescence spirit" of many Protestants and their churches. In this spirit people assume they can "go it alone" and that they "don't need anyone else in relating to God." It also tends to be highly judgmental, as are many adolescents. Such individualism produces exaggerated ideas of attempted domination of the self by other Christians, often "the central office" or "the bureaucracy" that is "trying to control us." In fact, the organized church may be depicted as "apostate," which makes it easier for some Christians to create independent "spiritual" churches and para-church organizations. At present there is a great appeal of "spiritual fellowships" created by the gathering of more or less autonomous individuals.

In the earlier era of the monopolistic Church there was a prevalent spirit of childishness and overdependence on an outside authority. Children love ritual and color and need the comfort of authoritative figures found in fathers and mothers. A childish spirit clings to these things. This could be called the "Catholic sin." However, there is an important, even an essential, need for Christians to have a "child-like" spirit as Jesus taught (Matthew 18:1-5). This may be considered the Catholic or traditional liturgical church contribution to the Christian Community. At the same time, it is important for Christians to stand for their beliefs, to have the right kind of independent spirit that is willing to "stand and be counted," and especially to have a strong voluntary spirit of initiative and participation. Both the childish spirit (Catholic sin) and the adolescent "go it alone" and judgmental spirit (Protestant sin) in the Christian Church are evidence that the Church has not reached maturity, namely "the measure of the full stature of Christ" (Ephesians 4:13). A major task of individual Christians and of the many churches in the New Age brought by Christ is to contribute to the maturing of the "Holy Catholic Church" or the universal Church of Jesus Christ. To do this it is essential that individual Christians be aware of their membership both in the local church and the universal Church. Many Protestant especially need a much stronger sense of the catholicity (universality) of the Church in its visible existence. This means incorporating the worldwide Church in their thinking, beginning with all the churches in their community. For those who may not have noticed, John Calvin (Institutes, Book IV, Chapter 1) speaks lovingly of the visible Church as "our mother" from whom we should never separate ourselves. There can be no private, free-floating Christians.

Jesus Christ gathered disciples around him at the beginning of his ministry and came back to them after his resurrection. On the Day of Pentecost, the Holy Spirit was given to the Church, not just to certain individuals. These facts are strong reminders that being a Christian means belonging to a larger body of believers—the body of Christ, the Church Universal, which exists in countless local expressions. It is not my purpose here to attempt to give a full blown ecclesiology or doctrine of the Church, but I would like to discuss some of the important characteristics that are needed in the Church in the New Age introduced by Jesus Christ, with the help of a social scientific perspective.

THE CHURCH AS BOTH MOVEMENT AND INSTITUTION

From the beginning the Church had the characteristics of a movement. However, any movement that is able to continue takes on additional characteristics associated with institutions. This happened to the Christian Church primarily after the period of the New Testament, even though signs of the developing institution can be discerned in the New Testament writings.

There is a tension between movement and institution characteristics. A major characteristic of a movement is that it is aimed at bringing about change and it contains people voluntarily committed, usually enthusiastically, to a cause. There is usually leadership by a charismatic leader or a small network of such leaders. In some contrast to this, a major characteristic of an institution is that it continues through time by the establishment of some routine practices with some on-going organization having officers and some mutually accepted written order or rules. Institutions are almost always attached to particular locations and to buildings. Institutions are needed in order to maintain the cause of movements over time. Key words here are "change" for movements and "continuing" and "routine" for institutions. Movements need to mobilize resources, but institutions are needed to regularize the receiving and use of resources. There are other characteristics of both, but clearly, there is a tension, which can often turn into a conflict between the movement and institution spirits. However, a movement will cease to exist if it does not take on at least some of the continuing and stabilizing characteristics of an institution. In other words, a movement must form an organization and if it does, the organization will become an institution in due time if it is to continue to exist. At the same time, what enables a movement to continue, namely institutionalization, may cause the movement characteristics to be greatly weakened or even cease to exist. When this happens the institution may become lifeless and without energy or enthusiasm. This will happen when the institution resulting from the movement loses the goal of bringing about change and makes self-maintenance its primary goal. The very important issue of the nature of the change and the kinds of change sought by the Church will be discussed in the next section.

The beginning of institutionalization of the Church is already seen in the New Testament, particularly in the Pastoral Epistles, where qualifications of officers in the Church are discussed. However, the Church did not lose its movement characteristic of bringing about change in the lives of individuals, households, and larger groups, at least in its first three hundred years. It was in the fourth century, when the Church became closely allied to the government, that the movement spirit of the Church was dealt a heavy blow. "Spirit" is a good word for movements because the goal of movements, namely to bring about change, must be carried in people's attitudes and not simply expressed in words and formal documents, the latter being especially important in institutions. The movement spirit never died, but it became dominated by the Church's institutional goal of self-maintenance, which can also become a kind of spirit, but the wrong kind of spirit.

Alliance with governments is particularly conducive to making institutional characteristics dominant because governments are primarily institutions, not movements. A primary goal of governments is self-perpetuation and continuity, often through dominating power. However, let it be said that democracies with their political parties help to maintain characteristics of a movement even in governments. Political parties usually advocate "change for the better." I have been very critical of the acceptance by Church leaders in the fourth century of state sponsorship and state imposition of religious requirements, especially the legal pressures for individual citizens to be members of the Church if they wanted to advance in the government. At this point I want to hasten to affirm the importance and even the necessity of institutionalization of the Church. What is particularly dangerous for Christian life in the Church is when institutionalization smothers much of the movement spirit of the Church. This is what inevitably takes place when the Church accepts and uses state power for religious purposes.

A second major characteristic of a movement, following the goal of bringing about change, is voluntarism. The voluntary spirit of the Church in its first three hundred years was greatly damaged by the alliance of the Church and state in the fourth century. The voluntary spirit was not completely killed because we can see that Christians undertook voluntary acts of faith throughout Christian history. We see this initially with the traveling missionary monks and the religious orders, but the voluntary spirit was greatly damaged for the broad Christian public.

In the United States, the importance of the institutional aspect of the Church has been reduced and the movement aspect of the Church strengthened by the formal separation of organized religion and the state. As a result, the voluntary spirit associated with the movement aspect of the Church has been greatly enhanced. This can be seen in comparing the American and European churches in which the latter existed or still exist in some measure as state churches. Voluntarism is generally more prevalent in the churches in the United States than in Europe. However, Christians in the United States and in other countries where there is formal separation of religion and state still have an important task to make sure that the movement aspect of the Church exists within the institution of the Church and that the institution is not captured by the surrounding culture.

Institutions usually make use of professionals. One place where the tension between the movement and the institution takes place is in the area of professionalism, which can conflict with the spirit of volunteerism. It is important to recognize that the professional is not automatically more effective than the volunteer, but neither is the opposite true. Developing professional specialists in an institution demonstrates taking the skills and tasks of these specialists very seriously. In the case of the Church, this means making excellence in Bible study, preaching, pastoral work and general leadership an important training goal for church leaders. Requiring seminary training for ministers of the word and sacraments shows the seriousness with which the Church regards the function of ministry of the word and sacraments. However, sometimes the emphasis on professional or specialized training has gotten in the way of doing the work of God.

The Presbyterian Church (my church) provides an excellent example. At the time of the American Revolution the Presbyterian Church was one of the largest churches. As people went westward into frontier areas they desperately needed ministers to bring them God's word and the sacraments. The Presbyterian Church leaders chose to make seminary graduation a primary requirement for ordaining ministers. They were not willing to make some adjustment for the special circumstances of western expansion. As a result some Presbyterians on the frontier separated to form the Cumberland Presbyterian Church, but an even greater consequence was that the

Presbyterians could not keep up with the growth of the Methodists and Baptists, who were willing to ordain lay people to be ministers. They grew much more rapidly and became the major Protestant churches in the land to this day. Some two hundreds years too late, the Presbyterians decided to establish the office of Commissioned Lay Pastor in order to meet the needs of churches unable to obtain or afford a regularly ordained minister.

In a broader sense, although seminary training has an important implication of taking seriously the study of the word of God and the work of ministry, there is an unrecognized danger by many in the church and the ministry of placing the profession of the ministry or "clergy" above the calling to ministry. (The Presbyterian Church does not use the word "clergy" in its Book of Order.) The emphasis on the ministry as a profession is an example in the modern world of the institutional aspect of the Church outweighing the movement aspect and endangering the voluntary spirit that is so important in the Church.

I have to remark in passing that the ordaining of lay people without full seminary training does not indicate necessarily any rejection of education. It is ironic that although the Presbyterian Church is rightly proud of its emphasis on education and its founding of many schools and colleges, the Methodist and Baptist churches both have larger and more influential universities than does the Presbyterian Church. I consider this a judgment of God on a misplaced institutionalism.

The tension between institution and movement appears again in the overseas missionary effort of the churches. The mainline churches have generally recruited and sent out career missionaries who were promised support by the home churches. I was one such missionary in Taiwan from 1956 to 1972. The Presbyterian Church, in fact, decided in the middle of the nineteenth century, when many missionary societies were being formed, to constitute itself as a missionary society with its own Board of Foreign Missions. Nevertheless, from the beginning of the missionary movement of the nineteenth and twentieth centuries, numerous independent missionary societies were continually formed. Many of these societies were characterized as "faith missions" because of their reliance on missionaries to raise their own support from as many sources as they could find. Although both types of missionaries could be considered as responding to a Divine call and as professionals or specialists, the missionaries who have had to raise their own support usually depend on a personal relationship with voluntary supporters to a greater extent than those who were promised support by a denomination. Although there are ways of emphasizing the voluntary participation of supporters in denominations, for example, allowing individual churches to support individual missionaries, there is a greater danger of allowing the institutional aspect of the Church to overshadow the voluntary aspect of the Church in the denominations than in the "faith missions." It is simply a fact that the "independent mission societies" or "faith missions" have tended to emphasize the voluntary aspect of missions to a greater extent than do denominational mission organizations. At any rate, significantly, over the last half century, denominational missionaries have lost ground in terms of numbers to the "independent missionaries" supported by "faith missions." However, an interesting development that is now taking place within denominations is a great increase of voluntary missionaries and mission teams going out from congregations and area organizations. There has also been an increase among denominations of sending missionaries who pay or raise their own support, especially those going for short terms. This type of mission activity obviously emphasizes the voluntary spirit that belongs to the movement aspect of the Church. At the same time, this approach may ignore the connectedness that should be manifested by the Church. Also, in some cases, the voluntary missionaries have not received proper orientation in how to relate to people in overseas churches, resulting even in harmful effects. The work of short term missions needs to be carefully evaluated and important improvements made in orientation of volunteers and in some cases in the kinds of work undertaken.

I was blessed in my experience as a missionary to see at least the latter part of a Christian movement in Taiwan among the aboriginal people. A large number of people became Christians over a period of two or three generations. At first the movement was underground under the Japanese occupation that tried to stop the spread of the "American religion," but after World War II the movement came out into the open. When I arrived to work among the Amis, one of the larger language groups, which had approximately 100 villages, there was a thatched roof church in practically every village built by local people. At that time there was not a single ordained minister among the Amis. I saw the excitement and energy of the new Christians. However, institutionalization took place relatively rapidly with the help of the Presbyterian Church of Taiwan. Unlike the United States, where Presbyterians required all ministers to go through the same seminary training, the Taiwan church ordained ministers with shorter training and made much use of lay ministers among the aboriginals. Most importantly, the aboriginals were enabled to organize their own presbyteries (district governing bodies) and conduct their worship and church business in their own languages. The aboriginal Christians have continued as a strong body of Christians, making up approximately forty percent of the Presbyterian Church of Taiwan membership, though constituting less that two percent of the Island population. As many migrated to cities, they have carried their churches with them. In the case of the aboriginal people, the great change that took place was the transformation of a non-Christian people into a largely Christian people and at the same time numerous social changes resulted from this transformation. Seeing this transformation has made me realize that given the right circumstances under God's providence, especially circumstances that do not associate Christianity with domination, people will receive the gospel as a powerful source of new life and hope.

The conclusion of this section on the movement and institutional aspects of the Church is that the Church for the Last Days, which is the New Age introduced by Jesus Christ, must be a Church that while making the best use of the institutional aspect of the Church inspires the movement aspect of the Church. I have particularly emphasized the importance of the voluntary spirit in the movement aspect. However, I return now to the first characteristic of a movement, which is to bring about change.

PROBLEMS WITH CHANGE AS A GOAL
FOR THE CHURCH

It is extremely important that the Church in the Last Days aims, not so much at bringing about change external to the movement (as typical social movements seek to do), but at being an instrument of God in bringing about the changes God desires to carry out in the world beginning with the Church itself and extending outward. This means that churches need to distinguish themselves from typical social or even religious movements because their first task is to worship God and allow God through Christ and the Holy Spirit continually to change those who are called believers or seek to be believers. Christians can never be satisfied with themselves as individuals and as the Church. They are also never satisfied with the world as it is, but in a secondary way because the changes in the world follow the changes in the Church as salt flavors a meal or light shines from a lamp stand (Matthew 5:13-14). If God wanted to leave humanity and the world as they were, Christ would not have come into the world.

First, in regard to changes that need to take place in the Church and the world, it is important to recognize that often God works beyond the planning and efforts of the Church. This is often missed by those studying missions. Circumstances or social conditions that were not intentionally created by Christians or anyone else may have a powerful effect on what takes place in the spread of the gospel of Christ and the building of his Church. An excellent example is the providential mixing of various denominations in the United States that led to the dethroning of the Church from political power. This dethroning has greatly enhanced the life and influence of Christians. This dethroning meant that the real meaning of belief – trust instead of assent – and the use of persuasion by the Church became more important than stressing "official authority" and the use of coercion in religion. Even beyond the ordinary providential work of God is God's use of "human wrath" to praise God (Psalm 76:10), meaning that God even uses human evil actions to bring about needed changes in the world. This could be regarded as God's judgment on humans, especially God's own people. An ancient example of judgment proclaimed by the Hebrew prophets is the destruction of Israel by Assyria and later Judah by Babylon. A modern example would be the collapse of colonialism caused by Japan (later also losing its colonies) and the self-weakening conflicts among European nations. The collapse of colonialism (unplanned and unaided by the Church) greatly aided the spread of the gospel. Another modern example working through human sin is the failure of Communism in the Soviet Union and Eastern Europe, which has allowed people to see the futility of government that ignores the human desire for personal freedom. In other words, God is not limited to working through the Church in history, but nevertheless the Church or the Community of God is to be a special instrument in the hands of God for fulfilling the prayer, "thy kingdom come, they will be done on earth as it is in heaven." However, this is not to be through coercion or gaining power in government, as some Christians still desire to exercise. The mission of the Church is expressed in the term missio Dei (mission of God), which means that the mission of the Church is to allow itself to be used by God in God's work of redemption. In short, the Church's goal is to be a part of God's work or "to fit in" as best as it is able, certainly with the help of the Holy Spirit, in God's mission in the world. At this point, we turn to a problem that has been with the Church for many centuries, particularly since the fourth century. This is the desire and attempt of the Church to use power to accomplish particular goals desired by church leaders or particular groups of Christians. The problem is that this attempt to control or manage history has brought untold suffering to many and enormous opposition to Christianity itself.

Although in the United States the Church has been divested of political control, the large numbers of Christians in the population causes many Christians to seek to bring about socio-cultural changes that they deem are just and righteous based on their Christian beliefs. There is certainly a place for influence, but not as a "Christian" political organization. Hunter (2010) has much to say about how Christians should think about and approach socio-cultural change. His first task is to disabuse Christians of some of the superficial concepts of cultural change as consisting of simply "changing people's hearts and minds." The task is not, therefore, simply trying to change people's "worldview," which is only one part of culture that is embedded in society. He (2010:32-45) sets forth the social scientific understanding of culture and society, which we have sought to use in this book. I will not repeat his seven propositions on culture and four propositions on cultural change. For my purposes here I will emphasize a few pertinent perspectives on culture that he brings out.

Although ideas are important in culture, they are closely linked to actual organizations and institutions in societies. This is why I have used the term "socio-cultural forces." Cultural change is generated within social networks and is not the creation of "great men," as so often thought by individualistically oriented Americans and others. One of the views that may be distasteful for Christians (I found myself looking for exceptions to this pattern) is that cultural change is usually generated by elites, namely from the top down. But it is also true that "change is typically initiated by elites who are outside of the centermost positions of prestige" and minorities and relatively small groups may have a disproportionate influence on socio-cultural change (Hunter 2010: 20, 42). (This made me feel better.) An important point made by Hunter (2010:45) is that "cultures are profoundly resistant to intentional change—period" and, in fact, "t[T]he most profound changes in cultures take place over the course of multiple generations." For me, the socio-cultural change brought about by the Civil Rights Movement raises some questions about Hunter's view, but the on-going problems of racism in the United States supports his view on how gradual change can be. Also, the Civil Rights Movement led by Martin Luther King and associates, unlike the movements to eliminate poverty or hunger, was distinctive as a struggle of an ethnic minority for rights ostensibly already guaranteed in the Constitution. In some ways it was a continuation of the nineteenth century Civil War, but by important non-violent means.

It is useful here to point out that religions, including Christianity, usually have a strong conservative tendency. That is, people typically see religion as a means of preserving what they value. The great problem for Christians is that this tendency has caused some Christians over the years to oppose needed social progress, including democracy, the abolition of slavery and then segregation, the elevation of the status of women, social security and socially sponsored health care, and the establishment of programs to overcome poverty and violence. This opposition has often included considerable anger and even violence.

Hunter (2010:99-176) faults both the left and the right among Christians, although especially the right, as well those between (those who seek change apart from state structure or "neo-Anabaptists"), for their tendency to politicize issues producing a struggle for power and domination. He discusses the problems that Christians have had in understanding power and the misplaced attempts to wield political power based on a sense of *ressentiment*, which includes our word, "resentment," but also involves a combination of anger, envy, hate, rage, and revenge. He argues that Christians on the right and left and even those who see themselves as "apart from the world" (Neo-Anabaptists) have politicized issues by seeking political power. The consequence of this has been "to reduce Christian faith to a political ideology and various Christian denominations and para-church organizations to special interest groups" (Hunter 2010:174). The tragedy of this is explained by Hunter:

> The problem is that many prominent Christian leaders and Christian organizations in America have been at the corrupting center of this kind of tribalism, Christian conservatives most prominently. Christians may not have created this tapestry but they are a fabric within it.

> What is even more striking than the negational

character of this political culture is the absence of
robust and constructive affirmations. Vibrant culture
makes space for leisure, philosophical reflection,
scientific and intellectual mastery, and artistic and
literary expression, among other things. Within the
larger Christian community in America, one can find
such vitality in pockets here and there. Yet where they
exist, they are eclipsed by the greater prominence
and vast resources of the political activists and
their organizations...What this means is that rather
than being defined by its cultural achievements, its
intellectual and artistic vitality, its service to the
needs of others, Christianity is defined to the outside
world by its rhetoric of resentment and the ambitions
of a will in opposition to others.

The purpose of the above discussion for Hunter, as well as for me, is to
clear the ground, for developing an appropriate and effective approach
of Christians to the world to bring about changes they may desire. In
this regard, Hunter (2010: 184) affirms that Christians cannot escape
the fact that they have power in the world and will inevitably make
mistakes in their use of it. However, the Church should focus on the
"social power" or "relational power" that "is exercised every day
in primary social relationships, within the relationships of family,
neighborhood, and work in all of the institutions that surround us in
daily life and therefore it is far more common to people than political
power" (Hunter 2010:187). The social power that Jesus exercised, that
disarmed and triumphed over worldly power, had four characteristics:
(1) It "derived from his complete intimacy with and submission to his
Father"; (2) It involved "his complete rejection of status and reputation
and the privileges that accompanies them"; (3) It was defined by
compassion for fallen humanity; (4) It was noncoercive toward "those

outside of the community of faith" and therefore "his kingdom was available to all...men, women, young, old, servant, master, slave, freeman, Jew, Samaritan, Gentile" (Hunter 2010:188-193).

In his last set of chapters, Hunter (2010:197-286) develops an appropriate approach for Christians, called "practicing faithful presence." Like all terms for describing an ideal Christian life, including the ones I used in the previous chapter (following, listening, receiving, loving), this one can be interpreted inadequately, for example, too much in individualistic terms and too much as a passive approach to the world. Nevertheless, as a social scientist, Hunter is able largely to avoid this by stressing that "presence" means "engagement with the world." I will seek to use his insights in continuing to think about the Christian Community in its movement characteristics.

CHANGE AS A GOAL FOR THE CHRISTIAN COMMUNITY AND ITS MEMBERS

Given the checkered history of the Church and the numerous times in which the Opposition has been able to mislead many Christians to seek dominating political power and thus deeply mar the witness to Jesus Christ, (including in the ways Hunter has shown the Christian flawed understanding of culture and attempted use of power), it is clear that we as Christians should be drawn to the emphasis on repentance in the New Testament. Both Old and New Testaments reveal God's purpose to prepare his people to be a fit witness to the truth, love, peace, and justice of God. For this to take place continuing repentance by individual Christians and Christian communities is required. Both the Prophet Amos (3:2) and the Apostle Peter (I Peter 4:17) teach that God's people are the first to receive judgment. This means that the Church's prayer should be, "Let God's will be done on earth and let it begin with us."

Jesus began his ministry with a call to repentance (Mark 1:15) and the Apostle Paul announced to the Athenians that God was calling on all people to repent (Acts 17:30). Since the Great Commission of Matthew 28:18-20 stresses "making disciples" and "teaching" all things that Jesus commanded, the question can be raised, "When is making disciples and teaching what Jesus commanded completed?" Repentance, being made disciples, and learning to follow what Jesus taught is surely a never-ending process in this world. This means that the first job of the Christian Community is continually to change itself to "conform to the image of the Son" (Romans 8:29), to live up to the criteria of discipleship, and to follow more nearly and fully the will of God as revealed in the life, death, and resurrection of Christ. As noted above, movements normally do not aim at changing themselves, but rather some external condition. However, the movement of the Christian Community is distinctive because it begins with continually seeking to change itself or rather allowing itself to be changed by God. This is the basis for the slogan of Reformed Theology, "Reformed and Continually Reforming." But this refers to more than theology; it refers to the whole life of the whole Community. Furthermore, this is to be done in the whole world ("all nations" in Matthew 28:19 refers to "all peoples") into which the Community of God has been sent. When this is done, the witness to Christ, which is also a way of expressing the mandate to the followers of Christ, will be continually clarified. From the review of Christian history and the examination of the work of the Opposition, it is the witness to Christ that greatly needs clarifying.

A very obvious change that has taken place in the world in the last 2000 years has been the spread of the gospel throughout the world so that approximately one third of the population of the world report believing in Jesus Christ. But how much larger would be the population that recognizes the Lordship of Jesus Christ if Christians represented Christ more clearly? The clarification of the witness to Jesus Christ must continue to be the central change the Church is seeking to allow to take place. So the question remains for the Church, "How best to witness to the gospel of Jesus Christ?"

I digress briefly to mention some changes that at least provide some encouragement to followers of Christ. Just as Christ constantly acted to relieve suffering, so as the gospel has spread, many changes have taken place to greatly lift and improve human life on earth. Christianity has not been the sole cause for these changes. In fact, Christians have often opposed them. But a very good argument may be made that Christians and Christianity were major contributors to a number of changes that have benefited people's lives. These changes include the development and spread of democracy with its concept of human rights and the rule of law, the institutionalization of science, the spread of modern medicine, the encouragement of literacy and general education for populations at large, and (I must mention) the development of beautiful music, dance, and art. Jewish people have been especially active in all these areas and people in general have been drawn to support these developments as they saw the benefits for life in general. All people share as creatures of God in God's common grace that makes them appreciate and support changes that make human life flourish. This is not to deny, as this book has emphasized, that some terrible events arose within the context of Christianity that were either encouraged or not sufficiently hindered by Christians. These include religious wars and persecutions. In spite of them all, but alongside them often in hidden ways, the witness to the value of every individual in the sight of God has spread around the world and brought enormous changes in the world's societies. In addition to these general changes that are benefiting human lives worldwide, in recent decades there has been an increasing recognition of the need to protect the world that God has entrusted to humankind. When the implications of the gospel of Jesus Christ are seriously considered and the life of compassion lived by Jesus Christ is seriously followed, then all the changes that lift human life and relieve suffering become part of what Christians undertake in response to the gospel.

It is not necessary for Christians to debate with others the effects of the gospel of Christ in history. What is most important is that Christians live out the gospel in ways that Hunter (2010:263) calls the "practice of faithful presence," which was mentioned in a quotation in the previous chapter in the discussion of the way of love. I quote him again: "The practice of faithful presence, then, generates relationships and institutions that are fundamentally covenantal in character, the ends of which are the fostering of meaning, purpose, truth, beauty, belonging, and fairness—not just for Christians but for everyone." It is important to understand that for Hunter, "faithful presence" involved active engagement with the world, especially through the social power that everyone has beginning with their own families.

I would like to add a point about the movement for change by the Christian Community: it is as it should be often "under the radar." As a son of missionaries in China and a missionary for sixteen years in Taiwan, as well as a reader of missionary history, much of what takes place in the spread of the gospel is unnoticed by the media and most secular observers. Many academics are among those who do not notice much of what takes place in the worldwide work of the Church. I mentioned in Chapter 6 Woodberry's (2012) study of the mostly unnoticed wide effects of missions in many lands. In contrast, many historians take much notice of the eighteenth century Enlightenment, but pay little attention to the important Evangelical movements, particularly in England and Germany in the same period that stimulated the modern worldwide mission movements. These movements have arguably had as important an impact on world history as the Enlightenment, which is actually given too much credit for the development of science and democracy, both of which developed strong roots in the previous century among Christians. A recent example from Taiwan with which I am familiar is the impact that the broad statement on human rights made by leaders of the Presbyterian Church in Taiwan in 1972 had on the development of freedom and democracy in that land. This was not a statement to gain political power, but to express the principle of the right of self-determination that was believed to be in the best interest of all the people. The contribution of Taiwan church leaders to the development of democracy is mentioned by Shelley Rigger (2011:73,107) in her book *Why Taiwan Matters: Small Island Global Powerhouse*. Another recent example is how the fall of Communist East Germany was precipitated by a prayer meeting in a church that spread into the streets. It began a movement that could not be stopped. The same could be said of the fall of the Romanian dictator, Nicolae Ceausescue. A church meeting sparked his fall.

Thus, given the major goal of the Movement of the Christian Community to improve and clarify its witness to Jesus Christ, many of these efforts will go unnoticed by the media and others who are looking for dramatic political or military events. Furthermore, remembering the characteristics of the "social power" of Jesus in his ministry, it follows that the Church will do much of its best work in humble and unassuming ways that are very different from the display of political and military power exercised by governments. Nevertheless, making the quiet and unassuming witness of the Church can be an exciting and very rewarding experience for all who participate in it. This is because the emphasis of social power will be on forming and working through human relationships. An excellent example of the social power exercised by churches is ministry to the hungry and homeless, whose numbers have been increasing in many communities.

Finally, to deal with perhaps the most sensitive question, should the Church as a movement or churches as movements seek to bring about political change? My own view, which may be a little different from Hunter's is that I believe Christians as individuals and in groups (not as churches) have a responsibility to be active in politics, which by nature is partisan, but it should not be with a spirit of hatred or resentment. Perhaps there may be anger, but it should be tempered by trust in the truth to prevail and by love for others.

I cannot forget Martin Luther King's expression of love for those who opposed him. Furthermore, his use of non-violence is extremely important for Christians and others working for social change. In the main, the Church and churches (having Christians with various political views) should focus on the long-range changes that come when people "conform to the image of Christ" (Romans 8:29; II Corinthians 3:18; Colossians 3:10). Consistent with that, the whole purpose of this book is to point to the "principalities and powers" affecting us largely as socio-cultural forces with which we have to wrestle, just as Christ wrestled with them. The Church can and should help with this on-going struggle by throwing light on these forces so that Christians may "not be conformed to this world" (Romans 12:2). This will help to bring about the long-range socio-cultural changes that are needed. Since, as this book has emphasized, we are all under the influence of socio-cultural forces that surrounds us and, especially in the United States, we are influenced to adopt a viewpoint or perspective out of several (right, left, or center) that may appeal to us, we should begin by considering ourselves biased. In other words, all of us have slanted views. This means we actually need to listen to those with other biases and viewpoints so that truth and justice will prevail, even if in the long run. Nevertheless, as we go forward political action and legislation can have important short-term and long-term effects. Social change influenced strongly by legislation regarding civil rights and against discrimination has certainly been important in the United States, although continuing social change that goes beyond legislation is certainly needed. Also, dealing with the very difficult problem of the root causes of poverty certainly requires legislation and important policy decisions. The movement to deal with the issue of poverty in the midst of plenty can and should include many Christians, but there will be non-Christians who will join and support the movement. In short, although Hunter warns Christians about the dangers of politicizing issues and seeking power through political action, as a Presbyterian Christian (from a long tradition of interest in social justice and just governments), I believe that involvement in political activity, including voting itself, is a Christian's duty. Also, seeking political office, in spite of the bad name of "politics," can be a Christian calling. Political power to affect change is a reality. However, I believe that the involvement in organizations with political agendas should be by individual Christians, not churches. At the same time, I believe churches and their denominational fellowships (judicatories) have a responsibility to point to the larger issues of social justice requiring government attention and action. It can be a delicate task not to politicize the issue or to support a particular political partisan position, but I believe it can be done by making a theological analysis of the justice issue and stating the principles of justice involved. At the same time, organizations with political agendas should not claim to be "Christian." I am glad that in the United States there are no "Christian parties." Thus, even though the major influence of Christianity is over the long-range through the spread of the gospel of Jesus Christ, the fact is that legislation and government policies can have important immediate, as well as long-range, consequences for humans and the world. It is important for Christians to think about these consequences.

An honest review of history requires the recognition that Christians and good people have often been divided on political solutions, with Christians often supporting causes that proved to be harmful or not supporting causes that proved to be beneficial. Christians will be involved on both sides of most political struggles. This shows us that the Church is not and should not seek to be a movement with a primarily political agenda. However, I believe that it should seek to be the seedbed, the inspiration, and the source of leaders for many kinds of movements to benefit human life, many of them not political. It is also important that the Church seek to lessen the anger and resentment that is apparent in some, if not most political campaigns. The central goal of the Movement of the Church will remain to spread the gospel of the love of God in Jesus Christ and bring about the change that grows out of faith in Christ. As is very evident, most of the African-American people involved in the Civil Rights Movement and poor people involved in movements to end poverty are religious people. Christians should seek to understand these movements and other movements and act in ways that support them. I believe this involves a deep study of root causes for social problems, a study which includes making use of the social sciences and the insights of both Christians and non-Christians. Christians can do a great deal as individuals and as communities of faith in the public sphere where truth can be lifted up and actions taken that change lives and communities. They can throw light on the "principalities and powers" (socio-cultural forces) that would rather remain hidden. This alone contributes to political actions. Requiring change and transparency in political power has been based on the important insight from the Bible regarding universal human sinfulness. Likewise, requiring regulation of the freedom of those with political and economic power comes from the same insight. In the end, to reiterate, the Church or individual churches ordinarily should not seek to constitute themselves as social or political movements. African American churches in the Civil Rights Movement were an apparent exception. In the current controversial struggle for gay rights, churches, including my own denomination, have been supportive (as they were to the Civil Rights Movement), but the movement itself has been primarily outside of the Church. The actions taken by the churches have been directed primarily toward church, not governmental policy. My denomination's support for both of these movements caused division in the church, but the majority of the church felt its actions were based on Scripture and therefore necessary. Time will reveal the truth about what is just for societies. The Church needs to take a long-range view point. When this is done, then it will be recognized that it was the social power of Jesus Christ through the Church that has had the greatest long-term influence. The Church is called to follow the Movement initiated by Jesus Christ for the last days. In the end, as Hunter (2010:285) stated, the Church should not be asking how to change the world in the sense of how should history be managed. Christ's victory over the "principalities and powers," which as we have found includes socio-cultural forces, "frees all Christians to actively, creatively, and constructively seek the good in their relationships, in their tasks, in their spheres of influence, and in their cities." As we honestly look at history, we can see that in spite of all the tragedy and sadness in human life brought on by humans, including Christians, human life can be made to flourish and life can have deep joy and peace even in the midst of suffering..

CONCLUSION

The doctrine of last things, eschatology, is extremely important in the New Testament. It claims that Jesus Christ introduced the Kingdom of God, what I am calling "The Real New Age," for the last period of history. This Kingdom constitutes the Real New Age for humanity. We are to be ready at any time for the return of Christ whether it is in relation to the "Coming of the Son of Man" as we experience Christ's Kingdom in the present or at the end of history or at the end of our individual lives. I personally believe that we will wake up after death and find ourselves to be at the end of history, but that remains a mystery. All whom we knew on earth may be there too. In other words, I believe that in a mysterious way to us, time may well be collapsed, namely, we will leave the dimension of time and enter another dimension. It has not been easy for Christians to avoid speculation about whether we are nearing the end of history or not. Nevertheless, Christians are called to faithful and expectant living characterized by the words, "follow," "listen," and "receive," directed toward Jesus Christ and "love" for the Triune God and all people and all creation. These words express the Movement that is found in ongoing joyous worship and humble service. In this we are following Christ who gives us access to the Father through his death and resurrection, listening to his word of grace, and receiving the Holy Spirit, all resulting in being changed for loving service in his Kingdom. In this way also we become part of a new People, a Community under God struggling to do the will of God on earth as it is done in heaven. In this chapter it was pointed out that the Community of God's people has both the characteristics of an institution, actually many institutions, established for ongoing life and the characteristics of a movement, aimed at bringing about change beginning with itself, but affecting the whole world. These two sets of characteristics are in tension with each other, but both have their contribution to make.

In the meantime, the increasingly rapid changes in the world, especially the bringing on of the "shrinking of the world," the "leveling of the nations," and the spread of democratic values adds to the excitement that we are seeing some of the signs of a coming climax of history, be it hundreds or thousands of years away. The latter would still be a short time in human history. I personally believe there are still large numbers of people who have not "heard" the gospel because they have not seen the gospel in Christians and Christianity. After all, Jesus did not simply speak to us, but rather he showed us God's way by how he lived. The words alone of Christians are not sufficient for people to perceive Jesus Christ. At least it is possible to say that the changes in the world are early signs that human history is moving toward a climax in which there will be a full revelation of both Jesus Christ, the "Son of Man" or the "Human Being," and of redeemed humanity, the children of God, recreated in the image of God (Daniel 7:13; Romans 8:18,19). This simultaneous event reveals God's great redemptive purpose for his creation.

CHAPTER 10

LIVING IN THE NEW AGE WITH FOLLOWERS OF OTHER RELIGIONS AND NO RELIGION

RELIGIOUS DIVERSITY COMES HOME

There has always been religious diversity among humans, but the diversity has been largely divided geographically and ethnically. Originally, there was relatively little direct contact between ethnic and religious groups. As civilizations developed and empires were formed people with diverse religious practices came in contact with each other. They often adopted beliefs and religious practices from one another or simply assumed that supernatural beings dealt differently with different peoples. The rulers of empires were usually considered as divine or semi-divine (at the encouragement of the dominant elite), but they tolerated diverse popular religions, as long as the official cult was recognized by the people. The Persian Empire and later the Roman Empire are examples of empires in which a variety of religions were tolerated as long as the official cult practices were observed by the people. Most religions in the ancient civilizations emphasized *particular practices* rather than distinctive beliefs and people often practiced more than one religion. Judaism and later Christianity were the first religions to emphasize the importance of distinctive religious beliefs in which commitment to the One True God was central. Then because of its tendency to actively seek converts, Christianity came into conflict with the Roman government until the famous change in the fourth century in which Christianity became the official religion and persecution by Christians of other religions became all too typical. (This shift in the status of Christianity was described in Chapters 3 and 4.) Actually, monotheism opens the way for a more religiously autocratic government enforcing the "one true religion," but fortunately the "hidden card" of monotheism can also justify opposition to those in power as being unfaithful to the "one true religion."

As Christianity spread, it tended to follow ethnic lines so that the older pattern of religions staying within geographic and ethnic lines was perpetuated. The formation of the Christian state church in Rome and later in Europe reinforced the lack of religious *diversity* within ethnic and national groups. The greatest shift in this pattern took place when people of various religious backgrounds migrated to North America. This was a momentous change in the usual pattern of non-religious diversity within given territories. Now in the rapidly shrinking modern world, religious diversity has increasingly become a local phenomenon. Less diversity is found in the lands where the ancient civilizations existed and where Christian state churches were established, but the least diversity is found in the lands where there are large Muslim majorities. Islam, of course, like Christianity and the mother religion, Judaism, recognizes only One True God, but also lands with large Muslim majorities, did not undergo the process of secularization of governments to the same extent as in the West. Turkey is the exception and some other lands with majority Muslim populations seem to be in the early stages of seeking to have secular governments. Religious diversity is especially characteristic of the United States and most of Western Europe (although in Europe there is nervousness about and restriction of groups deemed "cults"), but religious diversity is generally increasing around the world. Because of laws allowing freedom of religion, at least "on the books," religions with long religious traditions outside of the West, such as Hinduism, Buddhism, and Islam are increasingly being encountered by Christians in the West.

Christianity itself, in spite of the common assumption of many, should be considered a "non-Western" religion because it had its origins in the Middle East just as Islam. Christianity was highly influenced by classical Mediterranean civilization through the Greek and Latin languages and civilizations. Islam also was influenced by Greek learning and was a source for translation of Greek writings back to the West. Ancient churches continue in the Middle East, although there has been an out migration due to anti-Christian sentiment and pressures, sometimes active persecution, some of it stimulated by Western support of the State of Israel and the recent wars in the Middle East, but also by the rising influence of Islamic extremists. Christianity, of course, had a central influence in the forming of Western civilization whose major populations were originally illiterate tribes people.

In many Western nations, the rights of the non-Western religions are being recognized, for example to have chaplains in the military and in other public institutions, as well as to participate in public religious services. Islam, in fact, has never been that far from the West and interaction between Western and Islamic countries has been taking place for centuries, though immigration of Muslims to the West has increased in recent decades. Islam and Buddhism, and modern Hinduism, even have missionary traditions that cause them to seek and welcome converts wherever the religions exist.

In addition to traditional religions from non-Western societies, Judaism is a traditional non-Christian religion that has long existed within Western societies, though often being persecuted, sometimes quite severely. Many new religions continue to come into existence, some being recognized under the term "New Age," that draw from wide sources including pre-Christian religions of Europe. Not only are there many non-Christian religions in areas where Christianity has been predominant, Christianity itself is extremely diverse with three major divisions: Orthodoxy, Roman Catholicism, and Protestantism. This is in addition to the ancient churches of the East, such as the Copts and Nestorians. Then, Protestantism contains immense diversity of denominations with some groups, such as the Church of Latter Day Saints (Mormons), Jehovah's Witnesses, and Unitarian Universalists not being accepted by many Christians as belonging to the main body of Christianity.

With religious freedom in the West along with increasing religious freedom in the world resulting in widespread religious diversity, most people will have contacts with followers of various religions or of no religion at all. The last category of people professing no religion has been increasing, beginning in the West, but stimulated in the rest of the world by the spread of Communism, which also originated in the West. One phenomenon that has increased contact between people with different religious views has been inter-religious marriage, which creates families with more than one religion. There have also been increased inter-religious contacts in the work place.

The purpose of this final chapter is to deal with the question, "How should believers in Jesus Christ, who are beginning to live in the New Age introduced by Christ, relate to people of non-Christian religions or no religion, as well as to people in the various versions of Christianity?"

STARTING WITH JESUS CHRIST

It is important for Christians to start thinking about how to relate to others with different views on religion, as about almost all questions on how to live, with the recognition of the reality of Jesus Christ and the authority that has been given to him on the basis of what he accomplished by his death and resurrection. It is not said of anyone else that he or she died for the sins of humanity and rose from the dead to open a "new and living way" to God (Hebrews 10:20). For no one else, certainly not for the leaders of other religions, was the claim ever made that such a person was the sole Mediator between God and humans. For some, the Christian claim regarding Christ is a false claim and for others simply an unproven claim, but it is the basis of a faith and a religion which by this claim is set apart from all other religions. The gospel of Jesus Christ and the New Age, which Christ introduced, is known through this faith and the best evidence is that this faith is here to stay. Furthermore, the evidence of the last 2000 years is that the message of this faith will continue to be believed by increasing numbers of people around the world. The very great claim that Christianity makes about Jesus Christ means that it should never be necessary for Christians to resort to coercion in requiring faith in Jesus Christ or in keeping other religions from competing with Christianity. The claim only needs to be proclaimed and demonstrated in the lives of Christ's followers. Unfortunately, Christians have not always had such confidence in their own message, nor the needed humility that should go with the many failings of Christianity to live up to its message about Jesus Christ.

Some Christian missionaries would like to say that being a Christian is simply being a "follower of Jesus Christ." There is truth to this claim and if this claim becomes recognized more broadly it will open the possibility for "followers of Jesus Christ" to be participants in cultures which are closely related to other religions so that there might be Christian Muslims, Christian Buddhists, and Christian Hindus. (There probably long have been Christian Confucianists.)

Such people would be participants in the cultures associated with these religions, but be followers of Jesus Christ. Needless to say, this has aroused controversy. Having said this, it was and is impossible for Christians to escape creating a religion that has come to be known as "Christianity." This is because Christians are also humans and since religions are what humans believe and practice in relation to what they believe about God or simply what is beyond the empirical world, Christians inevitably created a religion with many variations. It is true that the term "Christianity" does not appear in the Bible and the name "Christian" is a nickname given by others to those who believed in Christ and spoke often about him. "People of the Way" was the original name for the followers of Jesus Christ. However, because human beings must organize to accomplish anything, followers of Jesus Christ formed the religion of Christianity. This is not simply a human characteristic, but the followers of Jesus from the beginning have shown a strong tendency intentionally to form enduring communities of believers, rather than simply be transient worshippers in designated places (temples) as in many religions. The initiation rite of baptism was practiced and rolls of members created. In certain respects, therefore, Christianity can be compared to other religions, both in beliefs and practices, but in other respects it has been distinct from other traditional religions. Nevertheless, Christianity represents the imperfect human response to the revelation of God in Jesus Christ. Although Christians believe that the Church of Jesus Christ is a Divine institution, which is like an extension of the body of Christ in history, the Church very clearly has a human side to it. It is a human institution, as well as a Divine institution. In fact it is made up of many institutions, all of which can be examined like any other human institution. Christianity not only exists as an institution, but as noted in the previous chapter, it is also a complex religious movement, which continually spawns new movements. However, Christianity was not established to be primarily a territorial religion as "Christendom." This was a distortion of its original movement characteristics.

Other religions all have areas of beauty and truth, not because they necessarily represent God's revelation as a way of salvation, but because they represent human responses to God and because human beings are created in God's image with inherent religious characteristics that makes them seekers after God, as Paul affirmed (Acts 17:27,28). The existence of a "religious nature" in humans is challenged by many in the modern age, but the evidence for it is rather strong. Still anyone is free to deny the existence of any religious nature in herself or himself or in anybody else. Whatever the case, it is clear that humans are free to escape God, at least in their own minds. Most importantly and significantly for Christians to note, the religious responses to God themselves, including Christianity, provide some means of escape from God and even opposition to God. A typical, if not predominant means of escape from and opposition to God is through the keeping of some rules and rituals to gain acceptance or some favor from God while not following God's will in relationship to other people. In other words, humans easily make a show of being religious. While all religions, including Christianity, contain means by which people can escape responsibility to God, people are more important than their religions with their mixture of truth and error. It is the people of other religions with which Christians must deal, not other religions per se.

The central task of Christians then is to focus upon Jesus Christ and to concentrate on representing (witnessing to) Christ to the world. This is to be done in a way that is consistent with the way Jesus lived, taught, and dealt with people. Nevertheless, it is useful to understand other religions as much as possible to see how they have influenced people and how they may express similar longings to those found in Christianity. In other words, understanding other religions is a way of gaining an understanding of the people who follow these religions and also of oneself. As far as understanding religions, it is most important that Christians understand their own religion, namely its origin and checkered history, in order to be able to witness to its central content and especially to witness in ways that are consistent with the Way of Jesus.

DOCTRINE—NOT BASED ON, BUT LEARNED THROUGH EXPERIENCE

Christianity, more than any other religion emphasizes the importance of doctrine, namely what we are to believe. In order to intelligently interact with other people of whatever faith or no faith, practice or no practice, Christians should know the key doctrines of Christianity that have been believed over the centuries, namely "classic Christianity." Christianity, after starting with faith in Christ, found it necessary to say what was meant by such faith and what is involved in such a life of faith. Typically, religious life for humans has meant carrying out certain practices related to what is above and beyond human life, primarily to gain some help in the face of many difficulties. As noted, the emphasis has been on "practices" since what to believe has been full of mystery.

The word "religion," coming from the Latin word "to bind" has the implication of obligatory practices, certainly not acceptance of God's grace and forgiveness. The early centuries of Christianity were taken up with defining the faith. As already seen, unfortunately, after the Church became allied with political power the struggles to define the faith led to violent struggles between various factions (Jenkins 2010). Separate historic churches were formed, which today would have been known simply as different denominations and, in fact, are coming to be known that way in the United States.

The struggle to state the meaning of faith in Christ is already seen in the New Testament, but in the following centuries divergent formulations of doctrines became quite pronounced. The doctrines of Christianity are not simply abstract statements of what Christians are to believe, although doctrines may appear to be this. They are beliefs that were worked out over time as Christians dealt with what they did not believe about the faith they were *experiencing.* This is why the meaning of the faith should not have been nor should not be imposed or coerced—taught or witnessed to, but not coerced. As they followed Christ they had to say to some people, "No, he is not simply a divine being masquerading as a human; he is fully human." On the other hand, they had to say to others, "No, he is not simply a human being; he is our Divine Savior." In this way, they came to define the difficult doctrine of the Incarnation as the expression of the reality of the One they followed. Even then, agreement was not reached on the exact terms to use, dividing those for and against the decisions of the various church councils. This was made all the more difficult because of different connotations of words in the languages of Greek, Latin, and Syriac. Nevertheless, almost all Christians agreed that their Savior was both fully human and fully Divine, and this became the classic view of all major branches of Christianity.

Similarly, Christians came to define the Trinity, one of the strangest of human beliefs about God, as the doctrine of the God they *experienced.* They came to know God the Father as their Creator and the one who sent Jesus Christ out of love for them. They found that they gained access to God, the Creator of all things, through Jesus, who died for their sins and rose again to bring them new life. They also found that God was with them and empowering them to serve

God and walk with their Lord Jesus through the Holy Spirit who was given to them. Without understanding it, the reality of the Trinity was brought home to them through these experiences.

Thus in the centuries after the New Testament the struggle to state the meaning of faith in Christ resulted in the emergence of the doctrines of the Incarnation and the Trinity. In spite of the struggles and disagreements over terminology, these doctrines basically represented the *experience* of Christians that required them to reject alternative doctrines. In the following centuries up to the present, Christians have struggled over many other doctrines, some of the most important being doctrines of the atonement, the Church, and the Scriptures. The present book represents the struggle over the doctrine of Eschatology.

Doctrines are not simply statements, although they obviously involve the use of words. In practice, doctrines or the theology of individuals and groups often turn out to be a matter of emphasis. The doctrine of the atonement is especially rich containing many meanings. Some Christians tend to emphasize one to the exclusion of others. Again, the doctrine of the atonement is very much a statement or statements that arise from experience, as Paul stated, "[He] loved me and gave himself for me" (Galatians 5:20) and "Christ died for our sins in accordance with the scriptures" (I Corinthians 15:3).

The statements of doctrines are particularly difficult simply because they require human thought and language, both of which are inadequate to represent eternal realities. It could be said that the doctrine of the Church is still being worked out, especially how the visible Church is to represent the invisible, universal Church of God. The visible churches (representing the invisible Church) have been influenced very much by the cultures that have surrounded them. This is seen particularly in how the churches have organized themselves.

For example, the older churches are more hierarchical, even imperial, in organization, reflecting the hierarchical social structures of the past. Protestant churches adopted democratic organizational forms that were developing through mutual influence between the churches and the societies in which they existed. Needless to say, the older churches have been influenced by the development of democracy and freedom of religion, for example, as evident in the Vatican II Council of the Roman Catholic Church, which supported democracy after a long period of opposing democracy.

The doctrine of the Scriptures has also proven to be difficult because of the relationship of the authority of the Scriptures to the authority of Christ. In many ways the doctrine of Scripture is analogous to the doctrine of the Incarnation, which can receive an emphasis either on the divine or human side. In the end, Christians experience God speaking to them through the Scriptures and thus know the Scriptures as Divinely inspired. Jesus Christ is the source of authority for Christians, as Christ said (Matthew 28:18), but in practice that authority is experienced through the Holy Spirit in the Church as the Scriptures are interpreted.

Eschatology, the primary subject of this book, is also especially difficult because it represents both what Christians heard from Jesus Christ and the Apostles and what has been *experienced* in human history that was not clearly envisioned in the Bible in spite of what some people may claim are the historical details foretold by the Bible. Basically, Christian eschatology is a distinctive view (philosophy) of history affirming that God is working in history, limiting the power of evil, and will lead history to a climactic end in which all things will be re-created. As already explained, the New Age in this book refers to the Kingdom of God in the last days in which believers obtain a foretaste of a coming New Creation of all things.

The purpose of this brief mention of various Christian doctrines is to make clear that as Christians encounter other religions or no religion, even though it is people they are encountering and not just bodies of thought, Christians carry a large and complex body of thought, which has come to be expressed through a large variety of traditions. The amount of literature concerning the Bible and the Christian faith is enormous. As the diversity of Christianities is confusing, it may be said that the diversity in nature is also confusing, but it is beautiful. Nevertheless, I want to stress that the witness of Christians is primarily to invite others to share the *experience* they have had in following Christ. That is the treasure they have to share. The witness they give to others should be based in their own experience, just as Christian doctrines, though found in Scripture, were attested in the experience of believers. However, it is important that Christians measure their experience by the experience of other believers found in the Bible and also respect and learn from the experience of Christians over the last two thousand years who developed the doctrines of their faith. Wise Christians will continually consult Christian literature, as well as other Christians, to gain clarity in their faith and ability to convey it to others. This does not base faith on experience, as some might say, but it does mean that experience is important as a means of learning and growing in faith.

ATTITUDES AND ACTIONS TOWARD FOLLOWERS OF OTHER RELIGIONS OR NO RELIGION

The most important set of attitudes of Christians toward followers of other religions or no religion is love combined with a humble confidence. Confidence, which is close in meaning to faith or trust, is based in the uniqueness of Jesus Christ and what was accomplished in his death and resurrection. It is personal trust in the grace of God received through Christ. Our confidence is certainly not based in our own strength and intellectual understanding of Jesus Christ and all that he did and all that he means. For Christians to have fear as in the case of recent Islamaphobia is to betray a great lack of confident faith. The desire of leaders in the Church to obtain official government support, as well as to use coercion against non-Christians, both of which were done in the past, also betrays a profound lack of faith in the inherent power of the gospel of Jesus Christ and of the Holy Spirit. Although in the United States the government has been formally separated from organized religion, there are still people who show their weak faith and lack of confidence in the gospel by seeking to promote the use by the government of outward signs of religion. God does not need the government to convey the gospel, nor does God bless the government on the basis of its outward show of piety. God expects governments to rule justly without covering their actions or seeking to justify them with religious language.

In interacting with people of other religious beliefs or no religious beliefs, it is most important for Christians to learn to listen. Actually, all people have beliefs, whether they recognize them as such or not. This includes the agnostics and atheists, as well as people who identify with particular religions. Sometimes people's views of Christianity are mistaken. It may well be appropriate to refer to Christianity, but it is more appropriate to refer to Jesus Christ. This should be done in terms of one's own experience and humbly. Thus confidence in the gospel of Christ makes it unnecessary and a bad policy to criticize the beliefs and practices of other religions.

Again, in combination with confidence in the gospel of Christ and the Holy Spirit there needs to be humbleness in any interaction with followers of other religions or no religion. Christians should recognize that Christianity itself is a religion, which is in the midst of being purified because of its many dark streaks. These "dark streaks" are well known as the association of Christianity with oppression, persecution, colonialism, and warfare. These are the large scale "dark streaks" (chocolate ripple effect), but there are also "dark streaks" in every Christian congregation and individual. Many of the "dark streaks" are hidden from Christians because they are sins of omission and neglect, sins of which individuals are hardly aware. They are often the taken-for-granted views and actions that earlier chapters have connected to socio-cultural forces. Thus the attitude of confidence in the gospel of Christ should be mixed with humility regarding Christianity.

The witness to Jesus Christ and his New Age has suffered greatly from the many misunderstandings and misbehaviors of Christians. This means that in relating to other religions and Christian groups, first attention should be given to oneself and one's own group. It is important to listen to criticisms of Christianity and of religions in general. Unfortunately, some Christians, particularly nominal Christians, do not want to hear any criticisms of their religion or of their country, which they assume to be "Christian." These are typically people who are not familiar with the prophetic tradition of the Bible with its strong criticisms of the People of God. (Jeremiah was considered unpatriotic, even treasonous, by his own people.) Often they are the people who see Christianity or some religion as a "good thing" and a general means of obtaining God's blessing on the nation. They are like those who cried in Jeremiah's day, "This is the temple of the Lord, the temple of the Lord, the temple of the Lord" (Jeremiah 7:4) believing that simply having the Temple guaranteed God's protection. As we know, this was not the case. Humility requires that Christians consider first what is wrong with Christianity.

The New Testament contains two remarkable examples of the

attitudes of the first preachers toward Gentile non-Christians. In fact, the accounts of dealing with Gentiles or non-believes in God are rather limited because the major focus was given to witnessing to Jewish people. When Peter went to the home of Cornelius, a Roman centurion and a non-Christian, he stated, "I truly understand that God shows no partiality, but in every nation anyone who fears him and does what is right is acceptable to him" (Acts 10:34, 35). "Every nation" includes all people and certainly people of many different religions.

When Paul preached to a group of idolaters and perhaps religious skeptics in Athens he stated, "While God has *overlooked* the times of human ignorance, now he commands all people everywhere to repent..." (Acts 17:30). This shows that Christians and hearers of the gospel should not worry about their ancestors in the past who had not heard the gospel, but focus on our present task of making known the gospel that enables people to turn (repent) and be accepted by God. Paul stated, speaking of all people, "In him [God] we live and move and have our being" and he quoted a pagan poet with approval, "For we too are his offspring." In an earlier message to Gentiles, which Paul did not finish because of the enthusiastic crowd, he indicated that God "allowed all nations to follow their own ways" and at the same time sustained them by treating them well (Acts 14:16, 17).

In these passages, Peter and Paul demonstrate that the early preachers did not consider it their responsibility to condemn other religions or to condemn their false beliefs. It shows that their focus was on people and what they needed in relation to God, which was to turn to God and receive God's grace. And this was a message not only to non-Christians. The numerous letters of the New Testament, which were written to Christian churches, demonstrate that a central concern of the apostles was that Christians continually change in the direction of becoming like Christ, a change only possible through God's grace in Christ. In fact, the Apostle Paul spoke of that as his own greatest need (Philippians 3:12-14). The purpose for such change did not end with the believers, but was to make them effective witnesses, as said in I Peter 2:9, drawing on Exodus 19:6 and Isaiah 43:20, 21: "But you are a chosen race, a royal priesthood, a holy nation, God's own people, in order that you may proclaim the mighty acts of him who called you out of darkness into his marvelous light." This is consistent with the messages of the prophets before Christ in which they said God's people should become worthy representatives of God. They saw that God's major concern was to purify his own people so that God would be well represented to the world. The last book of the Bible, the Apocalypse (Revelation) with its seven letters to the churches reveals very clearly that all of the churches have faults that need correction. The last letter contains the challenge, "Listen! I am standing at the door knocking; if you hear my voice and open the door, I will come in to you and eat with you, and you with me" (Revelation 3:20).

The major work of followers of Jesus Christ is constantly to seek the help of God to improve and clarify their witness to Christ. That can only be done by taking seriously the mistakes of the past and not repeating them. It also means that no group of followers of Jesus Christ fully represents him. It is always possible to learn from others, even if this means *not* believing or doing what they say and do. Nevertheless, it is important to understand *why* others believe and do as they believe and do. The social sciences are a great aid in this task. The many Christian groups in some way represent the many facets of Christianity and the great variety that is in God's creation, which is beautiful in itself. The New Age of Jesus Christ needs to be proclaimed, but it needs to be proclaimed humbly with the knowledge that no individual or group represents it perfectly and, in fact, it has been represented very poorly in the last two thousand years up to the present by followers of Christ.

Christian missiologists are in the midst of struggling with the issue of how to meet people of other religions and carry out the responsibility of missions. Stanley Skreslet (2012:97-134) gives a very useful overview of this struggle up to the present. In thinking how Christian mission should be carried out I found particularly helpful the recommendation of Terry Muck and Frances Adeney (2009) in their book, *Christianity Encountering World Religions: The Practice of Mission in the Twenty First Century.* The climax of the book focuses on the metaphor of gift with "giftive mission" as the best representation of our mission in presenting Jesus Christ and the gospel to the world. "Gift" catches up both God's act in creation and in the grace we receive through Christ. There is a great deal more to be learned about the meaning of gifting in the Bible and in all societies, which they discuss in detail. They state for Christians, "As people shaped by grace, we are in the giving mode all the time, and everyone we meet is a potential receiver of our largesse (actually, God's largesse channeled through us). In other words, we give all the time to everyone" (Muck and Adeney 2009:355). In case this should be misunderstood as our passing a gift from above to people below, they add, "Finally, the act of giving is a humble act. Both James and Peter use an intriguing phrase: 'God opposes the proud but gives grace to the humble.' (James 4:6 and I Peter 5:5)." They show that "giftive mission" is a two-way street in which the Christian who gives (or passes on) the grace of God in Christ also receives a special blessing from God through a new relationship with others in which there is give and take. There is new self-understanding as well as new understanding of the image of God in our fellow human beings.

The combination of confidence in the gift of God in Jesus Christ and humility about our full appreciation and acceptance of that gift allows the Christian time to receive and practice the fruit of love toward other people and to see them as fellow human beings with similar needs and experiences. The way may be opened then at an appropriate time for extending the invitation to share a common faith and blessing. As D. T. Niles (1951:96) the Sri Lankan Evangelist once stated, "Evangelism is one beggar telling another beggar where to get food." This expresses the proper attitude for Christians to have toward followers of other religions or of no religion.

FREEDOM OF RELIGION

It is confidence in the gospel of Jesus Christ that makes Christians become major advocates of freedom of religion. The gospel of Christ fares best when there is freedom of speech and freedom to make religious choices. Those who believe in the power of the gospel are not afraid of freedom. The attempt to restrict the freedom of other religions is a sign of the lack of faith in the power of the gospel with the Spirit of God to successfully appeal to the human heart. Christians also know that God wants to be freely chosen and trusted in by people. This goes beyond mere assent to what one is told by "the authorities."

Democracy in which people can exercise free speech and are free to make religious choices provides the best context for the gospel of Christ and the New Age. The gospel is such good news that it needs to be heard and people need the opportunity to believe. The gospel of Jesus Christ has proven to have an intrinsic power to draw people to a personal trust in the grace of God in Christ. The review of history, such as made in this book, shows that strange as it may seem people will believe the gospel, *given the right circumstances.* The best circumstances are not when the gospel appears handed down from a superior position as when associated with colonialism, but when it comes to people from alongside or even from an inferior position.

Throughout history, people have received the gospel most readily when it was not associated with domination, but rather with uplift and progress to those who are dominated.

God's providential work in history is bringing about first, a situation where most countries now claim to be democratic and to allow freedom of religion, even if true freedom does not exist. At the same time and even earlier, another important globalizing process now becoming clear is the leveling of the nations brought about by the collapse of colonialism and the increasing prosperity and power of many nations. The time when peoples of one nation, particularly a Western nation, could look with disdain on other peoples as "inferior" is fast coming to an end. Both the sense of superiority in the givers and of inferiority in the receivers is a hindrance to the spread of the gospel. The whole Biblical message and the message of the gospel in particular emphasize the equality of all people in the sight of God.

Another providential historical trend is increasing individualism in which individuals are obtaining many more opportunities, even often the requirement, to make choices. This means that increasingly people will be aware of their individual freedom and responsibility to choose to respond in faith to the unique revelation of God in Jesus Christ. For no other person was the claim ever made that he came into the world from God, died for our sins, rose from the dead for us, and continues as Mediator for us before God. Of course, the increase in freedom for making choices, including religious choices, means that there are increased opportunities for the Opposition to mislead, for example by appealing to selfishness and greed resulting in people ignoring the suffering of others.

There are many aspects of freedom of speech and religion that need to be guarded and promoted. This is often not understood in nations that have not experienced democracy for any length of time.

A free press, which is able to be critical of those with power, is highly important in order for a society to be self-corrective over time. In addition, an independent judiciary is necessary so that those with power are not able to oppress their opponents since their opponents will be able to appeal to the free judiciary for protection. It may seem a minor point to many people, but the freedom to publish political cartoons is extremely important to prevent those with political power acquiring a sacred or semi-sacred status. The Church itself needs a free press and other means of self-criticism. One of these is the use of the social sciences for self-examination. The Church, after all, is a human institution, as well as Divine.

Many Christians are not accustomed to the terminology, but the establishment of a secular government is important so that the government will not favor one religion over another and make difficulties for the non-favored religions. In this regard, it is important to distinguish clearly between secularism and secularization, as pointed out earlier. Freedom of religion and secularization make it possible for people to adopt secularism as an ideology and lifestyle, which sadly is self-destructive. However, it is important to listen to the criticisms of religion by secularists and even in some cases to work with them to curb religious people who would impose their religion on others. This is exactly what took place in American history, as Christian Smith with others (2003b) has pointed out. Nevertheless, secularism remains an ideology that considers God irrelevant to life and will lead to nihilism or a belief in the meaninglessness of life. Secularization, in contrast to secularism, is the process by which any particular organized religion is prevented from being able to use the power of government or of public institutions to coerce others or to have an unfair advantage over other religions. A secular methodology, therefore, is highly useful in government, as well as in science.

For some Christians and many Muslims to take organized religion out of government and the reference to God out of use by government officials is taking God out of the government and of public life. But organized religion and religious language are not the equivalent of God or God's revelation. They represent the human response to God, which is very imperfect. God is involved in all of life, including human government, but it is not the work of governments to use their power to seek to influence religious belief. The justice of government actions should stand on their own without the effort to give them a religious aura. Governments should not seek religious legitimacy, but they should seek the legitimacy of public approval by the governed through free elections. These are among the many subtleties related to freedom of religion that require constant attention from the advocates of freedom of thought and speech.

I would like to add notes on two points that can help in relating to followers of other religions or no religion or simply to people with other viewpoints.

LANGUAGE

Many religious people appear not to be aware of the basic symbolic nature of language, not realizing that language points to realities that are beyond words. This is especially true of religious language with its numerous metaphors. Much religious controversy is disagreement over words in which people use the same words, but give them different meanings or use different words with similar meanings. The Bible warns against disputing over words (I Timothy 6:3, 4) and also states, ..."for the letter kills, but the Spirit gives life" (II Corinthians 3:6). Unfortunately, the Christians who literally fought over doctrinal statements forgot the basic superficiality of words. Christians, who place so much emphasis on specific words in the Bible, need to realize the fact that the words of the original texts in Hebrew and Greek were not only not separated from one another (namely they were written in a continual line), but many words can only be translated through taking into account their context and even that is not always clear.

Theology or religious thought is really as much about the emphasis given to words, as it is the use of particular words. Much of religion is about attitude and feeling; particularly about God's attitude and feeling toward us and the attitude and feeling we should have toward others. There is an orthodoxy of the mind in each religion, particularly in each version of Christianity, in which doctrine is very important, as already discussed. However, there is also an orthodoxy of the heart, which is even more important. God looks at the heart and the intent behind the words. Christians need to seek to do the same. It is certainly important to remember the limitations of language when meeting with followers of other religions or of no religion.

One way of dealing with the limitations of language is through narratives or stories. The Bible is full of narratives and it is the stories of Jesus that convey to us most clearly what he was like. Especially because of its stories, the Bible can be applied across all generations and cultures. It is the stories of the Bible that remind us that our lives are to be made into stories that serve as witnesses to Christ.

THE SOCIAL SCIENCES

In relating to people of other religions or no religion it is very helpful to make use of the social sciences. The social sciences provide an excellent meeting ground for people of varying beliefs because beliefs and opinions, in other words normative perspectives, are set aside in examining data, including religious data. People with very different beliefs can search together for the facts on which theories or explanations of human behavior, including religious behavior, are built. Of course, in this search, only the human side of religions can be examined, but most religions believe that God or supernatural power acts through humans and human behavior may certainly be observed. Then religious though must go further to incorporate the valid findings of science. This is a dynamic process given the constant elaborations of scientific theory.

In accordance with what has been said above about the need for humility by Christians, it is in line with that humility for Christians to use the social sciences for the examination of Christianity itself, including churches as social movements and social institutions. There is a great deal about human thought and behavior that can be explained as influenced by particular social conditions and processes. This does not mean that God is not working through those conditions and processes, but recognizing the human influences on religion can be very humbling. In fact, God does work through many kinds of social conditions, beginning with our families. We are all subject to socialization by parents and others, but we are also subject to other strong socio-cultural influences as we grow older. The family and other social institutions together with social movements are very much important subject matters in the social sciences.

In the end, the social sciences themselves recognize (at least most scholars within them) that people must go beyond the observation and measuring of facts and the development of social scientific theory. This is where each religious group must recognize the right of other groups to formulate their own interpretations of God based on and expressing their beliefs. In addition, religions have the right to seek to make conversions, as long as the rights of others are observed. As long as a clear separation is made between the analysis of empirical data and the expression of beliefs, joint discussion and work can be fruitful and lead to greater understanding by individuals of both oneself and of others.

CONCLUSION

As religious diversity becomes more of a local phenomenon than ever before, different religious views and practices will become better known. Christians should welcome such a development because more than anything else they want the gospel of Christ to be known and understood without the hindrance of Christian behavior that discredits the gospel and does not reflect the character and Way of Jesus Christ. With this in mind, followers of Jesus Christ, who are seeking to live out the New Age of the Kingdom of God, welcome, in fact work for, the spread of secular democracy with its freedom of speech, press, gathering, and the protection of rights through an independent judiciary.

Followers of Jesus Christ should welcome the secularization of governments and public institutions, not as an exclusion of God from these areas of life, but as an exclusion of organized religion and ideologies and the politicization of religious beliefs, which are ever-present dangers. God does not need government officials as government officials to proclaim God's name, but rather to act honestly and justly. The work of proclaiming God's name and salvation in Jesus Christ is the responsibility of the Church, groups of Christians, and individual Christians. The Church and Christian families have not yet fully realized the enormous responsibility for Christian nurture and education placed on them by the secularization of public life. At the same time, Christians have the right and duty to work for the establishment of justice and freedom for all people. The secular is an instrument for self-correction, as the methodology of both science and of government. At the same time, humans need to live on a more profound spiritual level than can be attained through secular methodologies. This is the level at which beliefs and viewpoints are learned and expressed. Religions, cleansed of their propensity to seek to control and coerce human behavior, are set free to expose their messages to the world and people are set free to hear and believe. This is what the followers of the New Age of Jesus Christ want most to do because they have confidence in the incomparable beauty and power of the Triune God, who has acted and is acting for the salvation of humankind.

I cannot close this chapter without referring to a special document finalized in January 2011. It was prepared in a remarkable cooperative effort of the Pontifical Council for Interreligious Dialogue (PCID) of the Holy See and the World Council of Churches' Programme on Interreligious Dialogue and Cooperation (WCC-IRDC) with the participation of the World Evangelical Alliance (WEA). The six-page document is available on the internet at www.oikoumene.org. The production of this statement by such diverse Christian groups shows how facing the world of numerous religions has brought Christians together. I recommend this statement as incorporating all that I have been trying to say and much more. A short summary of the six recommendations at the end of the document are:

Study the issues in the document and where appropriate formulate guidelines for conduct...

Build relationships of respect and trust with people of all religions...

Encourage Christians to strengthen their own religious identity and faith while deepening their knowledge and understanding of different religions...

Cooperate with other religious communities engaging in inter-religious advocacy towards justice and the common good...

Call on their governments to ensure that freedom of religion is properly and comprehensively respected...

Pray for their neighbours and their well-being...

REFERENCES

Anderson, Irvine H. 2005. *Biblical Interpretation and Middle East Policy.* Gainesville, FL: University of Florida Press.

Arnold, Thomas. 2006 [1896]. *The Spread of Islam in the World: A History of Peaceful Preaching.* New Delhi: Goodword Books.

Baptist, Willie and Jan Rehman. 2011. *Pedagogy of the Poor: Building a Movement to End Poverty.* New York: Teachers College Press.

Berger, Peter. 1967. *The Sacred Canopy: Elements of A Sociological Theory of Religion.* Garden City, NY: Boubleday & Co.

Bonk, Jonathan J. 2009. "Africa and the Christian Mission." *International Bulletin of Missionary Research.* 33(2): 1-2.

Busch, Eberhard. 2010. *The Barmen Theses Then and Now.* Forward by Daniel L. Migliore. Grand Rapids, MI: William B. Eerdmans Publishing Company.

Calvin, John. 1559. *Institutes of the Christian Religion.* Philadelphia: Presbyterian Board of Publication.

Demereth, N. J. III. 2001. *Crossing the Gods: World Religions and World Politics.* New Brunswick, NJ: Rutgers University Press.

Ellwood, Robert. 2003. *Cycles of Faith: The Development of the World's Religions.* Lanham, MD: AltaMira Press.

Flory, Richard and Donald Miller. 2008. *Finding Faith: the Spiritual Quest of the Post-Boomer Generation.* New Brunswick, NJ: Rutgers University Press.

Froese, Paul. 2008. *The Plot to Kill God.* Berkeley, CA: University of California Press.

Fukuyama, Francis. 2006 [1992]. *The End of History and the Last Man.* New York: Free Press.

Gear, Felix B. 1944. Minutes of the Eighty-Fourth General Assembly of the Presbyterian Church in the United States, May 25-30, 1944. III. Reports of Ad Interim Committees. 123-127. "The Question as to Whether the Type of Bible Interpretation Known as Dispensationalism Is in Harmony With the Confession of Faith." Louisville, KY: Presbytrian Church U.S.A.

Gill, Anthony. 2008. *The Political Origin of Religious Liberty.* New York: Cambridge University Press.

Gribben, Crawford. 2006. "The Future of Millennial Expectation." In

Expecting the End, edited by Kenneth G. C. Newport and Crawford Gribben. 237-239. Waco, TX: Baylor University Press.

Hall, John R. 2009. *Apocalypse: From Antiquity to the Empire of Modernity*. Malden, MA: Polity Press.

Hunter, James Davison. 1991. *Culture Wars: The Struggle to Define America*. New York: BasicBooks, a Division of HarperCollins Publishers.

_____. 2010. *To Change the World: The Irony, Tragedy, and Possibility of Christianity in the Late Modern World*. New York: Oxford University Press.

Jenkins, Philip. 2002. *The Next Christendom: The Coming of Global Christianity*. Oxford, UK: Oxford University Press.

_____. 2010. *Jesus Wars: How Four Patriarchs, Three Queens, and Two Emperors Decided What Christians Would Believe for the Next 1,500 Years*. New York: HarperCollins.

Kane, Danielle and Jung Mee Park. 2009. "The Puzzle of Korean Christianity: Geopolitical Networks and Religious Conversion in Early Twentieth-Century East Asia." *The American Journal of Sociology*. 115(2): 365-404.

Kolb, William L. 1964. "State." In *A Dictionary of the Social Sciences*, edited by Julius Gould and William L. Kolb. 690-691. New York: UNESCO.

Kyle, Richard. 2006. *Evangelicalism: An Americanized Christianity*. New Brunswick, NJ: Transaction Publishers.

Lindsay, D. Michael. 2007. *Faith in the Halls of Power: How Evangelicals Joined the American Elite*. New York: Oxford University Press.

Marsden, George. 1987. *Reforming Fundamentalism: Fuller Seminary and the New Evangelicalism*. Grand Rapids, MI: William B. Eerdmans Publishing Company.

MacCullouch, Diarmaid. 2010. *Christianity: The First Three Thousand Years*. New York: Penguin Group.

Moffett, Samuel Hugh. 1992. *A History of Christianity in Asia, Volume I: Beginnings to 1500*. San Francisco, CA: Harper.

Montgomery, Robert L. 1991. "The Spread of Religions and Macro-social Relations." *Sociological Analysis* (now *Sociology of Religion*). 52(1): 37-53.

_____. 1996. *The Diffusion of Religions: A Social Scientific Perspective.* Lanham, MD: University Press of America.

_____. 1999. *Introduction to the Sociology of Missions.* Westport, CT: Praeger.

_____. 2002. *The Lopsided Spread of Christianity.* Westport, CT: Praeger.

_____. 2007. *The Spread of Religions: A Social Scientific Theory Based on the Spread of Buddhism,Christianity, and Islam.* Hackensack, NJ: Long Dash Publishing.

_____. 2012. *Why Religions Spread: The Expansion of Buddhism, Christianity, and Islam With Implications for Missons. Second Edition.* Asheville, NC: Cross Lines Publishing.

Muck, Terry and Frances S. Adeney. 2009. *Christianity Encountering World Religions: The Practice of Mission in the Twenty-first Century.* Grand Rapids, MI: Baker Academic.

Newport, Kenneth G. C. and Crawford Gribben, Editors. 2006. *Expecting the End: Millennialism in Social and Historical Context.* Waco, TX: Baylor University Press.

Noss, John B. 1949. *Man's Religions.* New York: The Macmillan Company.

Phal, Jon. 2010. *Empire of Sacrifice: The Religious Origins of American Violence.* New York: New York University Press.

Poythress, Vern S. 1994 [1987]. *Understanding Dispensationalists.* Phillipsburg, NJ: P & R Publishing.

Ricoeur, Paul. 1967. *The Symbolism of Evil.* New York: Harper & Brothers.

Rossing, Barbara. 2004. *The Rapture Exposed: The Message of Hope in the Book of Revelation.* New York: Basic Books.

Ruthven, Malise. 2004. *Fundamentalism: The Search for Meaning.* New York: Oxford University Press.

Ryrie, Charles. 1995 [1966]. *Dispensationalism.* Chicago: Moody Press.

Sanneh, Lamin. 1991. *Translating the Message.* Maryknoll, NY: Orbis Books.

Schweitzer, Albert. 1968 [1906]. *The Quest for the Historical Jesus.* New York: Macmillan Publishing Co., Inc.

Sharot, Stephen. *2001. A Comparative Sociology of World Religions.* New York: New York University Press.

Skreslet, Stanley H. 2012. *Comprehending Mission: The Questions, Methods, Themes, Problems, and Prospects of Missiology.* Maryknoll,

NY: Orbis Books.

Smith, Christian. 2003a. *Moral Believing Animals: Human Personhood and Culture*. New York: Oxford University Press.

_____. Editor. 2003b. *The Secular Revolution: Power, Interests, and Conflict in the Secularization of American Life*. Berkeley, CA: University of California Press.

_____. 2010. *What is a Person? Rethinking Humanity, Social Life, and the Moral Good from the Person Up*. Chicago: University of Chicago Press.

Stark, Rodney. 1997 [1996]. *The Rise of Christianity*. San Francisco, CA: HarperCollins.

_____. 2001. *One True God: Historical Consequences of Monotheism*. Princeton, NJ: Princeton University Press.

_____. 2003. *For the Glory of God: How Monotheism Led to Reformations, Science, Witch-Hunts, and the End of Slavery*. Princeton, NJ: Princeton University Press.

_____. 2007. *Discovering God: The Origins of the Great Religions and the Evolution of Belief*. New York: HarperOne.

Van Leeuwen, Arend Th. 1964. *Christianity in World History*. New York: Charles Scribner's Sons.

Verwer, George. 2008. *Drops from a Leaking Faucet*. Secunderabad, India: Authentic Books

Wallace, Anthony, F. C. 1956. "Revitalization Movements." *American Anthropologist*. 56(2): 264-281.

_____. 1967. *Culture and Personality*. New York: Random House.

Weber, Max. 1964 [1922]. *The Sociology of Religion*. Translated by Ephraim Fischoff. Introduction by Talcott Parsons. Boston, MA: Beacon Press.

_____. 1958. *The Protestant Ethic and the Spirit of Capitalism*. Translated by Talcott Parsons. Forward R. H. Tawney. New York: Charles Scribner's Sons.

_____. 1967 [1946]. "Politics as a Vocation." In *From Max Weber: Essays in Sociology*, edited by H. H. Gerth and C. Wright Mills. 77-128. New York: A Galaxy Book.

Weber, Timothy P. 1979. *Living in the Shadow of the Second Coming*. New York: Oxford University Press.

Wink, Walter. 1989 [1984]. *Naming the Powers: The Language of Power in the New Testament*. Philadelphia, PA: Fortress Press.

_____. 1986. *Unmasking the Powers: The Invisible Forces That Determine Human Existence*. Philadelphia, PA: Fortress Press.

_____. 1992. *Engaging the Powers: Discernment and Resistance in a World of Domination*. Philadelphia, PA: Fortress Press.

Woodberry, Robert D. 2012. "The Missionary Roots of Liberal Democracy." *American Political Science Review*. 106(2): 244-274.

INDEX

ABOUT THE AUTHOR

Robert (Bob) L. Montgomery was born in China of missionary parents. After graduation from Rhodes College and Columbia and Princeton Theological Seminaries, he returned to the Far East and served as a Presbyterian missionary in Taiwan for sixteen years. His work was among the aboriginal people, primarily the Amis language group. The movement to Christianity of the aboriginal people spurred Montgomery to obtain a PhD in Social Scientific Studies of Religion at Emory University. Through a number of articles and books, he has sought to develop the field of sociology of missions, while also contributing to the religious field of missiology. He sees missions as closely related to eschatology or the doctrine of last things, which is why he wrote the present book.

CPSIA information can be obtained at www.ICGtesting.com
Printed in the USA
BVOW011346061112

304792BV00001B/1/P